CALIFORNIA
CHILDHOOD

CALIFORNIA CHILDHOOD

Recollections and Stories of the Golden State

Edited by Gary Soto

Creative Arts
Book Company
Berkeley
1988

For information contact:
       Creative Arts Book Company
       833 Bancroft Way
       Berkeley, California 94710

Typography: QuadraType, San Francisco
Cover Design: Charles Fuhrman Design
Front cover photo of Catherine Mulholland by G. Edwin Williams, 1929

Library of Congress Cataloging-in-Publication Data

California childhood: recollections and stories of the Golden State
edited by Gary Soto.
       p.   cm.
ISBN 0-88739-062-5: $16.95
ISBN 0-88739-057-9 (pbk.): $9.95

       1. American prose literature—California.   2. American prose
literature—20th century.   3. California—literary collections.
4. Children—California—literary collections.   5. Authors,
American—California—Biography—Youth.   6. Authors,
American—20th century—Biography—Youth.   7. California—Social life
and customs.   8. California—Biography.   I. Soto, Gary.
PS571.C2C14 1988
818' .5408' 089794- dc19   87-30094

Printed in the United States of America   CIP

CALIFORNIA CHILDHOOD

Recollections
and Stories of
the Golden State

TABLE OF CONTENTS

Southern California

INTRODUCTION

I t would be wonderful if I could take a deep breath, clear my throat, and say something profound about California, this Golden State which, with the discovery of gold in 1848 and later the advent of the movie industry in Hollywood, provoked an image of wealth and paradise to those on the other end of America. In some ways it was wealth and paradise: Easterners were fed up with snow, Italians were tired of the tenement life of New York City, "Okies" were ruined by a three-year drought that brought on the dust bowl. And "Arkies," poor blacks, Armenians, Irish, Mexicans, Tejano-Americans, Pakistanis, and Eastern Europeans were all willing to say in their own idioms, "Hell, I don't like where I am now; let's give California a try." They scattered the Native Americans and made room for themselves.

There was quick money to be made in 1849. Gold nuggets lay like lost buttons on the bottoms of shallow streams, winking their dull yellow, and hid in rocks that could be washed or chipped down to grains of sand. But this get-rich-quick prospect faded within a few years. Many prospectors tossed aside their mining tools and eyed the land for the raw sources of life: logging, fishing, ranching, and farming.

With the 1930s, California saw an influx of poor whites, Mexicans, Filipinos, Japanese, all of whom came to California in search of that dream of prosperity. Instead they found themselves in the Golden State sweating in the fields. By the 1950s, the population moved from farms to the industries of the city. Paradise became that dream of an easy life: a union job, a bright sun and a lemon tree in the backyard, maybe a swimming pool, certainly safe schools for the children and free Saturdays to watch the barbecue sizzle with California-raised meat.

I could use figures to help define this state. Twenty-seven million of us call it home, including 44,156 who live in prisons. We harvest fifteen billion dollars worth of agricultural crops annually and bottle some four million gallons of beer. There are 765,924 full-time students, 6,150 veterinarians, 616 gun clubs affiliated with the National Rifle Association, 37 Nobel Prize winners (the first honored in 1927), and at last reading, one pair of California condors in the wild trying to propagate its species. The largest city is Los Angeles and the smallest is perhaps Minkler, population thirty-two (I say *perhaps* considering the perpetual debate among the small communities of who is really the smallest). In 1983, Fresno won the distinction of among 277 large cities as being the most unlivable in America; Modesto and Stockton wouldn't dare laugh at Fresno, for they were rated among the least desirable cities as well. At the University of California, Berkeley, where I happen to teach, the monthly utility bill is $1.2 million. My neighbor's bill for the month of June is $19.56.

I could drop my interest in numbers and talk in the abstract: the people from northern California tend not to like southern California. Those in the south tend to ignore the north and give their attention to the glories of immediate gratification, namely swimming pools, the beach, amusement parks, movies with special effects, and a speech pattern that is "totally" its own. Those from the San Joaquin and Sacramento Valleys cannot make up their minds which is the lesser of the evils. The north has the big-city "weirdos" and the south has smog and freeways where you can drive a full tank to empty before you can figure out how to get off. Those along the Sierra Nevadas tend to keep to themselves, hiding in the coolness of 100-foot redwoods.

This narrative is all casual conjecturing about California. I am here to introduce thirty-two recollections and stories about growing up in California, which is different from growing up in Rhode Island or Alabama or Utah. A child from northern Utah grows up much like those from southern Utah. A child from any corner of Alabama knows the summers are hot; everyone sweats in that state. But because of California's great size the climate varies. In June it's possible to eat a snowball in one place and only forty minutes away by car—and a five-thousand-foot drop—to drag yourself on your knees and beg for water. A California childhood is a peculiar assembly of religions, cars, subdivisions, and the inevitable 7-11s. It sees images of itself learned from TV and movies-made-for-TV, thinks nothing of poor people sharing the same sidewalk with the rich, or the daily bump against bump of people of different colors. In Garden Grove it's possible to walk two blocks and hear nothing but Spanish. Walk another two blocks and you hear Korean. In San Francisco, the Irish lived near the Italians and the Italians lived near the Chinese and the Chinese worked for the American whites in Pacific Heights who were suspicious of the enclave of two-generation Russians living in the better part of town, namely Russian Hill. The gays have made Castro Street and Polk Street all their own.

Aside from place, California childhood is about that imaginary landscape inside each child's mind. Childhood is not only place, but a response toward place. I am speaking of fear and boredom, the sense of resignation in a poor family, the utter joy of jumping into cold river water, the loneliness of no girlfriend or boyfriend, envy of the rich in "fresh" clothes, adolescent rebellion—human feelings that move beyond the borders of California to embrace all children.

The anthology begins with northern California. Floyd Salas calls up the memory of his brother and their world of boxing in the small towns of Buckeye and Boomtown, just outside of Redding. Bill Hotchkiss, too, remembers his brother, but the voice of his writing is poetic and the setting bucolic South Wolf Creek in Nevada County. Three selections recall San Francisco: Clark Brown writes about selling Christmas trees in the Sunset District for a latter-day pirate; Genny Lim learns about her father's momentary loss of pride in Chinatown; and Devorah Major meets up with a best friend. Palo Alto's Thomas Simmons writes about the death of his mother, Oakland's Reginald Lockett about his "going for bad" hip walk through adolescence, and Hayward's Valerie Miner about the teacher who haunted her for years in a love-hate relationship. Moving southward, Domenic Stansberry adds to the new dimension of the bored, troubled adolescents in San Jose, and James D. Houston, who has lived much of his life on a sliver of land west of Highway 1, raises from the past one gregarious uncle from his childhood. Louis Owens rounds out the north with a portrait of his father, a water witch, in the 1930s Salinas Valley.

Richard Dokey introduces central California with his boyhood on a farm near Stockton, and Maxine Hong Kingston, also from Stockton, taunts a "quiet girl." Frank A. Cross, Jr., portrays farm life as hard work against a backdrop of fun under a 106 degree sun. William Saroyan and I write about the orneriness of Fresno kids: Saroyan threw a cat off a one-hundred-foot structure and I (it was mostly my brother's suggestion, really) tried to burn down our house. Down the street—literally—Riverdale's Art Cuelho cocks his gun and goes off to hunt the blood of rabbits. Michael Blaine from Exeter, a small town then of two hundred folks among olive groves, confronts his feelings of Catholic guilt. Further south by Highway 99, in the small town of Oildale just outside of Bakersfield, Gerald Haslam remembers with awe and deep kinship his Spanish-speaking grandmother, and William Rintoul, in neighboring Taft, makes us chuckle about playing golf on a hot summer day in the Valley.

Further south, and inland on the edge of Los Padres National Park, Valerie Hobbs' story is about restaurant work and loneliness in 1950s Ojai. Backtracking up the coast to affluent Santa Barbara, Christopher Buckley provides a picture of a single-minded father who wants his child to succeed at local tennis. Southeast some hundred miles, Catherine Mulholland recalls her five generations of family who owned much of the San Fernando Valley. In nearby South Pasadena, Lawrence Clark Powell records those pleasant moments of a 1910 city muscling itself into prosperity; in Whittier, M.F.K. Fisher records pleasant moments, too, but with the feistiness of a young girl among prejudicial neighbors. Then there are the small cities that blend into one another and make up the sense of Los Angeles: we follow Mary Helen Ponce to the Saturday afternoon matinees in Pacoima, a restless Leonard Nathan up and down 1930s El Monte in search of a poetry for his life, and Michael Petracca into the arms of the Hollywood police. We are witness as Danny Romero's Catholic bazaar turns violent in Watts, and

Hisaye Yamamoto DeSoto's bittersweet reminiscence of living among the oilfields of Redondo Beach. Further south, in San Diego County, Richard Katrovas has written the most startling and original piece about homelessness. The final selection by Wakako Yamauchi is about everyday life during the depression in the Imperial Valley.

What brings these together is the liveliness of writing, the honesty, the personal histories which may speak for larger groups, and the peculiarity of incidents. These are convincing recollections and short stories, not faint remembrances that draw out the tragic with melodrama or charmingly sweet anecdotes that fail to convince. Moreover, in these pages, we bring together some of our most talented California writers; we wish we could have included others, namely Joan Didion, Richard Rodriguez, Charles Bukowski, Kevin Starr, all of whom have written about California. They were either busy with their own writing projects or—to be honest—their reprint fees were too large. Of course some will be missing because we didn't know about them. Probably they were writing quietly in places like Visalia and Compton, and we didn't know their genius was there.

Here then is a collection of thirty-two recollections and stories, from which southern California might learn about the northern California, and the north admit that it was wrong in its assumptions about the south, and the San Joaquin Valley learn to hold its opinions about either. It's also our hope that those east of the Sierra Nevadas will look upon urban California with new eyes. Dear reader, good friend who picks up this book, a *California Childhood* is in your hands.

Northern California

Brothers Keepers
Floyd Salas
Buckeye & Boomtown

Each tear is a crystal heart. Count them. Paper spots. Damp. Blurring print. Streaking my thoughts. But I'll spread them for you, give the why. Why? Because I ache in my guts. Because my intestines cramp with memory and that memory is greased with brain and blood, and this is the why of that.

His big plaster leg took up all the back seat and he held his crutches next to him. He was eleven and I was almost two. It was the deep depression of 1933. We lived in the small town of Buckeye near Redding, and my father was lucky to have a job. He had a job because he was a hard worker, the best, a rancher's son who knew how to get things done.

We were taking my brother Al home from the hospital where he had been put after jumping headfirst off a thirty-foot water tower. I stared at him. He was a spectacular sight to me. I remember the tower. My oldest brother, Eddy, who was thirteen and an intellectual prodigy, swung me around by an arm and a leg there and scared the hell out of me. I caught my breath, got dizzy and nauseous and saw a damp, dark spot on the earth beneath the water spout under the tower. Al had jumped headfirst from the tower when Eddy came to bring him home to get a spanking for selling one of Dad's rabbits for a big jar of marbles. That's my first memory of my brother Al and it set the tone for the rest of his life as I see it: tragic, meaning sad and noble, too. The nature of man at his greatest in the end.

Oh, he was fun, though. He took me to my first movie when I was three. It was in a red brick building across the dirt alley from our yard in the small town. It was only one story. He took me right down to the first row, where we sat looking up. I remember being astounded by the size of the big cowboys in front of me. And somebody behind us was shining a big flashlight down on them. I kept looking back and forth from it to the spinning

7

wheels of the stagecoach. It astounded me. I couldn't figure it out. It was real and not real, another spectacular sight.

Next, I remember this little suburb where my father worked in a packing plant. Al took me with him to a house where they stuck a rake under a front porch and pulled out little warm puppies. Then he taught me to shoot little green buds off a tree like spit wads. I was still three then. Then I remember him when I was four and we lived in a red brick, two-story building. We lived on the bottom floor. My birth broke my mother's rheumatic heart, then she had my little sister three years later so she had to sleep in the afternoons or she'd die, and I remember her lying down in the bedroom.

I had nothing to do and wandered around the house. Finally, rummaging around, I found my short-pants black suit and white silken shirt that my mother used to dress me up in when we went somewhere. I liked it and put it on and, since I was dressed, decided to go for a walk. I wandered to a big park with a swimming pool a block down. I stayed there all afternoon, had all kinds of fun. I remember playing with these bigger boys who carried me and another little boy piggyback and wrestled each other. It was great fun.

Then I wandered onto the other side of the park, where a woman in an alley told another woman I was the brother of Al Salas. He must have been 13 at the time. Then I went back to the park and it was getting very late, almost dark already, and Al appeared on the lawn. He said he had been sent to find me and that I was going to get a beating when I got home. I can still see him lying down on the lawn next to me: dark, wavy hair, strong-boned face, telling me very seriously that I better put a book under the back seat of my short pants so the whipping wouldn't hurt so much. I took him very seriously, but the book was too big and didn't fit. Though I needed it, because the next thing I knew, I was running around in a circle in the kitchen, hollering, while my mother held onto one of my hands with hers and switched me with the other. My brother even then knew how to lighten the punishment you got for being too free.

He put the first pair of boxing gloves on me then. Some little blond kid who lived next door was in the kitchen with me and he had to watch us, so he taught us how to box, or rather, put the gloves on us and had us slug it out on the linoleum floor. My opponent was a cute little blond kid. And we punched and punched at each other, getting all sweaty and red-faced. For some reason, I remember it as a rainy day. We didn't go outside, that's why. He kept stopping us and pouring hot water on the gloves so we could hit harder. I accepted this as kids do, but it did make the gloves heavier and it did splat more when we hit each other. I didn't know then how many fights he was going to get me into before it was over.

He taught me to tie my shoes, sort of. I don't know how old I was but I didn't go to school, not even kindergarten, so I had to be five or less, about 1935 or 1936. It was a pretty house and bigger than the other one, more lighted, too. It must have been cold outside because we were inside again, and again he was watching me and my little sister, too, as I recall. But I kept going up to him to get my shoe tied. It kept coming undone. I watched him as he did it. He was getting tired of tying it. I knew he was annoyed. But a little while later, it came untied again. So I sat down and tied it myself. I never asked him or anyone to tie my shoes again. He taught me that without even trying. He'd teach me a lot of things without trying before it was over, some good, some bad.

He protected me, too. I had a little dog by the name of Trixie, a little deerhound–rat terrier kind of dog, very pretty, black with perfect markings. A natural white collar around her neck, white feet, a white star on the back of her head, white tip at her tail and a white throat. I had a little bicycle my father bought me. She started barking one day at some Mexican kids about ten or twelve years old who had come into the backyard and grabbed my bicycle. When she threatened them, one of them hit her in the nose with a Vaseline jar and she started yelping and ran back to the house across the big backyard. I yelled, "They hurt Trixie!"

Al ran out of the house and, with all the neighborhood kids, chased those guys down to the ballpark on the next block where he tackled the guy who had hit Trixie. He then held him down and let me hit him in the face for hurting my dog. I leaned over the big kid, who stared at me with wide eyes, and touched him with my little fist. Then, satisfied, my brother let him up and he ran off across the baseball field and never came back to our neighborhood. My brother was a hero to me that day and would be on many other days.

The next thing I knew, my father was taking me to a boxing match. As a small child, things seemed to suddenly materialize before me and there I was sitting next to my father watching the Golden Gloves. I was astounded again. Another spectacular sight. I saw a great big brown man get into the ring. Heavy flesh filling him out, rounding him off, black hair, black, narrow eyes. He was fighting a pink man, with hair on his chest. The bell rang and they ran out at each other. There was a big thud and the pink man flew backwards and landed on the mat, and everybody yelled and some stood up and some man on the other side of my father said, "Who's that? He knocked him out." Another man, in a white jacket with a bony face, who was selling beer said, "He's an Indian!" and suddenly the cowboy movies I'd seen came to strange life again. Another spectacular sight. But that wasn't all. Then they brought out Albert, my brother.

I saw him go into the ring and stand opposite some kid with light brown hair, built husky like him. I got worried. He looked tough. Then the bell rang and they ran at each other. My brother hit him but he hit back. I jumped up on my seat and, standing on it, started swinging my arms like I was fighting, shouting, "Come on, Albert! Hit him, Albert! Hit him!"

He needed all my help, I could see. I forgot all about the people around me and threw all the punches I could, shouting all the time for him, shouting so much my father told the man on the other side of him, "That's his brother! That's his brother!" He said it a couple more times to other people who turned to look at me. Little kid, five years old, standing on a wooden seat, throwing punches for his brother. It paid off, though. When it was over, they raised my brother's hand. I was really happy. He won.

I found out that he would fight again at the end of the week and waited to go see him again. For some reason, we didn't. But the very next morning after the second fight, as soon as I woke up, I went into my brother's room and touched him, my eyes wide, my mouth open, and asked, "Did you win?" He shook his head and said, "No," then laid it back down, wavy hair dark against the white pillow, his handsome face looking sad. I was disappointed and lowered my eyes and shut my mouth and walked out. I was going to be disappointed in him a lot, too.

I did well in school. I could read before I even went to kindergarten. I remember my father reading the funny papers about a little kid about my age riding down a snow slope on a sled, screaming, "Eeeeeeeeeeeeeeeee!" all the way across the page. My father made the sound and followed it with his finger, and picture and sound and letter came together and made words for the first time for me. The corner grocer's name was Freeeee-man. I could see that "e" in the word. I read it out after that. So, when I went to school, I could already do that part.

One night, when I was six, I went out into the backyard with Albert to get wood for the stove. I don't remember why I went with him, maybe because my mother didn't trust him out alone. Maybe she wasn't home and he was supposed to stay with me. But when we were out by the woodshed, he suddenly said, "Do you want to go to the gym with me?" "Yes," I answered, right away, thinking of another spectacular sight.

So, off we went on his new bicycle. My father bought it new for him because he had stolen one and gotten in trouble over it. It cost a lot of money for those depression days of 1937, sixty-five dollars. You could buy a decent car for that, then. He sold all the fancy parts off it, a piece at a time, until it was stripped bare, without even fenders. That disappointed me, too, because it had been so pretty. But off we went across town to the gym, which was near the park where we used to live and where I had so much fun the day I went for a walk. I never did that again. But here I was with my brother. He was fifteen and a good athlete and took me inside. I remember playing around a while, even though I didn't know anybody. But then it came to be seven o'clock and all the little guys had to go home and the man put me out. I told him my brother was inside and that I had to wait for my brother. It got cold and the man kept telling me to go away and I kept saying I had to wait for my brother. But he didn't come out and I waited there for two hours before he did. I remember how worried I was that he might run off without me, and it was nippy, too, and I got bored besides. Two hours is a long time for anybody to wait, let alone a six-year-old kid. But he finally came out with all the big boys at closing time. The next thing I knew he said to this other big kid about his age, "My brother can whip yours!" and I looked up at this tall, skinny kid, at least a head taller than I, who had come out with the big boys.

They made a circle around us in the dark, just the glow of streetlights on the residential street, and Albert told me, "Fight!" I turned to face the tall kid, who immediately smashed me in the nose, made blood spurt out of it and stars fill my head. He almost knocked me down, and then hit me a few more times and Albert stopped the fight, tried to wipe the blood off my face. Finally, the blood stopped and he said, "Here!" and gave me a buffalo head nickel. I took it and thanked him and got on the bike again. He pumped down the dark streets for a long time. I remember how cold it was and that my nose kept dribbling blood. I liked my brother, though. He had finally come outside at closing time, had stopped the fight, and had given me a nickel. But when we were almost home, he told me not to tell my mother that we had gone to the gym or that I had been in a fight. I was a little guy even for six and fit handily on the bar in front of him. I said, "Okay," and he said, "Good," then asked me, "Floyd, could you give me that nickel back? I need it." "Sure," I said and handed it over to him. He'd do that a lot to me, also, before it was over.

He sure was fun, though. He'd take me with him when he had to go get a gallon of fresh milk from the dairy about six blocks away for our Sunday breakfast of pork chops and eggs. That was fun, walking hand in hand with him to pick up the big gallon glass jug with the thick yellow cream caked at the top. We'd stop and take a sip before we got home, and he'd say not to say anything. I didn't.

Maybe I thought he owed me something for the nickel or maybe I was just naturally a predator because I remember my older sister Dorothy, who was seven years older than I and two younger than Albert, giving my little sister Annabelle and me dinner, then saying that she was saving a small bowl of preserved plums for Albert and putting them far up on a pantry shelf. I don't know. Maybe she thought I was a thief or maybe she just wanted to get them out of sight and out of mind. But, in any case, later, I very stealthily sneaked into the kitchen, and, using a chair, climbed up into the pantry and took down the bowl of plums—I can still see them, pale purple plums swimming around in the juice—and ate them down. I was a sloppy crook, though, because the next thing I knew, Al was home, all fifteen-years-old, boxer brother of him, and Dorothy, who was a good housekeeper and baby-sitter, substitute mother, was showing him the empty plate and Al was right on me.

"Stole my plums, huh?" he said and slapped me right across the face. I yelled and started crying and felt the blood gush out of my nose again. But he didn't try to comfort me this time and neither did my pretty sister, Dorothy. I was a crook and, feeling sorry for myself, went into my bedroom, where I stood at the back window that overlooked the backyard and cried for myself, for the sting and the hurt, and dabbed at the blood with my mother's lace curtains. Then I got bawled out for that when she came home, and when I told her, feeling full of self-pity, that "Albert hit me!" she said, "You shouldn't have wiped your nose on the curtains, anyway!" She knew I was a thief and didn't feel sorry for me either. That hurt a lot. Maybe that's why I never became a thief.

Albert did though. I sensed it was about him when I came home from school and saw Mom walking back and forth in the kitchen. Her green eyes were all wet and pink as she walked back and forth from the table to the stove, cooking dinner. Her cheeks were pink, too, but they often were because she had high blood pressure and her skin was so pink and white it was almost transparent. This and the heat of the stove could make them burn. But next to her eyes, her cheeks looked worse now. She sniffled every once in a while and I looked up at her. But she avoided my eyes when she turned back from the table and stepped toward the stove. I was drawing on my chalkboard with the colored chalks my father got me, right next to the warm stove, between it and the back door. I didn't want her to hurt, but she kept me out of her world and I didn't say anything. I was well trained. Yet, I knew it was about Albert. He didn't come home that night. Often, he wouldn't be around for days at a time. The world was still a wonder to me. I didn't question its turning. My mother took care of all that. My life was well-ordered and I never asked when Albert disappeared or where my father was when he left somewhere for months at a time. She and he kept the worries of the world away from their children as much as possible. She kept a six-year-old child out now.

Soon after that, we took a Sunday drive some fifty miles away, I believe. Again, nothing was said to my little sister and me. But we saw Al there, in a blue dungaree uniform with a hundred other boys sitting out on the lawn talking to their families in front of a big yellow building. I remember my mother making sure that she gave him a carton of cigarettes. Then, later, all the boys lined up and took down the flag and we got in our '31 Model A Ford, and drove back through the settling darkness and I told my father all about how the Indians lived on the plains, which I had learned in school, where I had gotten an unbroken string of A's. I never asked where Al was. I wasn't told and I didn't question. But I knew he was locked up, though it didn't look like those reform schools for dead-end kids I had seen in the movies.

The next thing I knew, it was summer and I was skipping the last half of the third grade to enter the fourth at eight. I was taken to a ranch where my grandfather and grandmother lived in an old, long bunkhouse without separate rooms, with their sons. The house was on land, I heard, that my grandfather had owned before his brother, a college graduate, who was county auditor and had power of attorney, got syphilis of the brain, went crazy, and lost the family fortune to his cheating bank partner, then died in 1927. This was twelve years later in '39, and now my grandfather worked with his sons as a picking crew on other men's land. I didn't know this and thought it was my grandfather's ranch and that all the horses were his.

I was surprised to see Al there, with his head shaved bald. It didn't take me long after my mother and father left me there to learn that Al had escaped from reform school. I found this out because he stole my grandfather's new car for a joyride and wrecked it. Al was always pulling some kind of trick. I liked him, though, but I must have had some reservations already because my Uncle Willy saw how much I liked my little dog, Trixie, and smiling, asked, "Floyd, who do you like the most, Albert or Trixie?"

I looked up into his soft, gray eyes, then at Al, who looked away, and said, "Trixie!" and Uncle Willy burst out laughing.

I didn't see my brother again until late September, 1939, in Boomtown, an original boomtown from the gold rush days, near the Shasta Dam, where my father and his two brothers had gone to find work in the summer. Its legal name was Central Valley, but it still had the original boardwalks and Silver Dollar Saloon from the gold rush days of ninety years before, and it was called Boomtown by everyone who lived there. All Albert's hair had grown out and was wavy again, and he was seventeen years old.

It was fun being with Al and Dad again and the whole family, living together in an old cabin with unfinished pine walls inside. It nestled in the pine trees like all the other cabins. My Uncle Tommy and Aunty Dolly lived right behind us with their daughter, Hope, from my aunt's first marriage, who was fifteen like Dorothy; and their son, John, who at five was three years younger than me.

All the neighborhood boys used to gather in a clearing in the forest and play tackle football on the red earth. My brother was one of the stars and he chose me for his team. The next thing I knew, somebody centered the ball to him, and he gave it to me and grabbed my hand and took off running down the sidelines. My feet hardly touched the ground. I was flying and all these big boys were running at me, throwing their big bodies at me, but he blocked them off and ran down the field, with me sailing along behind him. That was scary and I got some bumps, but it sure was fun. Like when I was five and he had taken me to the city park near the lake, where he put me on a roller coaster with him. It was so scary, I caught my breath and couldn't even scream as the ground rushed up at me and my heart flew out my mouth above me. He put his hand over my eyes to help me, but, now blinded, too, I fell in the darkness towards the ground. Just about when my face was going to pop with red blood, I finally screamed.

In Boomtown, I remember Al getting the boxing gloves out and all the boys boxing in a clearing under the pine trees. Some boy's mother came by and said to her son: "You can't box him! Don't box him!" meaning my brother. She was being friendly but she didn't want her son getting hurt. I can still see her. Dark-haired woman about thirty-five trying to keep her tall, slim, dark-haired son with a large nose from boxing. Now, I'd think they were Italians. Then, I didn't think anything, just felt a great sense of pride out there under the pine trees on the red earth that she feared the prowess of my brother. He was a hero to me.

He was also handsome. My mother told him to take me to enter school on the very first day. We walked down a red dirt road under the pines a half mile or so to the school, which was a commandeered union meeting hall on a hill on the other side of the narrow paved road, the only paved road in town, which led to the Shasta Dam eight miles away. The unions were strong up there in the late thirties. There had just been a battle between the CIO and the AFL over jurisdictional rights at the Shasta Dam they were building when we got to Boomtown. I heard other boys talk about how the men went around town carrying clubs for a while. I was a child and knew that my father was with the CIO and so was on his side. But the battle was over when I arrived there with my mother and older brother, Eddy, who just finished his first year at the university on a four-year scholarship; my sister, Dorothy; and little sister, Annabelle, who was five and would enter kindergarten.

A pretty, young blond teacher sat at the desk. When she saw Al, she smiled and showed her pretty white teeth between her red lips and stared at him with her blue eyes. I knew right away she loved him. I could see it. That's when I realized he was handsome. Dark, wavy hair combed straight back from his big forehead, strong bones to his rounded face. Good nose bridge, full lips, large, bright front teeth. Well-built, husky, with thick shoulders and chest. Flawless complexion. His brown eyes, set far back, peered out intelligently at you. I found out later he was supposed to be a good dancer. That's after my father bought a house on the other side of town, in the southeast, which was barely populated; whereas when we first moved there, we lived in the older part of town under the pine trees.

In the new place, the forest was right behind us, but there was only an oak tree in our front yard in which my father put an old car door for a treehouse for me. One morning, I was out on the back porch where Al slept and he showed me this paper flower and I asked him where it came from and he said he paid fifty cents for it.

"Fifty cents? Wow!" I said, really impressed that he had fifty cents to waste on a frill. The only movie in town cost a dime for kids and a quarter for adults so to spend fifty cents on a paper flower at a dance was grandiose to me. I found out much later that they gave the flowers out when you paid the price of admission. So he was pulling my leg all the time. At that time, Eddy, my oldest brother, had bought me *Tom Sawyer* for Christmas and my older sister, Dorothy, teased me and asked if I loved Becky, Tom's sweetheart. She embarrassed me because I did love Becky. Dorothy, by the way, after only a month in town was picked out at a dance to run for Boomtown Sweetheart and finished second to a very pretty girl called Elaine Garber, whom my brother Eddy said, quite seriously, won only because she was better known. Though Dorothy thought Elaine was as beautiful as a movie star and always said, with awe in her voice, how pretty Elaine was.

That Christmas of '39, I saw Al put on the gloves with my Uncle John, who later won fifteen straight professional fights by first-round knockout before he lost one decision to a fancy boxer, quit, and became a rich contractor. The next thing I knew, my brother was lying on the front room floor facedown, eyes closed, arms stretched above him. He never forgot that beating and neither did my father, who had raised John, his younger brother, since the age of seven when their parents died of the Spanish flu in 1918.

Not long after that, Al asked me how much money I had saved in my bank and I answered I didn't know. "Get it and I'll help you count it," he said, and I ran to get it. We sat on the bed to count all the pennies and nickels and dimes, but he kept moving his hands so quickly, while smiling at me, that I couldn't keep count. I finally saw him filling his palm with pennies and not counting right and I shouted, "Albert! You're stealing my pennies!"

"I am not!" he said, still smiling, showing those big front teeth, making me smile, too. He kept snitching them until Dorothy ran in from the kitchen, took the bank away from him and put it away. He did cheat me, but he was funny. I didn't want him to take my money, but I couldn't stop laughing. He was funny.

I heard that he also got into a fight with this guy called Bozo, who was an old acquaintance of my father's. Because Al, who was now eighteen, beat him up, Bozo came to our house on the outskirts of town, where the dirt road ended up against the railroad right-of-way that loomed like a levee a block's distance from us, woke my father up, and threatened to stab him with his knife.

Now, my father was a big-boned man who weighed two hundred pounds and was very strong. I heard the ruckus outside and the next day learned that my father had talked Bozo, who was drunk, out of it. It's odd, because twenty years later, this same Bozo would live a couple of blocks from my sister Dorothy. I met him by coincidence one time when I was twenty-nine—not having seen him all those years. During the course of the conversation, he would pull a big, sharp, pointed knife out of his pocket and tell me what he would do if somebody ever bothered him. So evidently the threat was real. My father was no coward but was also no fool.

I remember walking in the rain into town for some reason, maybe to go to the show, with Dorothy and Albert. When we got near the business section along the paved road, where the post office and the soda fountain called The Big Dipper were, Al wouldn't carry the open umbrella anymore because he felt it made him look like a sissy. I was impressed and made sure that I didn't carry one like a girl, either.

A carnival came to town that hot summer of 1940, where 110 degrees in the shade was not unusual, with a traveling boxing show, run by a big black man, really a brown man, who looked like Joe Louis, then the heavyweight champion of the world. The carnival was pitched on a vacant lot across the street from the post office and The Big Dipper Cafe.

It was a big deal to me. I got to go there every night for a whole week or so. One of my big brothers or my sister or older cousin took me. I walked on the swords the sword lady walked on because the soles of my feet were thick with callouses from running barefoot all summer. The fire-eater man used to let me and my little sister into the sword-lady show free. I didn't like the whirling octopus ride at all when my older cousin Manuel, who was fourteen, took me on it. It was almost as bad as being on the roller coaster with Al. But I liked the fluffy pink cotton candy and the greasy hamburgers and the red soda pop. And I liked the boxing matches, too.

The big brown negro man, who looked like Joe Louis, puffy face and cute, pouty lips, narrow eyes, liked me, too. He always told me he was going to give me a nickel but he never did. Though he did let me in to see the fights free every night. He was an ex-pug, a heavyweight, and he had this black, wiry fighter, whom, I'd guess now, would be a welterweight of a hundred and forty-seven pounds. He was long and lanky and muscles rippled on his black body. He didn't wear boxing trunks but a close-fitting bathing suit. When he was already in the ring, his manager, the big heavyweight, would shout something like, "Boogie, Baby, boogie!" and the fighter would snap his hips in a pumping motion like he was screwing and make all the men laugh. Then he'd fight all comers.

"Would any man in the audience like to fight my fighter?" the big negro would ask from the middle of the ring and local men in the audience would put on the gloves and take the guy on. A local man would also be chosen as referee. I don't remember right now whether there was some kind of prize offered if you could beat him. There must have been, or, except for some crazy young men, nobody would fight him and they had to present entertainment every night. So there must have been a prize for beating the black welterweight.

In any case, I saw a few men try. I saw my Uncle John, who later turned pro, give it a try. It seemed to me like my uncle was winning when, in the first round or at the break, they stopped the fight because my uncle's eye was cut. When they gave a TKO to the black fighter, all the local people booed, and some girl in my class at school told me my uncle won, too. I agreed, but my father said my uncle, the one who'd beaten up Al with the gloves at Christmas, was chicken and quit.

I went to the carnival with my brother early one night. He was taking his own boxing gloves to the manager, who wanted to use them. I didn't know if Al was paid for it or not. We were sitting by the ring in the big tent and there was only the brown manager and his black fighter, Al, my cousin Manuel, who was in high school, and me, until the men in the gypsy family that told fortunes came in. The oldest gypsy had two string bean sons, one my size and the other a head taller. Al said a couple of words. The gypsy man said a couple of words, and the big brown man said a couple of words. The next thing I knew, I was in the middle of the ring with big boxing gloves on, facing the tallest gypsy boy, my heart pounding.

Now, I wasn't exactly a sissy. There was an Indian reservation near the Shasta Dam and my father's brother John, the fighter, was a dark, handsome man who looked like the movie star George Raft. He told somebody in town that he was an Apache Indian so everybody started calling him Chief, even though he wasn't an Indian. Then the local people called every man in my family (except for my college brother, Eddy) Chief; including my father, my brother Al, and my Uncle Tom. I was called Chiefie by all the kids. It was great, but I had to live up to it.

The first day I went to school in Boomtown, when they unloaded all the new desks for the union hall school on the hill by the right-of-way, all the boys attacked each other with the straw padding, sandwiched between cardboard. Evidently, I could hit hard. When I hit some blond kid on the head, he turned and attacked me with his fists. I saw a blond, fifth-grade teacher watching and I assumed that she would break the fight up right away like they did in my old school, where the only fight I ever saw was between two kindergarten boys. But she only stood on the porch and watched us fight. A big blond woman, she didn't make a move. I put up my guard, like I had been shown by Al, and jabbed and blocked and countered and made the boy quit.

I had two more fights for the same reason that day and won them both, too. I quickly became known as a scrapper, who was handy with his fists, and was asked by the other boys to join their clubs. It was a taste of athletic glory, even if of the bootleg kind. My cousin, Paul, who went to Denver University and was later shot down in a fighter plane over the Philippine Islands during World War Two, taught me how to wrestle and bring down bigger guys by tackling them low on the legs. I was a good rough-and-tumble fighter, the kind of kid who sometimes chased other boys home. The new school principal thought I was too small to play in organized games with the older, bigger boys in my grade though, and always put me on the sidelines with the other misfits: tall, skinny, awkward boys; round, roly-poly fat boys, and tiny boys like me. But he was mistaken, because I could fight, and here I was in the center of the ring, facing a kid a foot taller than me.

The tall gypsy boy came at me and I didn't get a chance to dance and box, he was too big for that. But I knew how to keep my head down and stay in close so I wouldn't get hit in the face and hook to his head and body with both hands. That's what I did, nonstop, while he pounded on the top of my head and arms. I felt like I was suffocating, but I kept punching and was getting the best of it. I kept driving him backwards toward the ropes, determined to knock him through them, like I had heard a great fighter like Dempsey did to Tunney. My brother had put me in there and, though I was scared, I wasn't afraid, and if I couldn't box and dance around the ring like Billy Cohn, I could slug, and I did. I drove the gypsy kid back toward the ropes, determined to knock him through them. I put all my will and power into it and was doing it, too. I had him almost to them and through them— he was so small at nine or ten, he could have fallen between the strands, even though he was taller than I—when my brother shouted, "Hey! Get away from the ropes! Move back into the center of the ring!"

I stopped and stepped back, did what I was told, and Al stopped the fight, but he had ruined my plan for a spectacular victory.

The dark-skinned gypsy father then pointed at me and laughed and said, "Your face is all red!" and all the gypsies laughed, as if for this reason I had lost. But I was pale-skinned and my face got red from sheer effort, not from punches. I knew I won because I drove him back around the ring and almost knocked him through the ropes. Even my older cousin, Manuel, who was about fourteen or fifteen, said right after the fight: "Gee, Floyd, I didn't know you could fight like that!"

So, even though my brother got me in another fight, this was legal and I won without getting hurt. Sometimes, he did me some good. I wish it could have stayed fun like that, but my brother got in trouble again and we moved to Oakland.

South Wolf Creek

Bill Hotchkiss

Nevada County

In October wild grapevines that have climbed fifty feet and more, drap-
ing creekside alder and fir, blaze tapestries of gold, almost identical in
hue to spreading creek maples. Leaves shimmer in afternoon sunlight,
dance when a breeze comes, and a few detach, down and back and forth,
settling on boulders or upon slowly moving water yet cause no ripples. In
some legal sense this land is mine now—brush, timber, rocks, and cascad-
ing stream—but actually I belong to what I own, a bond struck at some indeterminate moment during boyhood. Now I have built a cabin and come
here often, as if waiting for something I know is supposed to happen, or
else searching. . . .

*   *   *

South Wolf Creek runs through Woodpecker Ravine, starting at Mel's
Pond and wandering fifteen miles through interlaced canyons to the bridge
on Highway 49, then joins Wolf Creek. From our parents' house on
Screwball Hill, we boys cut down through Smith's field to Fall Creek and
thence a mile or more to meadows and an abandoned orchard at the point
of confluence—a few bricks beneath locust trees, all that remained of a
homestead from half a century past.

The stream twists southward, its canyon tangled with grapevines and
dense groves of fir, past the old Antonovitch mine: rusted ore cart, heaped
tailings, windowless cookshack, washed-out earthfill dam. Then the long

21

meadows and juncture with Dry Fork, Dog Bar Road, Dunn's Dam impounding a small lake, big pike in the water, blue herons, a family of beavers. That was as far as we ever walked except twice.

The first time, my brother and I were in elementary school. We set out to explore the entire creek, but the canyon reached on seemingly without end, past glistening falls beyond the boundaries of the world. We turned back too late in the day, and darkness had already filled the canyon by the time we reached the broken dam. Fear took hold of us, but we stumbled up the ravine, groping our way, and reached home under starlight.

For months I had nightmares of finding myself so far down the canyon there was no way back. I'd awaken those nights, breath short, clutch at my bedboards and wait for the vision, slowly, slowly, to fade from my mind.

Later, in high school, we walked it down (to conquer the nightmare) clear to the bridge on Highway 49, stood fascinated to watch two big creeks, both swollen after autumn rains, rush silently into a single torrent. That day our father came to pick us up—we phoned him from a bar a mile north of the bridge.

*   *   *

But by then we owned the creek, were owned by it. We'd long since built a lean-to four miles down from our parents' house, our own house hewn with boys' axes, its roof moss-covered. We used rocks to dam the creek and lay a bridge across it, two lengths of downfall cedar.

Once on a summer afternoon, swimming naked in the only deep hole in the ravine, we glanced up to discover a black bear shuffling toward us. We shouted and ran a mile, stumbling over vines and logs, my brother cutting his knee on jutting stone. Two hours later, bare-assed and still frightened, we crept back to the pool and got our clothing, ran again, pursued by unseen swarms of bears and mountain lions.

The next year we found a horse the cougar had killed: neck broken and hind quarters eaten at, paunch laid open as well. When the cat had finished, vultures came to feast. A dozen or more of the big birds rose in a cloud of wings as we approached. We traced a progress of hoofmarks, vivid in torn turf, to an oak from which the lion must have leaped. A week later countless flies, almost like moss, covered gouged-out wounds, and smell of death was permeant and raw in the canyon.

It took three years for the bones to whiten, be hidden by grass, scattered by coyotes. During that time I hunted the cougar, my single-shot .22 rifle grasped tightly. One autumn morning, dense fog and light rain, I followed track up a lateral ravine until monsters glared at me from behind each boulder. I stopped, stared about through mists, could hardly breathe, my sweating hands as if welded to the beechwood stock of the gun.

I turned, scrambled down the ravine, while sounds of panting reeked through thickening, gray-white fog.

*   *   *

Windstorm and driving rain ripped through the hills, tearing limbs from pines, breaking off tops—then clear sky, sunlight, almost unreal warmth. We followed South Wolf Creek to its source the first time; dense woods, steep canyon, and there, as a bridge spanning the creek, a whalelike trunk of a huge live oak thrown down by the air, great roots reaching out, knotted. We felt as if in the presence of some ancient deity, but after a time our religious awe diminished, and we climbed upon the moss-draped horizontal trunk and ate our lunch, breathing odor of riven oak wood and basking in pleasant spring sunlight.

*   *   *

Traplines: for three years during winters, each night I walked Fall Creek, from there up Woodpecker and the offshoot meadow where redbuds grew, thin skeletons at winter sunset, past an old stone fireplace huddled beneath oaks where someone had once built a little house. Only heaped stones remained, rising from leaf-covered earth as if from the first creation. Thence through chaparral and over a power line right-of-way to Fall Creek again, uphill through Cosgrove's gulch, where on the hill above, in a tar paper shack, a withered old man and his wife lived with three tall and beautiful daughters.

I caught skunks, civets, foxes (sometimes a chewed-off foot alone remained in the sprung trap), raccoons, and once even a mink that may have gotten loose from Glen's mink barn, and sometimes possums—many of these, and once in a while I'd put one in a burlap sack and bring it home for a pet until the foot healed, and the creature could be turned loose. The other animals I clubbed to death, and my brother skinned them behind the chicken house. In April we'd bundle the pelts and mail them to Iowa, two weeks later receiving a check that barely paid for steel traps and bottles of scent.

At last, after beating a raccoon to death (that refused to die) and after thoughtlessly shooting a rabbit (I found it dead on the trail, stomach moving with unborn young), I dreamed of being trapped myself and vowed never to do such a thing again. My game, henceforth, would be a creature neither larger nor smaller than myself.

Do fur-bearing animals feel joy and fear and sadness and excruciating pain and sense of loss precisely as human beings do? I knew the answer, had known it all along but hidden it from myself. Yet a boy who spends all his time wandering the woods, isn't he expected to bring something back, something to justify his wandering?

*   *   *

I climbed an oak that roots to the summit of Screwball Hill, could see to the east the long white line of High Sierra rising above a welter of blue-green ridges—and west, Woodpecker Ravine, beyond that Osborne Hill and Wolf Mountain, beyond those the huge Central Valley, dim blue of the Coast Range—and westward still, though I could not see it, could feel it, the pulse of a coast-chewing ocean.

Once, at three in the morning, I left my bed to climb the hill through wind and rain, climbed higher—to the top of a tall pine just down from the hill's crest, the branches slippery, top lashing wildly in wind. And I cried, too excited, too astounded to be afraid; dark earth reeling more than a hundred feet below me with the fifteen-foot sway of the tree that might fling me, as I imagined, toward unseen stars, and a rich smell of rain and storm-tattered foliage raged confusion and wonder in my brain.

I was seventeen at the time, graduation from high school not far away, and my world would change. A new path lay ahead, not through woods, but to the city, to the university in Berkeley and to situations and people with whom I knew I shared nothing at all.

Even as the wind and rain swirled about me, and I clung to the top of this tree I had climbed many times, a living thing, old friend, I could envision my life altering, I wondered if I would ever again be—what?

Myself?

I prayed to the night, to whatever God had set South Wolf Creek to winding through wooded hills, had laced the mountains with river and canyon, had arched up the basalt and granite spine of the Sierra:

Do not let me forget, do not let me ever forget all this beauty or fail to remember rain in my face, sough of the stream, a water ouzel dipping, phantom deer gliding through dew-glistening chaparral in the mornings, blue-gray haze on oak-yellow hills in October, ladybug swarms near the creek when the snow melts out in late February, do not let me fail to worship rising springtime sap, clusters of wild grapes in autumn, explosions of snow-weighted branches in winter (my muffled steps as I wandered through ultimate softness and stillness of falling snow), the green riot of summer and sun gleaming up, just flickering from the point where water holds at the top of the falls, a heron standing like rock in the shallows and mist at sunrise at Lost Lake, butterfly swarms at the sandbar where Clipper Creek forks, or the bleached bones of that horse the cougar killed in the long meadows close beside the alder-lined current of South Wolf Creek.

*   *   *

Now it's October again, another birthday, a long while since that night in the wind and rain. I was seventeen then, and another seventeen years have slipped past me. I lean against the side of my cabin and stare down into slow-moving water, remembering, remembering.

A few years back loggers ravaged this canyon, but the Demon heals all, rich growth of saplings, seasons smoothing even the scars of bulldozer and winch line, and one day, I suspect, no human presence at all will trouble the Ravine.

For me, though, that's meaningless. I stand here at the midway point of my life, when I had nearly forgotten, and now from paper days of lectures and meetings and continual arguments with colleagues and more meetings and readings, now this afternoon in October I've come back to Wood-pecker Ravine once again, having bought a bit of land and built myself a cabin.

I stride into the stream, step out into it, stand ankle-deep and exult as water fills my shoes—a man escaped from the wreck and pattern of his life, I stand and feel cold wetness about my toes and shins, listen intently, listen to birdsong and creek sound, other noises inchoate and strangely familiar arising at dusk toward cloudbars that begin subtly to pulse redness, and I pray in this fashion:

Sir, you mad sonofabitch, you almost let me forget. . . .

A Christmas Story

Clark Brown

San Francisco

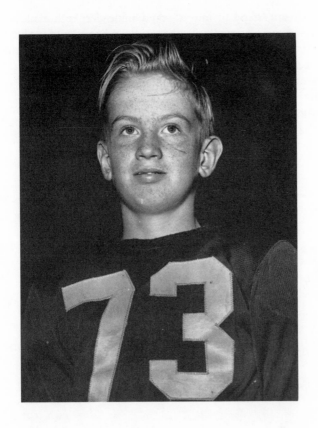

E ach Christmas, when the furor of present opening has subsided and bushels of wrapping paper blaze in the fireplace, I go the bookcase, and—with the awkwardness of a man who distrusts gesture—pull down the battered old volume of Milton and read again the "Nativity Ode." I do this not because I like Milton (though I do like Milton) or because I admire the ode (a stiff creaky thing out of the poet's youth), but in a contrived attempt to capture a Christmas long ago. But to explain that I must go back to a Christmas older still.

I was fifteen. With the Morgan brothers—Paul and Pete—I went looking for work. We tried a Christmas-tree lot in San Francisco's cold and foggy Sunset District and were hired at once.

There were two bosses—Joe and Mr. Moss. I never learned Joe's last name or Mr. Moss's first, and I still think of the men that way. Joe—short, wiry and strong—looked something like a monkey and was always in motion, pounding stands together, stringing lines and tying trees to them, carrying shaggy loads of pine and fir. His grin and the watch cap, pulled low on his brow, made him seem good-natured but dim. Actually, he could hustle a customer as well as anyone but preferred to leave the talking to Mr. Moss, who did a lot of it. It was he who hired us.

Mr. Moss, too, was short—sallow-faced and long-nosed, with quick shrewd eyes. He kept his hands in the pockets of a plaid wool jacket, and a square-billed cap of the same stuff was tipped back on his head. Joe was the brawn—until we arrived—and Mr. Moss was the brains and the mouth. He never did a bit of work but he missed nothing.

Mr. Moss applauded our enterprise. He could see at once, he said, that we were good hardworking kids (we beamed and flushed). We could start right in, he declared, and our hearts leaped. He seemed to have taken an enormous liking to us; we couldn't believe our luck. Then one of us (Paul, I think) cleared his throat and bashfully asked how much we would be getting.

A gleam came into Mr. Moss's eyes. He threw back his head and guffawed. By God, yes! We weren't working for nothing, were we? Of course not. We were smart damn kids who wanted to know just where we stood. He shook his head in admiration. Then he leaned forward, winked and lowered his voice (though no one was around). "Tell you what, boys," he said. "You do a good job for me, I'll take care of you!" Another knowing wink, and he slapped somebody on the shoulder. Our hearts, as they say, took wing.

We did a good job. Every day after school and all day Saturday and Sunday we toiled in the miniature forest, our hands numb and swollen, pricked by needles and sticky with sap. We stole clotheslines and strung them between stakes bludgeoned into the frozen ground. We hammered stands and banged them onto oozing trunks. We sawed and clipped. We toted great loads of limp, cold trees, and—most of all—we *sold*, becoming, under Mr. Moss's agile direction, glib little con artists who despised the people on whom we fawned.

"Now," Mr. Moss would instruct, "when somebody asks for a Silvertip, don't *say* we don't have any. Just tell 'em, 'Now *here's* a nice tree!' You're not actually lying, you see. You're not *saying* it's a Silvertip, and if they don't know any different what's it matter?"

We got the idea. Secretly chuckling, we "moved" the lopsided white fir and the scrawny Douglas (always referred to as "old-fashioned"). It was great fun, and sometimes when business got slack, Mr. Moss would invite us into the aluminum trailer at the rear of the lot—a big silver egg half-buried among trees like a fairytale cottage. There we would thaw out, sipping coffee and hot chocolate and feeling deliciously grown-up. Outside, above the chicken-wire fence, strings of electric lights gave the whole place a lurid enchantment.

I suppose it wasn't perfect and we must have had our doubts, but when the Junior Prom approached and we needed capital, we shyly informed Mr. Moss, who took us into the trailer and with great solemnity handed each of us a ten-dollar bill. We were reassured and eager to show our gratitude.

Our chance came the next week when the wholesaler backed his truck into the tiny lot and we climbed aboard to throw down trees. Mr. Moss came over and winked. "Say!" he whispered, "When nobody's looking, why don't you just throw some off the side?" We grinned. Then, while supplier and boss stood at the rear, bending over clipboards and tallying together, we would toss a couple trees at their feet and another to the left or right, where nobody was looking. Drunk with brazenness, we overdid it, and the young man grew surly.

"Hey," he said, "I had more trees than this. I think those kids threw some off the side."

Mr. Moss was aghast. "What?" he cried. "Those boys? They wouldn't do that. They're fine boys!" And smiling and laughing, he talked us out of trouble, though our pulses thumped.

So it went. We would come home dead tired but happy. I would sit down for dinner with my mother and sister, ready to drop but at peace, enjoying what Conrad claims work holds—the chance to find yourself. I asked for nothing more.

All this changed abruptly.

One afternoon while I was at work, my mother, a widow, collapsed with a heart attack and was rushed to the hospital. Whether she would "make it," as my uncle delicately put it, remained in doubt for several days.

Terror numbs and dazes. I remember little of that time, only a fist clenched in my stomach and my feverish prayers, shameless offerings of feats of churchgoing and other displays of piety. It was the Old Testament God who had seized my imagination in my Sunday-school days years before, and I understood all too well the need to propitiate the divine.

God seemed to accept. My sister went to stay with my aunt and uncle. I remained in the lonely little house, going to school and to work and traveling across town by bus to see my mother. She was weak but alert and good-humored. I dared to hope. As always, she preferred to talk about *me,* a good sign. I had told her a fair amount about the Christmas-tree lot, but she failed to share my admiration for my employers.

"Did they give you a tree yet?" she asked.

I said they hadn't.

"Well!" she said. "The bastards!"

Even cardiac arrest couldn't blunt her frankness.

It seemed to me—and to her too, I thought—that I should have a Christmas tree up and decorated when she returned, but I was reluctant to ask Mr. Moss. Paul and Pete felt the same, but we all agreed the bosses should have offered us trees by now.

Then one Sunday morning we were opening the lot by ourselves (Mr. Moss and Joe distributed newspapers to carriers in the early hours) when a station wagon pulled up, and a woman and a small boy got out. The woman said she was Joe's wife—separated and divorcing. She wanted a tree for "the kid" but couldn't afford one. Could we let her have one, before anyone showed up?

We were distressed. We wanted to be loyal, and besides, something whiny and nagging about her smothered our compassion.

"Look," she said, "have they given you guys a tree yet?"

"Um—"

She nodded toward the station wagon. "They should have given you trees," she announced. "Why don't you take a couple and I'll drive you wherever you want?"

She knew us all right, and Mr. Moss and Joe as well.

I picked out a tree, the Morgan boys took another, and Mrs. Joe selected a third. We stuffed them into the wagon, and while Pete guarded the lot, Paul and I rode with Joe's wife and son to my house, then hurried back. She thanked us and drove away. We believed we had brought it off.

On weekends a gang of kids hung around the lot, not exactly "urchins" but vaguely Dickensian. Moss, a latter-day Fagin, paid them a quarter for each wreath they stole off people's doors. These prizes he sold the customers for $2.25 each. We had forgotten the kids, but they had taken notice, and when the bosses arrived somebody finked. Mr. Moss spoke loftily of The Principle Of The Thing and the need for trust. We apologized, and everyone seemed to feel better, as though we had all undergone some painful but healing therapy. But things were *not* the same, and we knew that Mr. Moss would try to cheat us too, and as Christmas came on we gave each other little pep talks. "Whatever they offer us first," Paul would growl, "we won't take it!" Pete and I agreed.

Showdown came, in the trailer of course. Mr. Moss, grave once more, pointed out that he had *already* given us ten dollars each. We cited the long, brutal hours after school and on weekends—a solid month!

"So!" he said, suddenly jolly, "what say we make it another ten each and call it quits?"

"Okay," Paul said and shrugged, but something like a howl broke from me.

"What!"

"Only kidding, boys! Only kidding!" Mr. Moss winked. "Tell you what," he said. "We'll make it *twenty* apiece. How's that?"

I'm afraid that we agreed, wandering off and trying to convince ourselves we hadn't been robbed.

But maybe we hadn't—or I hadn't at any rate—for leaving Mr. Moss and seeing my mother come home, I had the sense of miraculous survival. The long, cold hours of numbing work had come in some strange way to be like the numbness and strain inside me. Yet I'd emerged. My mother was home and the tree was up—an explosion of tinsel, lights and colored glass. The clenching had eased in my stomach. It was as though a great wing had passed over my head in the darkness. It was gone now, and daylight was back, though I had lost forever some childish peace.

A *Juk-Sing* Opera
Genny Lim
San Francisco

I had this dream where I was inside a museum surrounded by ancient Chinese artifacts. The feeling of reverence and exaltation was great each time I discovered a precious object retrieved from memory or association. Silk garments with hand-embroidered dragons and phoenixes, porcelain cups, opium pipes, a hand-carved camphor chest with intricate motifs, jade and ivory carvings, vases once touched, possessed or seen in the past and long forgotten. Discovering an old rattan trunk, the type my uncle might have brought to Angel Island, I am moved to ecstasy and suddenly break into song.

The music that emerges from my mouth, however, fills me with amazement. I am singing Cantonese opera! It's as if I'm possessed by another being. My voice rises and falls in a familiar falsetto. The only time I have heard such virtuoso singing like this was as a little girl at the Great Star Theater, where the traveling operas came once a year. They, too, had to stay on Angel Island each time they came to tour. In fact, they entertained the detainees to alleviate their depression and boredom. The crowds in *Die-Fow* (San Francisco) loved them so much they would shower them with fabulous collars made of dollar bills. Now I become their idol, singing like a Hung-Sung-Nui, the famous opera star, with every soul rapt in my hand's palm. My phrasing and timing are precise, my tone clear and shrill like a flute as my voice slides through a series of varying pitches on the same syllable, turning vocal cartwheels in steep-falling rhythmic cadences.

I awaken and the opera vanishes. The illusion of transcendence and

33

self-mastery is suddenly gone. I'm still a tongue-tied *hu-ji nuey,* an American-born Chinese girl in San Francisco.

But I can still hear the opera echoing in my ears. Its lyrical melody lingers, leading me like the zigzagging line on a highway map to a destination unknown.

As the youngest of seven children, I often felt removed from any sense of a cultural past. As a second generation American-born Chinese, I was often a living contradiction of dual values and identities. At home, my Chinese-ness gave way, much to mother's sadness, to American-ness; and outside, my American-ness always belied my Chinese sensibility. If the twain theoretically never met, they certainly often collided for me.

As a little girl, I bristled with shame and outrage as I heard people call my father "Chinaman." Yet his erect, proud bearing never betrayed any anger or humiliation. And I now realize the alienation that pride cost him. Because of his need for the secure kinship of fellow villagers, father never left Chinatown. He would not hear mother's constant cry to leave the ghetto for the suburbs of the city. One of the very few places where he did take us was the Sacramento Delta.

In the old days it would take Pop about four hours to wind his way through the highways to the delta. Perhaps the trip took so long because of his growing confusion over the new freeways that kept springing up overnight. Our out-of-town trips trickled to about one a year for only special clan occasions, like the Bomb Day celebration in Marysville, where a frenzy of over-zealous young men vied for the coveted prizes that signified the appeasement of the goddess, *Bok Kai,* thrown into a crowded square. Sometimes fights would erupt over the cylindrical, red-wrapped prizes, which contained a gold ring, and sometimes we would get jostled or stepped on. Once in the melee I cried in terror as I was knocked to the ground. Maybe *Bok Kai* could ward off floods, but she didn't seem effective against stampedes.

Father was part-owner of the Golden Lantern Restaurant in Sacramento. All I remember of the place were the golden lanterns strung from the ceiling, the green matchbooks with gold lanterns embossed on the cover, the steamy, bustling kitchen where we kids were not allowed, and the dark storeroom where we spent hours rolling around on a dolly and climbing up boxes stacked almost ceiling-high. I enjoyed the summer trips to Sacramento, if only as a departure from the daily existence of Chinatown. Once, we slept in an unairconditioned hotel room and I could hear my brother and sister having a water fight in the bathtub next door as I tossed and turned in bed. Once, we discovered an empty storefront and spent the morning impersonating mannequins to the amusement of passersby.

The banquets were memorable. Unlike today's banquets where people eat and run, they were all-day family affairs. Cases of Bireley's orange sodas, sparkling cider, Seagrams 7, mounds of *gwa-chi* (melon seeds), candy kisses, coconut candy, were always on hand. In the screened-off area, the men and very often the women, gambled and talked loudly, among the din of clacking *mah-jongg* tiles, dominoes and Cantonese opera blaring from the loudspeakers. One elderly woman passed water right in her chair, she was so engrossed in her game! The men liked to drink and make speeches. They toasted from table to table during the nine-course banquet, ignoring their wives' worried glances.

The Cantonese people that I knew were very different from the Chinese people I read about in newspapers or books. They did not resemble the fawning stereotypes I saw on television or films. The Cantonese I had grown up with were vibrant, adventurous, passionate, courageous, proud, and fiercely loyal family men and women. The men were given to bouts of drinking and gambling, often as their sole escape from a lifestyle of virtual exile. The women embraced their rituals and superstitions as a talisman against harm, appeasing the gods with chicken and wine on Chinese New Year's Day, consulting soothsayers and oracles from yarrow stalks and chanting to ward off evil spirits.

I am sitting in Mrs. Wong's living room in the town of Locke, which is near Sacramento, and am looking up at her wallful of memories—children, grandchildren, husband, young wife. . . . I am touched with sadness. I want to bring her oranges once a month, sit and chat with her about the size and brilliant color of her *gwa,* her infallible fishing technique, her expert knitting which she proudly holds up for my inspection. A white vest for her only son who lives in Sacramento with his family. I do not ask how often he comes because I know it is not often enough.

I become that son, sharing in his guilt. I am that generation of Chinese-American who fled the Chinatowns. The invisible breed. The shamed, who like the Jews, bury the scars of the diaspora; but unlike the Jews, we cannot escape our yellow skins behind masks of white.

She brings me an ice-cold can of 7-Up. I am not thirsty, but I graciously accept. It is safe here, better than the city. I think about my mother wandering like a frightened child in the darkness; my thoughtlessness had sent her unknowingly into the new underground metro-muni subway. The train never emerged from the tunnel and she could not read the English signs. She could not even return to her departure point because the train had switched routes at the end of the line. Mother wandered the length of the city, looking for a familiar Chinese face, any face.

It does not matter that my mother and Mrs. Wong have been in this country a majority of their lives. Their lot as Chinese women had been circumscribed, preordained here as it was in China, except that now there was no need for bound feet. Like mother, Mrs. Wong has never learned to speak English. Life in Locke and other American Chinatowns was self-sufficient, insular. You toiled in the fields, orchards, factories, sweatshops, and came home at night to your own teacup, bowl of rice, and four walls. There was a curtain that hid you from the outer world. . . .

"You hold his hand right now!" the white kindergarten teacher scolded, as the children filed out in pairs for recess. How could I explain to her what the other Chinese children had told me—that skin color was transferable. If I held the negro boy's hand, I too would turn as dark as a *see-you-guy* (soy-sauce chicken). Deep within, I sensed my attitude was perverse, yet I still spent the remainder of recess in the lavatory, scrubbing the ubiquitous mark of Cain, which the Mormon missionaries who came to Chinatown spoke about, from my palm.

I used to hide my lunches from the other kids because they laughed at my *joong* (sweet rice with a duck-egg yolk, pork and peanut filling, boiled into a glutinous lump wrapped in banana leaves), or they would wrinkle their noses in disgust at my greasy deep-fried Chinese New Year's dumplings and other such incriminating un-American concoctions. Being Chinese in America always seemed a liability to me until much later in my youth when I realized the lack of any identifying American culture.

Before father died, I tried to convey to him the importance of reclaiming our Chinese-American history. My father, like so many of his first generation cohorts, however, always felt that what history was lost was not worth retrieving. "What's the use?" he used to say with a helpless shrug. Years later, as I talked to an old man in Locke, I was to hear the same words repeated over and over. *"Mo-yoong, mo-yoong . . ."* he kept repeating bitterly. "It's no use, it's no use . . ." He tells me his family was slaughtered in the war (Sino-Japanese), and blinks back tears. "Nobody's left here," he says, gesturing around the crumbling wooden house with an age-peppered hand. "Mo-yoong-ah . . . And I'm too old."

I dreamt father was alive. I nuzzled against him the way I did as a small child, and felt his warmth. The hands that held me were smooth, gentle, unlike the tensed veins that stood on the back of his hands and the tapered fingers that tapped nervous rhythms on tabletops, the calloused palms once swollen white with pus and sores from beating flames out of my hair and clothes when the sash of my dress caught in the open gas fireplace while thumbing through the pages of a Montgomery Ward catalog (my favorite pastime).

Like watching a fading dinosaur, I watched father's strength give way to age. This handsome, worldly, natty *gum-san-hock,* this guest of the Gold Mountain with the impish grin, who once boasted he owned the first La-Salle in Chinatown; the Arthur Murray dance expert who could rhumba, swing, and out-fox-trot any *bok-guey* (white demon) since Fred Astaire; the droll Chinese Jack Benny who refused to age beyond his long-past thirty-nine years; the hot-tempered septuagenarian who bellowed Cantonese opera around the house and who once challenged a rude young clansman less than half his age to a fight for turning down the Cantonese music during a banquet—had become the inevitable victim of a dying breed.

The twinkle in his eyes disappeared into two cloudy cataracts and soon into two distant gray moons blinking behind Coke-bottle thick lenses. I saw the once quick, reptilian grace slow to measured, halting steps intermittently punctuated by coughs and breathlessness. But most frightening of all, I saw him sleeping corpselike but still breathing in the winter before his death. My four-year-old daughter whispered as we peeked into his room, "Is *Gung-Gung* (grandfather) going to die?" I hushed her and quickly closed the door.

Father came to *Gum-San* three times in his lifetime. He came as a young boy with grandfather. He returned at sixteen to China, then came back. It was on his third trip to China that he married mother. He lived with her in *Chel-kai* for four and a half years before coming back to the states for the last time.

He always threatened that when I turned eighteen he was going to return to China. Then his duties as husband and father would have been fulfilled. Like many of his kinsmen, however, the communist takeover in China destroyed the dream of retiring in wealth to their native villages.

It has taken me many years to reconcile my father's pain with my father's pride. I remember as a little girl holding my big Poppa's hand as we walked into his sewing shop on Powell and Vallejo. We were greeted by the hostile presence of a towering redheaded white lady. She stormed at him, "Mr. Lim, if you do not finish this lot by next Wednesday, I'm going to give the next shipment to another Chinaman, is that clear?"

I remember how I waited with anxious anticipation for my fearless father to tell that ugly old white lady to shut up and then hit her. I remember how stunned and confused I was when my father did nothing; instead, head bowed, he answered under his breath, "OK, Ci-Ci."

I feel rage spilling into me as I think of how on that day Ci-Ci towered above us like a redhaired ghost, reducing my beautiful, shining, mythological father into an insignificant Chinaman.

That was twenty-five years ago. I have not had to make such compromises in my life, thanks to my father. His legacy of sweat and hard work has left me with a richer life and is still very much alive. It is the Cantonese opera. I hear it in my sleep, in my dreams. It awakens that part of me which lies buried deep along the Pacific route to America decades before I was born. I can sing it perfectly in my sleep. The Cantonese flows out of my lips like the Pearl River.

I might have been a diva in China. It used to frustrate me that the moment I awakened the language would be lost. Now I see the loss can be taken as a gain. The trick is to render the opera in English when I awake. In spite of what the critics and skeptics say, I know it can be done. It's like learning a whole new language. I rather like my *juk-sing* phrasing. Who says a hollow bamboo can't sing?

Little Girl Days
Devorah Major
San Francisco

The first time I met Lora she was getting her hair pressed. Her mother had just singed a lock, and the bright yellow kitchen smelled of oil and dry smoke as it crackled. Whining, Lora pulled away as her ear collided with the thick slate-gray comb. I was a welcome relief, if only so her mom would put down the comb and complete the introductions. We would be, we were told, good friends because we were almost the same age. Charlotte, already preened with an air of knowing sophistication I would later envy, seemed to see me as snot and bruises, two characteristics I did seem always to carry, one from allergies and the other from my determination to prove that "pretty" and "awkward" were not self-canceling adjectives. After the brief introductions were ended and the birthdays arranged in a linear fashion, we were done. That was it. No, I was not to play with the landlord's children that day, just to meet them. Anyway, Lora had seemed to immediately lose interest in us as her mother reached over the stove again, brandishing the smoking hair iron.

Lora had more than a little spunk. While the hot comb made her mean, the music in her home made her swirl. She was for me a wonder. She could hula-hoop from her neck, do one-arm cartwheels, and blow gum bubbles as large as her head. All of this at six or seven. I, with rash crevices at every fold of skin, counted dancing and jacks as my only accomplishments. The dancing was mostly in mirrors and hallways, waiting for lessons that hadn't yet come, and the jacks were played along on the linoleum flowered

41

kitchen floor. I could run fast, too, but I wasn't supposed to because of my lungs, so I didn't let many people know.

Lora knew more than me about most things. When she and David and Charlotte pushed me into the closet with Junius, she knew what kind of kissing we were supposed to be doing, and it wasn't bird pecks. When we only hugged and giggled, she also knew we didn't do our part and tried to push us back. Instead we decided to write love letters full of hearts and flowers. Of course, Lora colored better than me too. She always stayed inside the lines, making a thick hard border, and was undeniably neat.

Lora was always game and I liked to play. So we became adventurers, light and dark caramels running through Golden Gate Park, rolling down hills, chasing White Russians (weren't they all white?) and calling them "pasty" and "whitey"—tame words against their ugly screeches of "nigger." At the park we found seventeen different ways to get to the glass house and disturb its humid silence with races across the wooden bridges. Sometimes on the way home, when we were lucky, we would see an almost-grown-up guy laying on top of his girlfriend and getting ready to do it. We, wanting more than anything to be noticed, would pretend to sneak closer until, unable to deny our presence any longer he would jump up and shake his fist and growl, and occasionally even start to chase us. We would bellow out laughter as we ran for the safety of our homes to share a grape soda and laugh at how red they got.

We knew the best hills to roll down and where to fly kites without having them snatched by trees, and we had traveled through time in the furniture rooms at the De Young, becoming princesses and madams as we debated stepping over the red corded rope to actually sit on the shrunken hard bed. We were asked to leave the museum by a gray guard with a face that would crumble if it remembered youth.

It was the two us, bored with a long, fogged-in summer, who elected to investigate the local Russian Orthodox Church. It was big and lovely and opened to a large somber chapel. We walked around the room, being overly quiet, looking at the windows and icons that lined the walls, and commenting on the women who spent the day on their knees praying for unknown miracles or at least relief. When we found ourselves seduced by the flickering candles, we began with care and young-girl ritual to light them one by one. Taking a new one, as we had seen others do, we leaned its tip to the fire and made a wish and then another wish and then another. Some of the women grabbed up their prayer shawls and looked at us with scorn, but we ignored them. They were, after all, the same ones whose children called us hurtful names. They certainly had no more dominion over magic and candles than us! So we lit each golden fire, making a little more heat with each until a halo of light appeared, when a slim wrinkled hand reached out and touched mine. A nun in long dark clothes and wire-strung top said, "No more."

"We weren't hurting anything."

"These are prayer candles."

"Well, we were praying."

And then I could see it coming. Lora expected us to just get kicked out and was ready for the Hop-Along-Cassidy run. But I had a mother who gave me long sorrowful looks whenever I erred and rarely raised a hand. So I knew the very serious look-at-me-when-I-talk-to-you lecture. The litany rolled over me, full of reason and patience and far too much religion. I knew we hadn't sinned or made a "scalidge." Finally when we had twisted and flinched enough, the nun led us to the door, and we bolted out with wind-blown "sorrys." The fog was thick and cold by that time and the try-and-be-cool skip home wasn't quite worth all the trouble. But Lora and I had, as our parents directed, become friends—get chicken-pox-together, watch-for-signs-of-growing-titties, and talk-about-preferred-forms-of-punishment friends.

I was what was later to be named a "latch key" child, while Lora had a mother who made magnificent cakes with an electric mixer that even turned the bowl by itself, and then heaped them with thick frothy icings, even when it wasn't anybody's birthday. Lora always had desserts, ice cream, cookies, jello, something. Even though their vegetables came from cans, eating at her house was a special treat with sugar and forbidden Wonder Bread. They also had television. My parents listened to jazz; later I discovered that her dad actually played it. Her mom looked at Jack La Lanne and Ed Sullivan and Disney, and we were allowed to sit on the floor and marvel. Lora always spoke on my behalf as we invaded her parents' bedroom while my parents sat upstairs debating the wisdom of no television set against the reality of children who seemed to be trying to relocate downstairs.

Lora and I never fought, or when we did, it wasn't for long. I suppose that could have been because we were two of the few black girls in the neighborhood, but I think it was because I was peaceable and she was fun. Other than our hair—mine was wild and "good," impossibly messy most of the times; hers was kinky and "bad," excruciatingly neat even on the windiest days—we really had little about which to argue. But one day we found something which was just big enough to set up a spark and we, with cajoling from my brother and hisses from her sister, entered the garage where we began to wail at each other, pulling hair and circling around each other as our siblings rooted us on, offering tips for tight punches, hard kicks and good slaps. They laughed and would not allow us to stop the fight although I stood biting my lips and wincing, forgetting what the issue had been but knowing I was supposed to be mad and trying hard to show it.

And then we didn't speak for a long time. She must have won because I wasn't serious and really couldn't fight unless enraged to the point of insanity, in which case I foamed at the mouth, cried, and in my usual smart-mouth way, let loose with a shadow of the verbal epithets I heard flowing from my father whenever his steel lightning-fast hand collided with the side of my equally hard if fragile head.

After a respectable spell it was over. After a number of days of not playing together at recess, not walking home with each other, not skating together, not borrowing each other's skate key, not searching the gutters for lost pennies, and not having a best friend, we were friends again. We were sitting on the stoop. I finally had gotten the wide petticoat I had pined for. Lora already had three. "Come on," she said as I lifted my dress to show the lace, and she took me by the hand to her dining room at the back of the flat, where no one seemed to ever eat, except on Christmas or Easter, and where the record player lived. She put on a forty-five and we began to dance. First we twirled around the table as the cloth swirled and floated above our ashy legs. Leaping and prancing we performed circles around the wide oak table and began to spin each other under and around each other's arms playing the record again and again, melting in giggles at our fantasy dance hall. Oiling the floor, we were little girls reaching to be women, laughing as our skirts flew around our spindle legs as her father's record beat out lick after lick of happy talk.

How I Started Writing Poetry

Reginald Lockett

Oakland

At the age of fourteen I was what Richard Pryor over a decade later would call "going for bad," or what my southern-bred folks said was "smellin' your pee." That is, I had cultivated a facade of daring-do, hip, cool, con man bravado so prevalent among adolescent males in West Oakland. I "talked that talk and walked that walk" most parents found downright despicable. In their minds these were dress rehearsals of fantasies that were Popsicles that would melt and evaporate under the heat of blazing hot realities. And there I was doing the pimp limp and talking about nothing profound or sustaining. All I wanted to do was project that image of being forever cool like Billy Boo, who used to wear three T-shirts, two slipover sweaters and a thick Pendleton shirt tucked neatly in his khaki or black Ben Davidsons to give everybody the impression that he was buffed (muscle bound) and definitely not to be messed with. Cool. Real cool. Standing in front of the liquor store on 35th and San Pablo sipping white port and lemon juice, talking smack by the boatloads until some real hoodlum from Campbell Village (or was it Harbor Homes?) with the *real* biceps, the shonuff triceps and sledgehammer fists beat the shirt, both sweaters, the T-shirts and pants right off of Billy Boo's weak, bony body.

Herbert Hoover Junior High, the school I attended, was considered one of three toughest in Oakland at that time. It was a dirty, gray, forbidding looking place where several fights would break out every day. There was a joke going around that a mother, new to the city, mistook it for the Juvenile

Detention Center that was further down in West Oakland on 18th and Poplar, right across the street from DeFremery Park.

During my seventh-grade year there were constant referrals to the principal's office for any number of infractions committed either in Miss Okamura's third-period music class or Mrs. George's sixth-period math class in the basement where those of us with behavorial problems and assumed learning disabilities were sent. It was also around this time that Harvey Hendricks, my main running buddy, took it upon himself to hip me to everything he thought I needed to know about sex while we were doing a week's detention in Mrs. Balasco's art class for capping on "them steamer trunks" or "suitcases" under her eyes. As we sat there, supposedly writing "I will not insult the teacher" one hundred times, Harvey would draw pictures of huge tits and vaginas, while telling me how to rap, kiss and jump off in some twanks and stroke. Told me that the pimples on my face were "pussy bumps," and that I'd better start getting some trim or end up just like Crater Face Jerome with the big, nasty-looking quarter-size pus bumps all over his face.

Though my behavior left a lot to be desired, I managed to earn some fairly decent grades. I loved history, art and English, and somehow managed to work my way up from special education classes to college prep courses by the time I reached ninth grade, my last year at Hoover. But by then I had become a full-fledged, little thug, and had been suspended—and damn near expelled—quite a few times for going to knuckle city at the drop of a hat for any real or imagined reason. And what an efficient thief I'd become. This was something I'd picked up from my cousins, R.C. and Danny, when I started hanging out with them on weekends in San Francisco's Haight-Ashbury. We'd steal clothes, records, liquor, jewelery—anything for the sake of magnifying to the umpteenth degree that image of death-defying manhood and to prove I was indeed a budding Slick Draw McGraw. Luckily, I was never caught, arrested and hauled off to Juvenile Hall or the California Youth Authority like so many of the guys I ran with.

Probably through pressure from my parents and encouragement from my teachers and counselors, I forced myself to start thinking about pursuing a career after graduation from high school, which was three years away. Reaching into the grab bag of professional choices, I decided I wanted to become a physician, since doctors were held in such high esteem, particularly in an Afro-American community like West Oakland. I'd gotten it in my head that I wanted to be a plastic surgeon, no less, because I liked working with my hands and found science intriguing. Then something strange happened.

Maybe it was the continuous violence, delinquency and early pregnancies that made those Oakland Unified School District administrators (more than likely after some consultation with psychologists) decide to put a little Freudian theory to practical use. Just as I was grooving, really getting into this fantastic project in fourth-period art class, I was called up to the teacher's desk and handed a note and told to report to a classroom downstairs on the first floor. What had I done this time? Was it because I snatched Gregory Jones' milkshake during lunch a couple of days ago and gulped it down, savoring every drop like an old loathsome suck-egg dog, and feeling no pain as the chump, big as he was, stood there and cried? And Mr. Foltz, the principal, was known to hand out mass suspensions. Sometimes fifteen, twenty, twenty-five people at a time. But when I entered the classroom, there sat this tall, gangly, goofy-looking white woman who wore her hair unusually long for that time, had thick glasses and buckteeth like the beaver on the Ipana Toothpaste commericals. Some of the roughest, toughest kids that went to Hoover were in there. Especially big old mean, ugly Martha Dupree who was known to knock out boys, girls, and teachers when she got the urge. If Big Martha asked you for a last-day-of-school kiss, you'd better give it up or make an appointment with your dentist.

When Miss Nettelbeck finally got our attention, she announced that this was a creative writing class that would meet twice a week. Creative writing? What the hell is creative writing a couple of us asked. She explained that it was a way to express what was on your mind, and a better way of getting something off of your chest instead of beating up your fellow students. Then she read a few poems to us and passed out some of that coarse school-issue lined paper and told us to write about something we liked, disliked, or really wanted. What I wanted to know was, did it have to be one of "them pomes." "If that's how you want to express yourself, Reginald," she said. So I started racking my brain, trying to think about what I liked, didn't like and what I really wanted. Well, I liked football, track and Gayle Johnson, who would turn her cute little "high yella" nose up in total disgust everytime I tried to say something to her.

I couldn't stand the sight—not even the thought—of old monkey-face Martha. And what I really wanted was either a '57 Buick Roadmaster or a '56 Chevy with mag wheels and tuck 'n' roll seats that was dropped in the front like the ones I'd seen older dudes like Mack's brother, Skippy, riding around in. Naw, I told myself, I couldn't get away with writing about things like that. I might get into some more trouble, and Big Martha would give me a thorough asskicking for writing something about mashing her face in some dough and baking me some gorilla cookies. Who'd ever heard of a poem about cars? One thing I really liked was the ocean. I guess that was in my blood because my father was then a Master Chief Steward in the Navy, and, when I was younger, would take me aboard ships docked at Hunter's Point and Alameda. I loved the sea so much that I would sometimes walk from my house on Market and W. MacArthur all the way to the

Berkeley Pier or take a bus to Ocean Beach in San Francisco whenever I wasn't up to no good. So I wrote:

> I sit on a rock
>   watching
> the evening tide
>   come in.
> The green waves travel
>   with the wind.
> They seem to carry
>   a message of
> warning, of plea
>   from the dimensions
> of time and distance.

When I gave it to Miss Nettelbeck, she read it and told me it was good for a first attempt at writing poetry, and since there was still some time left in the period, I should go back to my seat and write something else. Damn! These teachers never gave you any kind of slack, no matter what you did and how well you did it. Now, what else could I think of to write about? How about a tribute to Miss Bobby, the neighborhood drag queen, who'd been found carved up like a Christmas turkey a week ago? Though me, Harvey and Mack used to crack jokes about "her" giving up the boodie, we still liked and respected "her" because she would give you five or six dollars to run an errand to the cleaners or the store, never tried to hit on you, and would get any of the other "girls" straight real quick if they even said you were cute or something. So I wrote:

> Bring on the hustlers
> In Continental suits
> And alligator shoes.
> Let ladies of the night
> In short, tight dresses
> And spiked heels enter.
> We are gathered here
> To pay tribute to
> The Queen of Drag.
>
> What colorful curtains
> And rugs!
> Look at the stereo set
> And the clothes in the closet.

On the bed, entangled
In a bloody sheet,
Is that elegant one
Of ill repute
But good carriage
Oh yes! There
Was none like her.
The Queen of Drag.

When she read that one, I just knew Miss Nettelbeck would immediately write a referral and have me sent back upstairs. But she liked it and said I was precocious for someone at such an innocent age. Innocent! When was I ever innocent? I was guilty of just about everything I was accused of doing. Like, get your eyes checked, baby. And what was precocious? Was it something weird? Did it mean I was queer like Miss Bobby? Was I about to go to snap city like poor Donny Moore had a year ago when he suddenly got up and started jacking off in front of Mr. Lee's history class? What did this woman, who looked and dressed like one of them beatniks I'd seen one night on *East Side, West Side,* mean? My Aunt Audry's boyfriend, Joe, told me beatniks were smart and used a lot of big words like precocious so nobody could understand what they were talking about. Had to be something bad. This would mess with me for the rest of the week if I didn't ask her what she meant. So I did, and she told me it meant that I knew about things somebody my age didn't usually know about. Wow! That could only mean that I was "hip to the lip." But I already knew that.

For some reason I wasn't running up and down the streets with the fellas much anymore. Harvey would get bent out of shape everytime I'd tell him I had something else to do. I had to, turning punkish or seeing some broad I was too chinchy to introduce him to. This also bothered my mother because she kept telling me I was going to ruin my eyes if I didn't stop reading so much; and what was that I spent all my spare time writing in a manila notebook? Was I keeping a diary or something? Only girls kept diaries, and people may start thinking I was one of "them sissy mens" if I didn't stop. Even getting good grades in citizenship and making the honor roll didn't keep her off my case. But I kept right on reading and writing, looking forward to Miss Nettelbeck's class twice a week. I stopped fighting, too. But I was still roguish as ever. Instead of raiding Roger's Men's Shop, Smith's and Flagg Brothers' Shoes, I was stealing books by just about every poet and writer Miss Nettelbeck read to the class. That's how I started writing poetry.

The Last Word
Valerie Miner
Hayward

Rain is threatening. It's a chilly autumn evening. The sun is setting in pale pink and I had hoped for coral to blaze my spirit after a long day of teaching. The grocery store is drafty. One of the back lights is broken, giving the impression that the grocer is going to close before I finish shopping. The grapefruit look as rotten as they have tasted for the last two weeks. I recall Allen Ginsberg's euphoric poem, "A Supermarket In California," and begin to question seriously the things we learn and teach in school.

Next door, even the donuts in Redimade's window—even the French chocolate twists—seem to be drooping. I remember the Redimade shop on the road home from Dickson High School and how I had to use every ounce of willpower to pass by the French chocolate twists, ("One ounce of willpower equals one pound of fat," warned my gym teacher, Miss Mendoza, who seemed to subsist on carrots.)

Around the corner from Redimade's now, my favorite shop has a sale. "Some items half-off." I find the sign depressing rather than enticing. I think of Alexa out of work and all those newspaper stories on the declining economy. So I don't stop to check the snazzy purple suit I've been coveting. Instead, I walk home, fiddle around making a cup of coffee and try to figure out what is depressing me. It is more than a lost sunset.

Of course the first days of school are always unpredictable. Sometimes the weather is stormy. Sometimes the students are too. I sit back on my living room couch and regard the last shards of pink sky through the drizzle. First days of school. I can still taste the finger paints from St. Matthew's kindergarten and smell the egg salad from the damp basement which served as our cafeteria and fallout shelter. Again, I feel the nervousness of my first week in high school, where I seemed like a fraud, the only person in my family to move past eighth grade. I was silent throughout freshman year and astonished to hear myself speaking Latin and geometry as a sophomore.

"Sister Marian, Mrs. Wilson, Sister Antoinette, Mrs. Richter, Sister Cora, Miss O'Leary."

Sipping my coffee, I realize that I have recited this litany every autumn as the sunsets dissolve in drizzle. I am long past believing in rosaries, but I still practice meditation on teachers past. What happened to them, I wonder, fingering the heavy beads of those years. Sister Marian channeled all my guilt feelings into possible offenses against the Ten Commandments. I spent the entire second grade scared that she would write more commandments to terrorize me. Sister Antoinette looked as frightened as I was. And she was so tactful. Upon hearing my squeaky alto, she promoted me to "page turner" as the other seventh-grade girls sang "The Happy Wanderer." Then Miss O'Leary. Why couldn't I forget Miss O'Leary, for godsake? I wasn't that impressionable—a senior in high school—when she did her deed. It wasn't exactly a deed, rather more like protracted torture.

The torture began one late September day during the third week of my senior year. By then, not only was I speaking Latin and geometry, but I was making A's in English literature. While other teachers had reached out to me, Miss O'Leary seemed to dare me. She even drew out my secret ambition to become a writer. In those days I thought she was old and wise. Now I realize she was only about forty. Every day of class was exhilarating.

I was excited as Miss O'Leary handed back the Matthew Arnold assignments—until I saw Donna wince. I knew I was done for because Donna was ten times smarter than I. Besides, we had talked after submitting our essays and I had learned—much to my delight—that we had made the same points. Now I sat peeling the aluminum off a chewing gum wrapper, knowing I must have failed terribly. Miss O'Leary stopped at my desk and waited for me to look her in the eyes before handing back the essay.

"A" it said. At first I thought she had made a mistake. Should I report it? We were beginning our discussion of *Tales From a Troubled Land* and I was conjuring Sister Marian to inquire what sin I was committing by not reporting the error. Suddenly a note was slipped under my notebook.

From Donna, "What did you get? She gave me a C, the old battle-ax." My first reaction was relief. No matter which commandment I was sinning against, at least it was only the difference between an A and a C, not an A and an F. It would be a venial sin. I managed to concentrate on *Tales From a Troubled Land.*

After class, Miss O'Leary rushed over to the faculty lounge where she drank the coffee and smoked the cigarettes which stoked her mighty breath. She didn't notice Donna and me lagging behind, indifferent to our seventh-hour gym class. (P.E. wasn't interesting until October, when Miss Mendoza had purged herself of the required month of hygiene lessons and allowed us on the softball field.) Scrupulously, Donna and I examined each other's papers without finding any real distinction. Donna had made the same arguments. I had one more spelling error. Still, I had received an A and Donna a C. At the bottom of her paper was Miss O'Leary's meticulous Palmer penmanship, "Simplistic and general." At the bottom of mine was the comment, "Creative potential." Whatever the definitions of these phrases, they couldn't mark the distinction between an A and C. I didn't know what to do.

"Why do you have to *do* anything?" asked Donna as we hurried into our gym clothes. Technically I didn't have to dress down because I had my period, but the least I could do was keep Donna company.

"Because it's . . . unfair," I managed. Donna didn't disagree.

The next morning during study hall, I dropped by Miss O'Leary's classroom. She sat camped over her papers with a distressed, resolute posture that reminded me of Dad camped over the bills in our living room. Embarrassed at catching her in such an intimate moment, I walked out of the room and then knocked with loud formality on the doorsill.

She looked up, her face a blur of motion as if she couldn't decide which expression to adopt. Finally, she said, "Yes, dear," with a sympathy that reminded us both that she was the authority and I the supplicant.

"I came about my paper," I managed.

She smiled more kindly.

"I, I got an A." I stammered, struggling to recall the speech which had kept me awake the previous night. "And," I spoke more rapidly, "Donna Gomez got a C."

Her face blurred again, the kindness fading to confusion and then disappearing into affront. Her eyes darted briefly to the faculty coffee room and then back to me. "And what would you have me do about this?"

"Well, we made the same points in our papers," I went blank, forgetting just what I *would* have her do about this. "So, I, uh, guess it would be fair if we got the same grade."

"Fair. I suppose you 'uh guess' you're qualified to make such decisions," she said with reflective softness.

I glanced over at the faculty lounge, remembering how awful Dad behaved before his morning coffee. ("Timing," Mom often admonished me, "it's all in your timing.")

"What is this," her voice swelled, filling the empty classroom, "teenage tyranny?"

"No . . . sorry . . . fair . . . only . . ." my words scattered between us like spilled Scrabble letters. I sucked them in with a quick breath, struggling to reassemble my thoughts. Miss O'Leary coolly flipped through the green-marbled grade book, biting her Bic pen and repeating, "Fair. Fair. Well, I can adjust the situation right now."

As I watched her long finger travel past Gomez, to the bottom of the alphabet, I knew just how she would adjust it.

My grades remained C's for the rest of the year. No matter how many times I rewrote an essay, no matter how much creative potential I tried to tap, I always got a C. This class could have lost me a scholarship, but luckily I was sailing through social studies where we were doing a long section on ethics. And the funny thing—I think it's odd even now—is that she didn't stop me from loving English or from wanting to be a writer. I worked twice as hard trying to get out of C. Writing and rewriting rewriting. Doing extra work. Miss O'Leary went through my papers with a microscope. My spelling cleared up as if I had swallowed a dictionary. Donna somehow made her peace with Miss O'Leary and emerged with an A-. I was C all the way, right up to the final report day, which was also the afternoon that Miss O'Leary signed our yearbooks. "Keep in touch," she jotted in mine, "and send me a copy of your first book." The report card said C.

Actually, I did intend to invite her to the first book party. But something stopped me. The dialogue was a little stiff. And the descriptions were imperfect. She might find a punctuation error. "Funny," Donna smiled over the champagne, "this would have been a good way to show Miss O her place." I was relieved to know I wasn't the only person haunted by the old witch. I also realized that I hadn't yet made the mark I wanted.

Several years later, with my second book published and a new job at the state college, I found myself driving out to Dickson High School. I got to the campus at 3:15, after class but early enough to find her there. As I walked down the Lilliputian corridor, past the teachers' lounge, I sensed that something was wrong.

No, I sighed, her door was ajar as usual. Already smelling her nicotine and caffeine greeting, I knocked rapidly. Inside, a strange voice called, "Door's open." It was the same room. Matthew Arnold still presided from his battered frame. The "most misspelled words" were listed in her perfect handwriting next to the window. Apparently, kids continued to have problems with "manila." The tattered posters of the Lake District hung over the chalkboard.

"Help you?" inquired the young woman who was packing boxes. She looked remarkably like Angie Truman, our head cheerleader, but just as she was too young to be Angie, she was too old to be Angie's daughter.

"I . . . look . . . long . . . time," the whole Scrabble game spilled before us.

"Looking for Miss O'Leary?"

By the cheerful way she asked, I could tell Miss O wasn't dead. I hadn't considered the possibility. She seemed indomitable.

"She's OK, now . . ." I heard fragments of the young woman's voice between my memories, "hospitalized last month for emphysema." ("An ounce of willpower . . ." Miss Mendoza had, no doubt, also advised her.) "She took an early retirement and I'm helping to pack up." *Cry the Beloved Country. Culture and Anarchy.*

"A former student?" she persisted with implacable cheer.

"Yes," I nodded reluctantly. What did she know about it? Perhaps she, too, was one of Miss O's former students. Suddenly my discomfort crystallized in rivalry.

"Her students are her life," she spoke with a detachment revealing she had never had the privilege. "See over there, the scrapbooks."

I was lost at that shelf for an hour. Yearbooks. School newspapers. Albums. John Cotello passing the bar. Martha Killam singing in New York. Donna Gomez getting married. I was nowhere.

Until I found the rose notebook. All about me. Clippings describing my scholarship and graduate fellowship. My early articles in the *Standard*. Then reviews of my books, all meticulously situated under glossy plastic. My own mother couldn't have done better if she read newspapers.

"Got to close up now," said Angie Truman in her school spirit voice. "I'm sure Miss O would love to hear from you."

"I'll be in touch," I answered brusquely.

"Who shall I say called?" she continued.

"I'll be in touch." I left, eager that she not see the red around my eyes or hear the bewilderment in my voice.

I drove back from Dickson High School puzzled. Puzzled at my own sadness, at my reluctance to give a name. I was irritated that after all these years I was still baffled by Miss O while she knew my whole story, had organized it in plastic, for godsake. What effect did she really have on me? Had she intended to provoke, to draw me further? Did she know that for years, still to this day, I rewrote for the precise phrase, the deeper description, to get beyond the C; for what, to stay afloat on the sea? Did she know that nothing had ever compelled me more than that little phrase on my first essay, "Creative potential"? Or was she simply a sadistic, cold woman who found rough consolation breathing smoke and drinking stale coffee?

Of course I recognized that I was taking this too seriously. I resolved to visit her. But I had only been able to make that one trip on the spur of the moment. Could I ever be spontaneous again? Perhaps I would phone. Finally, it occurred to me to dedicate my third book to Miss O'Leary. Yes, I would wait for this, wait to hand her *our* book.

The publication was delayed a year because I had a complicated term at school and a very rough time with the final draft.

When Donna phoned, I was more surprised by the sorrow in her voice than by the news itself.

"Did you know that Miss O died last week? Lungs."

We made plans to see each other. However, like so many plans that year, they fell through until the book appeared. At the book party, Donna was taken aback by the dedication.

"To Miss O'Leary, who may have had the last word."

My coffee is turning cold now. The whole apartment is cold. It's almost dark. The rain sputters. Yet there is always creative potential. So I am drawn back to the typewriter, ignoring the gurgling in my stomach and the familiar craving for a French chocolate twist.

Siddhartha
Thomas Simmons
Palo Alto

Once, when I was a child, our cat Siddhartha disappeared. I knew that he had injured himself a few days earlier when he tried to leap from a tree branch to my parents' third-story bedroom window. I did not see him fall to the ground, but I did see him shortly afterward, running sideways with an odd and slightly horrible awkwardness. He stayed near the house for several days, more or less eating, more or less all right. Then he vanished.

In an unusual moment of candor, my father explained to me that Siddhartha had probably gone away to die. Something inside him told him he couldn't survive, my father said, and he wanted to go where people wouldn't pester him by trying to help. The explanation astonished me. It had never occurred to me that a living being, a cat or even a person, might sense that it was time to die. My mother was devoutly religious, believing in her heart what my father only professed, and she belonged to a religion which asserted the unreality of death. My first taste of religion came through her: she told me that I was spiritual, not material, and that when people left the earth, they didn't really die; it just seemed that way to us, though we could learn to know better. I'm not sure if, at the age of four or five, I really had any conception of "spiritual" or "material." The world was still whole to me, a welter of experience not yet forced into theological categories. Yet I had already begun to sense that fatal anxiety of things not being as they should be. I had been born into a world that was playing a nasty trick on me. In Sunday school I was told that I had to protect myself from this illusion. But this was not always easy.

I remember, for example, when my grandfather—my father's father—died. I was perhaps six. My father cried during and after the funeral, although he tried not to. My mother remained impassive—though perhaps slightly solicitous toward me—and reminded me that death was something that only *seemed* real. In reality, she said, the perfect identity of my grandfather was eternal. What that meant, she explained, was that he was still alive, although we couldn't see or hear him. As I talked with my mother about this, I glanced frequently toward my father, whose tears awed me. I had no idea what to say to him. Yet I felt the greatest sympathy for him, as he clearly summoned all his husbandly devotion to support, with his silence, my mother's authority.

When, a couple of years later, my father explained to me about our cat, I again felt a rush of sympathy for him—and, oddly, of gratitude. There was something unexpectedly comforting about the view of the world that his explanation implied. Somewhere in himself he knew that no tricks were being played: creatures did what they did from an instinct deeper than fear, from a kind of intelligence at once simpler and more profound than the Mind I was introduced to in Sunday school. His words soothed my sense of loss; I was almost happy. A day or two later he came into the yard with Siddhartha's matted body, which he had found by a hedge while walking the dog. He buried him right then. My mother came out later and, in line with some superstitions which she admitted to having and refused to relinquish, did a little ritual of Christian burial which she herself had created.

Siddhartha's instinct to die alone, as explained by my father, came back to mind about twenty years later, when my mother had grown incurably ill. We were, of course, not supposed to admit her incurability. She had spent so much of her life denying the reality of whatever was animal or material that my father, brother, sister and I were all supposed to be ready to witness her own great realization of her spiritual being, which would also restore her "temple," her body. But I was not to be preached to—nor were my brother and sister. We knew we were witnessing the ravages of cancer, and before that solemn pain we held to our sense of the real—real pain, real love, a depth of feeling that moved from my mother's shrunken body to the blessed fact of our own corporeal existence. What astonished us, however, was my mother's slowly increasing, unmistakable desire to die alone. At first she would tell us what ideas and encouragement the practitioners were giving to heal her. Then she began, so gradually, to complain: How these practitioners would not come to visit her but only talked to her over the telephone, how their ideas were trite or simpleminded, their prayers ineffectual. Then she refused to discuss her faith at all. Finally, when it had become difficult for her to speak, and to lift the telephone receiver, she announced without a trace of either pride or sadness that she now refused to talk to the practitioners when they called. After that, she said very little. For a couple of months I sat regularly in her room, occasionally speaking, earning silence in return. On my next-to-last visit to her, when I arrived, she suddenly pointed, in an act of almost scorching clarity, to the full moon outside the window. From then on she acknowledged no one.

I have never gotten over how this woman, so attuned to the world as illusion, and this cat, utterly absorbed in an instinctual world in which illusion cannot be conceived, should die the same death. My mother was a crusader for the spirit; in her healthy years, had someone suggested that she would want to die the way her animals died, she would certainly have scoffed. In both these deaths—but of course most obviously in my mother's, since it was hers that brought me to these thoughts—a terrible affirmation staked out its claim: the dying took place in defiance of all our strategies for smoothing the transition from the known to the unknown. We who were alive, who might have wished to comfort the dying as a solace for our own souls, were banished; the lines of communion between the dying person, the dying animal, and death, were infuriatingly intimate and profound. They left us speechless even at an enforced distance, from which we might have been expected to pass judgment.

Yet, after the initial shock, even our speechlessness became a kind of comfort. There was a point beyond which—for us, as for my mother—the language of wretched theorizing and solemn dogmatism could not go. There was a time when we could say, with the full authority of the heart, this death is not illusion; this communion between the dying and death is not some metaphysical sleight of the hand. There was no room for euphemism or clever jargon; this death guaranteed at least one taste of what was real. Though our whole intelligence resisted it, it was there. It was the fundamental instinct resolving itself into a kind of pure presence—cat and prey, cat leaping, sheer experience which no external portrait can capture.

Animals crawl toward the privacy of their death from this instinct. I believe my mother, too, was finally in the hands of this fundamental directive, so much more powerful and straightforward than the spirituality she preached to us, and had preached to her. The heresy that my father once confided to me, regarding the seemingly small matter of a cat, became at last my mother's faith—or, I find myself hoping, something simpler: a way, a quality of light, a full moon in the dark sky.

Fire Season
Domenic Stansberry
San Jose

I

That summer my father went to the desert. He took his books, and he took the papers he had filled with obscure numbers and symbols. We did not know exactly why he had left. The travels his job took him on, as well as much else he did, were always a mystery to us. Once, he sent home a picture of himself standing dwarfed among a field of steel towers; tracking devices of some sort, used to guide the paths of missiles. I found out, years later, he was working on a way to heat material from the inside, deep at its core, until it disappeared in a quick flash.

With my father gone, my older brother and I found ourselves free to wander the streets as we pleased. We spent the nights in his truck roaming over the hard valley floor outside San Jose and listening to the radio, its static shifting with the pitch of the engine. The parade of lights often followed us into our dreams; from our beds we heard the cars coursing on the roadway beyond. I often fell asleep with the blurred images of the roadside in my head.

I remember the mornings cool, the sun and sky an almost shadowless white, my brother's bed empty and rumpled. He worked stocking the shelves at a store in Argonaut Mall. I stayed home with my mother and sister, watching the morning cartoons, the thinly sketched animals chasing one another across the television. When these cartoons finished—the animals never caught one another, instead they disappeared in a frenzy of light—we switched to a show where women ran through the supermarkets gathering as much as they could fit into their baskets: pieces of roast and

65

slabs of bacon; cans of bright, syruped fruit; boxes of cereal and detergent. I watched without interest, except for an occasional attachment to something the women put in their baskets. I thought ahead to the evening, to my brother's return.

I waited while the day heated—the day always heated—and a warm wind rushed down the slopes filling the neighborhood with the smell of gardens and fertilizer. The neighbors' yards bloomed with flowers and trees. Our backyard, different from theirs, stood much as it had when we first moved in, the same tired dirt a fruit grower had sold to a local developer. Aside from a few California poppies, the drained and cracked mud supported only weeds, thistles, and a pale sort of butterfly.

In the afternoon, my mother left the television and went to the courtyard in front. My sister followed her. On my mother's insistence, my father had built a tall plank fence to separate us from the street. My father had covered the ground, first with a dark plastic tarp, then with colored stones and gravel, so nothing could grow. In a few places he had cut holes in the tarp for cactus he never planted.

It was hotter in the courtyard than elsewhere on our small property. The fence blocked off the breeze, and the gravel collected the heat. My mother liked to lie in her chair for hours, taking the sun into her chest, while my sister played with the warm stones at her feet.

I hate that man, my mother said once—maybe it was that day, I don't remember—and she wiped the perspiration from her olive-colored face. My sister looked at her dully, and I turned away, back inside to the television.

When my brother came home, we made ourselves dinner and then took the truck out into the evening. My brother was like my father, always casting his glance about on everything but never speaking, as if probing some deep mystery. We went many places, riding together in silence, my brother guiding the broken shadow of the car over fence posts and spreading lawns. When the sun went down—that was my favorite moment—the familiar shapes of houses and street and people became less distinct, casting unruly shadows on the asphalt.

I enjoyed watching these shapes, feeling the hot August breeze in my face and imagining them leaping to life—animals, soft underbellies covered with leaves and dirt—yet I felt safe since the truck moved so rapidly, the shadows changing with it, that none of this other world had time to become real.

That night we drove to the old park. Around us the suburban houses seemed to sink, windows and all, into the heat. Large weeds grew through the asphalt. My brother's truck cranked sorrowfully over them, billowing exhaust. Behind us, the lights of the city illuminated the sky, and I imagined a rocket—an invention of my father's gone out of control—plummeting nose downward, its light searing the sky, turning us into radiant creatures without substance, without shadow.

II

The creek gave off the cool smell of wood and rushing water. We walked down the embankment holding the bottles to our chests, then crossed to a park the city had developed and abandoned. Poison oak grew in clusters about the rusted tables, and frogs croaked at our feet. Streets bordered the park on all sides; the penetrating smell of exhaust reached all but the most remote places. We came here to drink. Later we would go visit Scott Powers, a friend of my brother.

Until then, we sat under a small overhang, an alcove made of rocks and overhung with a thatchwork of wild ivy. In this place, where high-school lovers wrestled in the crackling leaves, Tom Rosa had shot out his heart. My brother and I listened to the frogs and the more distant rumble of cars over the bridge. A pair of girls walked by, their laughter muffled behind their hands. I was nervous here close to the trees and rustling bushes. My brother handed me the liquor, warm and almost sweet tasting.

Tom Rosa, the suicide, had gone to our school, a sad and obese boy whose flaccid looks scared the girls. At first, he had tried to be polite. Then he had changed, maybe realizing that, bearlike and sweaty as he was, they would never want him. So he had begun to call obscenely from his car window, yelling as he drove by. Sometimes, he had parked on a corner near the high school across from where the girls loitered, and he had yelled out the brand names of products: perfumes and deodorants, kitchen utensils and panty hose. This aggravated the girls' boyfriends more than the girls, but Tom was big and the boyfriends could do nothing. Often my brother and I sat with him in his car, smirking and sullen, while Tom gunned the engine and shouted.

After Tom died, I had dreams about him. He was always pulling me into darkness. He would appear—outside a classroom at school, or a window at home, or next to my brother's truck—and pull me into the shadows, holding me down with his heavy, animal-smelling body. I would suffer under him until I could no longer breathe, then wake up staring into the white morning, the cool fiberboard. I still have such dreams, but it is no longer Tom who holds me down.

Once I went with my brother to visit Mrs. Rosa, Tom's mother. It was after Tom's funeral, and my brother felt badly because he had not been able to go.

Mrs. Rosa lived in a neighborhood, off El Camino Real, where the houses were small and close together. That afternoon was hot and glaring, early in spring, the air filled with an unusual humidity. Someone had left the door to the house open, but no one answered our knocking. So my brother stepped in and called the woman's name. Later, my brother told me it was her fault Tom killed himself because she tried to make him different than he was. Buying him clothes. Arranging dates. Talking to teachers.

The house smelled moist and cloistered. A picture of Tom, laced with flowers, stood on the mantle. A framed group of newspaper clippings about Tom's brother hung on the far wall. The brother had died in Vietnam. At the center of these clippings someone had pasted a picture of him with his arm around one of the local girls. He was heavy-set like Tom, but his flesh was firm and solid.

We waited, but Mrs. Rosa did not come. We went to the back screen before we saw her. A large woman, she wore clothes that did not match her looks: a tight, wide-belted skirt like the fashion magazines. She knelt in front of a statue, a shrine of the Virgin crushing the head of a snake with her heel.

Mrs. Rosa bent lower, her elbows cradling her large breasts. She bent until she lay flat on the grass. The Santa Clara Valley bloomed under her thighs: the rectangular lawns, the endless streets of Cupertino and Los Gatos and Milpitas; the telephone wires lacing all San Jose together, holding everything in its place. When she cried "My boys, I tried to give you everything," my brother and I hurried through the house back into the bright profusion of the day.

III

The Powers' house grew out of a scarcely tended lawn, its property lines marked off with a cyclone fence. Mr. Power's car sat parked in the driveway. A low, shining car, I thought I saw starlight glimmering in its windshield. The neighborhood—the shadowy smell of damp grass, of clothes hung out to dry, of children playing and sweating—made me wish we were back in the truck, moving with the other cars.

The front room was dim, hot, filled with the sweet-sick smell of sweat and grease. From his chair against the wall, Mr. Powers watched the football game. It was not football season, but this game was an exhibition for the pros. Mr. Powers sat before it with his bottle of whiskey. I was not comfortable with him: his small and gnarled looks, the gray workshirt, and the grease beneath his fingernails. He was not the sort of man my father would like.

Mr. Powers was divorced. He talked in a way my father seldom did, at least not in our presence. He gestured absurdly at the young women on the commercials. He laughed at the way they held their lips parted as they spoke. Though he seemed to hate these women, he could not resist watching.

A young quarterback got smashed hard into the ground, the ball slipping from his fingers and rolling into the end zone. An opposing linebacker picked up the ball, then spiked it in the dirt. Mr. Powers was drunk. His philosophy embraced everything.

"I'm a fatalist, you know. When your time comes, you'll know it. There's no sense worrying about dying. It's like worrying about shitting. When your time comes, it comes. It's like that young hotshot quarterback. He knew what was coming, he saw it, but there was nothing he could do. It's the same with everything. When the time comes—before your car flies off the road or your wife screws the guy next door—there'll be a second when you know it's over. The sooner the better, you ask me."

Mr. Powers went on while the two teams struggled with one another. He laughed as the players limped off the field. He laughed more when they came back to continue the fight. When the camera flashed to a sun-drenched young girl or an excited cheerleader, he laughed again and yelled at the women.

I tried to ignore him, as if he were an unpleasant voice on the television. I did not know what lay behind his brash voice and vulgar talk, though in the years since, I have heard my father speak in the same tone to my mother: when I die, don't bury me. Have my body burned.

Mr. Powers' daughter, Cindy, came into the room. She was thirteen, a few years younger than myself. She was heavily made up, wearing jeans and a sleeveless blouse, its ends tied together in a knot above her stomach. She seemed to notice little of what went on around her, though she did raise her eyes to glance at my brother. He did not look back, but he was conscious of her, just as I was, of the thin and vaporous heat that seemed to rise from her body. Sometimes he used to follow her into the other room where they sat quietly, neither looking at the other.

Scott was the one we came to visit. Like Tom, he was my brother's friend more than mine. Though older, he was not much taller than me, small but wiry and tough. I admired him for the distance he kept from everyone, the deliberate and dispassionate way he surveyed the room. He had a soft look to his face and a moonlike cast to his eyes that attracted the girls. Even so, he disliked them and kept his distance.

Scott stood by the refrigerator. Though I was afraid of him, I half hoped he would make a gesture to draw me towards him. Once before, while my brother and Cindy sat together, he took me down the street to watch while he smashed a windshield out of a neighbor's car. The glass had sparkled when it broke, but no one heard the crash. No one had chased us when we ran.

Maybe Scott guessed what I wanted. He made a motion with his head, beckoning me to the kitchen. Cindy and my brother looked up. Mr. Powers paid no attention.

I followed Scott to the garage. He picked up a gas can and gathered a bundle of old, sweet-smelling rags, torn blouses, and faded skirts.

"Your brother's turning into an asshole," he said while handing me the rags. I did not know what he meant—I thought of my brother and Cindy sitting in the other room—but I nodded my head, not wanting to make him mad just as I had won his attention.

Outside, we no longer talked. We walked past the street where Mrs. Rosa lived. Nothing distinguished her street from any other. All the roads were straight, laid out in a grid.

After a while the street changed, no longer going straight ahead but curving slowly, a wide arc. The neighborhood began to resemble my own, the houses large and set back. Finally, I followed Scott up a long driveway into an open garage. Scott seemed to have chosen the house at random, maybe because the garage door was open, or maybe because one of his old girlfriends lived there, I didn't know for sure.

The garage was used as storage. An old couch and chair. An extra refrigerator with food inside. Some shelves holding cardboard boxes, broken gadgets, plastic toys. I knew we were making too much noise, but the night was so still and warm the sound did not seem to travel. We were in a quiet place, the center of all motion. Then there was a smell like Tom in my dream, and I became frightened. I wanted Scott to hurry. He may have felt my fear because he began to move, scattering the rags over the furniture and pouring gasoline about the room, over everything, even the refrigerator. He took out the matches and motioned for me to stand back.

I do not know how long the woman had been there, but when I looked up, she was standing at the far end of the garage. The door to the house stood half-open. A slim bit of light came in behind her. She had a sleepy look, as if she had just awakened. Though I could not see her distinctly, I remember her gentle features, her warm-colored robe like a blanket over the hills, the dusky smell of grass.

"Boys?" She spoke without alarm, as if addressing her own children. Her voice was husky and reminded me of when I was younger and played in the leaves and dirt. Maybe all this was my imagination; maybe we had caught her at an odd moment, between sleep, when the earth was a gentle place. I do not know if Scott noticed anything about her. There was no time for him to look. He threw the burning matches into the rags. The room filled with fire, the flames bursting out more quickly than I could imagine.

We ran. We did not take the streets this time but climbed over the backyard fences, kicked at the backyard dogs. As we ran, the night spun in my head. I felt as if the entire valley—the Argonaut Mall, the house, the streets filled with cadmium lamps—I felt as if everything were a maze and I was a tiny flame shot through its blackness. I heard the woman's voice again, coming from somewhere beneath the valley, but more remote now, unable to reach us, locked under the asphalt.

I abandoned myself to Scott. I stayed a step behind him. Light flicked on in the houses. A man appeared in one yard and yelled at us in his underwear. But no one chased us this time either.

We reached Scott's house and then slowed our pace. We were too excited to go inside the house, our hearts beating unevenly. Together we climbed on top of Mr. Powers' car and sat on the roof.

Later, Mr. Powers would come out and yell at us. My brother and I would drive home, walk into the silent and sleeping house, quiet except for the hum of the appliances. My father would still be in the desert, working where the towers glinted in the sun. I'd wake up to the cool white of the plasterboard in my room. Nothing would be changed.

But for now we sat with the warm night air against our sweating backs. I was afraid and exhilarated, almost happy. Scott lit a cigarette, twisting his hand to hide the glow of the match. I heard a siren, but I thought it must be too far away to be coming in our direction. Then we heard another engine, then another, until it seemed the night filled with their crying. We stood up on the hood of the car—tonight they'll show her picture on the news, I thought, with the murders and the suicides; she'll be a photograph, pure light—and as my brother came out, Mr. Powers behind him, we saw a tremendous glow in the sky, the kind that happens late in summer when the hot winds blow west through the canyons, catch spark, and fill the neighborhoods of California with a brilliant fire.

The Dangerous Uncle
James D. Houston
Santa Cruz

He was the renegade, the one who could not be tamed or domesticated, the wild card in the family. Was he my favorite uncle? No. But he was by far the most attractive, a man who could not hold his liquor or his money or any of the numerous women who passed through his life. Among my father's four brothers he was the closest in age, so they had grown up together in east Texas, Dudley and Anderson, companions and cohorts, two years apart. I have seen my father rigid with fury at something this brother had recently done to him. I have also watched him laugh as he recounted a boyhood stunt that foreshadowed the kind of life Anderson would lead. I mention this because my father was not what I would call an outgoing or expansive man. He was not given to shows of pleasure, yet Anderson could make him laugh aloud.

"I remember a day we were down along the creek," he told me once, "and back in that part of Texas the creek was the only place where you could cool off in the summer. I guess I was around twelve and Andy was around fourteen. He had this trick he liked to do, just to show off. He used to do it at school until the teachers made him quit. He was always real limber, you see. He had a way of putting one foot up behind his head, like a Hindu, and he was mighty proud of himself whenever he got his foot up there, since he was the only one in our family who could do that.

"Well sir, on this particular day, just about the time we had our shirts pulled off, but still had our trousers on, a couple of girls came walking along the creek trail. Anderson decided he would show them something

73

they would never forget, and he commenced to shove his whole foot and ankle up behind his head. The girls saw that and they got to giggling and ran on down the creek. Anderson got to laughing so hard he fell over. He'd been standing on one leg, ya see, like a stork. For a while he was laying there in the dirt by the creek laughing til the tears ran down his face. Then he quit laughing and looked up at me with this funny look, and he said, Hey Dudley, come over here and give me a hand, will ya, while I get my foot down.

"I went over there and pushed and pulled a while, with him telling me what to do and where to grab hold. But it turned out there wasn't much either one of us could do because his foot was just plain stuck. He had shoved it over too far and got his neck turned some kind of way, and I had to leave him there and run back home to get my dad and our oldest brother, who was already grown, and stronger than anybody else too, because he did push-ups and lifted weights, and bring them down there. It was a mile to the house and a mile back. Before we got near where he was we could hear Anderson yelling. His leg had cramped up. He thought he was going to die alone by the creek bank with one foot locked behind his head."

The way dad told it, that was the prelude to Anderson's entire career—the family clown and a born nuisance, always leaving a mess behind that someone else had to come along and clean up. It was also the longest story I can remember hearing him tell. He was not a talkative man, yet he would talk about Anderson. I think he had to, there was so much to get off his chest. Anderson called things out of him no one else could call out. My dad was not given to shows of anger. Yet this brother could make him curse and slam a fist into the side of the house. He was not a violent man, but one day Anderson made him angry enough to kill.

This happened after we moved south into Santa Clara Valley, where dad had picked up a few acres with a house and outbuildings. During our years in San Francisco, before and after World War Two, one of his dreams had been to get out of the city and back to the land. In the late 1940s, the valley had not yet begun to bulge and multiply and become the high-tech head-quarters it is today. It was still one huge orchard. Out near the western foothills we had a small piece of it, with some fruit trees, a barn, a greenhouse.

Not long after we made this move, Anderson started showing up three or four times a year. He liked it there, since he shared dad's taste for the rural life. They shared a few other things too, but in certain crucial ways these two brothers were like day and night. Dad was a quiet and inward man. Anderson was a compulsive talker. Dad was anchored. Anderson was not. He had gone through five wives and countless jobs, and now he was drifting back and forth between Texas and California. Dad would allow him to stay, sometimes for months, because they had grown up together, and because he was the brother with nowhere else to go, and because Anderson would talk him into it, and because Anderson, when sober, was a man of many talents. Perhaps too many.

He was a carpenter. He was a gardener. He was a mechanic. He could sink postholes and erect a fence that ran straight and true. One summer I watched him take over a picking crew, become foreman for a rancher we knew, and get twenty acres of apricots gathered in record time. For a number of years before the war, Anderson made a good living as a hairdresser in Los Angeles. He changed his name to *Andre,* and he took advantage of the fact that in their boyhood section of Texas the nearest town of any size had been Paris. He became "An-dray from Par-ee." With his wavy hair and his rascal's grin and his gift of gab, it worked. He made and spent a lot of money.

When World War Two came along he joined the army and traveled the Pacific with a construction battalion: Hawaii, New Guinea, the Aleutians. The heavy drinking started then and led to a stomach ulcer that finally put him in an army hospital. No one could say it was the army or the war that disabled him, but he left the service with a disability pension and a chronic condition that had him moving in and out of V.A. hospitals for years. Mostly out. He wouldn't sit still for treatment. He would check himself in on a Monday. By Tuesday night he would be sneaking out the side door, carrying his shoes.

If medicine was prescribed, he wouldn't take it. If advice was given— such as Stop drinking—he would listen a while, then forget. Twice he joined A.A., and twice he backslid. By the time we were installed in Santa Clara Valley he was living on his pension checks, which he tended to blow as soon as one arrived in the mail. His monthly binge could end with a phone call from a bar in Salinas. Or it could be a call from an all-night service station in Reno, someone saying, "Mr. Houston? We got a fella here out of gas and out of money sittin in a vegetable truck that isn't his and he can't remember where he got it, who says you're his brother and not to call the police til we call you first . . ."

Dad would slam the phone down and say that as of today Andy would have to take care of himself because this was absolutely the last time he was going to bail him out of anything!

The next day they would both appear in the driveway side by side in our pickup; my dad stoic, the survivor who had come west during the 1930s with seven dollars in his pocket and now had seven acres with a house in the country, and Anderson, disheveled, hangdog, the prodigal brother with nowhere to lay his head.

We would soon learn he had promised dad something. We would usually learn it from Anderson himself, as we sat around the supper table. And I should point out that in those days I did not yet know the broken pattern of his life. I only heard his Southern Comfort voice, saw the crafty eyes of the garrulous uncle, the colorful uncle, the uncle you hoped would stay for a while.

"Some people are slow learners," he would say, as he dove into his first solid meal in a week, talking between mouthfuls of biscuits and gravy, pork chops, black-eyed peas. "And you people are looking at the slowest learner of all time. But I'll tell you right now, ol Andy has learned his lesson at last. I have taken my final drink. I swear it. Dudley here is my witness. You are all my witnesses. If it wasn't for Dudley, I would be a goner. I would be breathing my final breath in the darkest gutter of the skid rows of Los Angeles, and nobody knows that better than I do. I tell ya . . ."

Now tears would be glinting in his red-rimmed eyes, as he paid tribute to all the many ways my father had saved him from himself. "I tell ya, I am going to make it up to you, Dudley. I am going to make it up starting tomorrow. Starting tonight! We've got a couple of hours of daylight left. Soon as we finish supper I am going to go out there and get started on that chicken house roof. Yes sir. I am gonna get a new roof on your chicken house, so them white leghorns will sleep cozy. Then I'm gonna run that fence down along to the end of the property line like I started to do last spring. And listen. Let me tell all of you right now, help me stay away from the mailbox. I mean it! I don't want to *see* that pension check. I don't even want to see a calendar. That way I'll lose track of time and won't know which day of the month it is and won't even know when to look for that check, because that check belongs to *Dudley!* You all hear me now? You are talking to a man who is making a fresh start!"

I should also point out that dad's vision of how things could look around the place ran far ahead of his available time. There was always brush to be cleared or the barn to be patched, a chimney to rebuild, a bedroom to add on, an acre of trees to prune. He was working fulltime as a painting contractor, and the weekends were never long enough. My mother, meanwhile, had her hands full managing the house, tending her flowers outside the house, keeping me and my sister in school clothes, and giving any spare hours to the vegetables. In this little world Anderson's skills were much appreciated, particularly when it came to the chickens, which played a key role in my father's dream. A well managed chicken pen would provide the eggs and the meat to complement the tomatoes and the corn and the greens that would emerge from the year-round garden. Building up his flock little by little, he had accumulated thirty white leghorns and a few Rhode Island Reds. He had recently widened the pen with new fencing. Anderson must have known, consciously or unconsciously, that the henhouse roof was right at the top of dad's long list of chores, and the very offer that would soften his heart.

So once again he stayed, and two months went by without incident.

Fresh loam soon darkened all the flower beds. New gravel appeared in the driveway. Borders of brick and river stones had encircled the fruit trees nearest the house. At night, around the table we would listen to him talk, and this in itself was worth a lot. Dad never talked much at the table. He ate in silence, thinking about what had to be done tomorrow.

Two months like this, then one night the supper table was quiet again. My father, home late and coming in from the garage just as the food was set out, looked around the kitchen and said, "Andy lost his appetite?"

My mother said, "I thought maybe he was with you today."

"Why would he be with me?"

"I sure haven't seen him around here."

He thought about this and started to eat. After a while he said, "What day is it?"

"Thursday."

"What day of the month?"

"The second."

He thought again and ate some more. "I suppose if you brought in the mail yesterday there is no way he could have got his hands on that pension check."

"I thought you brought the mail in yesterday," my mother said.

"How could I bring in the mail when I wasn't here."

"I told you I had to go shopping."

"You don't have to go shopping right when the mailman is coming up the road."

"I can't spend my whole life walking back and forth to the mailbox, Dudley."

This came out sharp. When he didn't respond, she softened. "One time that check didn't get here until the third or the fourth. The way he keeps changing addresses, it's a wonder it ever gets here at all."

"He wouldn't take off by himself if he didn't have any money."

"Did you look in your clothes closet?"

"I'd better do that," he said, pushing his chair back.

If anything was missing, a jacket, or one of dad's favorite shirts, it meant Anderson was gone and did not plan to return for quite some time. But nothing was missing, which meant the phone could ring at any moment. Dad sat down at the table again and pursed his lips and narrowed his eyes and looked out into the dusk, waiting for that call, already bracing for it.

For three days he waited, then he began to worry that something might have happened, something worse than drunkenness. On the night of the third day he drove around to the nearest saloons. No one had seen Andy.

The next afternoon I was out in front of the house trying to straighten the handlebars on my one-speed when he reappeared, carrying what looked like a square cage. He wasn't staggering. He was very erect, walking with his shoulders back, planting his feet like a mountaineer starting a long climb, though there was no mountain. The road was flat.

He called out, "Jimmy! How you doin, son?"

"I'm doin fine, Uncle Anderson. How you doin?"

"I got somethin for ya," he said.

As he approached, I looked again at the cage, trying to see through its close wire mesh. There was something alive inside, eager to get out. But that was not what he meant. From his scuffed-up leather jacket he withdrew a photograph and handed it to me with a wink. It was a folded and rumpled but still glossy eight-by-ten of a young woman in a skimpy white swimsuit, early Jayne Mansfield perhaps, or someone of her proportions. I don't have a clear memory of the face. I was fourteen, and I was transfixed by the cleavage. I glanced at Anderson and saw him watching my hunger, the depraved uncle, the outlaw uncle, the uncle you wished would take you somewhere.

He winked again. "I got somethin for your daddy too," he said, lifting the lid of the cage an inch to reveal a beak, a glittering eye. Half a head forced its way out, black and fierce. Anderson pushed the lid shut.

"Your daddy is big on hens, but he is short on roosters. This is a little rooster I picked up over in San Jose. Fella I ran into raises em to fight. So they got plenty of spunk. This little black one here is the spunkiest chicken I have ever seen. It is just what your daddy needs to pep up his flock. You know what I mean? Crossbreeding is what I'm talking about. Hybrid vigor."

Though I knew next to nothing about raising chickens, even less about fighting cocks, I knew this sounded like a dangerous idea. I also knew better than to stand in his way. There was whiskey on his breath, and smoke in his clothes, and in his eyes a glint just like that rooster's, somewhere between mischief and madness. Once before, when he was this far along, he had challenged me to a fight. With clenched fists swirling, he had demanded that I punch him as hard as I could, to try for the face. If I was afraid to punch my own uncle in the face, he had cried, I was a yellow-bellied coward and no nephew of his. Today he was on a kind of automatic pilot, he was walking and he was talking, but he was hearing no one, seeing nothing but some crazed vision of how this bird was going to transform his brother's flock—which of course it did.

Holding to his own straight-and-narrow course he moved past the house, past the barn, around a corner of the pen. Once inside the gate, he set the cage down on its side and unlatched the lid.

The cock rushed out, with an impatient lift of sleek black wings, so black, in late sun, the close-trimmed feathers had a purple tinge. As if surprised to find no adversary there, it stopped in the middle of the yard, muscular and nervous, its head twitching, its tense legs ready to spring.

Anderson had probably picked up that bird right after a fight. Spurs were still tied to its heels, little knives that looked dark with what might have been blood, though I wasn't sure. He only stood still a few seconds. These cocks that have been trained to kill, they must feed on fear. It must bring out the worst in them. The leghorns had scurried for the fence, clucking and bunching. This black rooster went for the other males first, then started after the hens, ripping and slashing, jabbing at eyes, sometimes lifting off the ground to drive spurs into a defenseless breast or wing or rump.

I remember Anderson poised in the half-open gateway, for a long moment of stupefied horror, while a few birds made their escape between his legs. He began to kick at them, warning, "Look out now! Look out!" Then he was a barnyard dancer, waving his arms at the flurry, shouting, "Hyeah! Hyeah!" Wary of the rapier beak, he made some half-hearted lunges. Finally he yelled at me to go inside and get my .22.

Loading it took a while. The rifle stood behind my desk. The shells were in another room, one dad kept locked. By the time I came bounding through the back door, his pickup had pulled into the driveway. I watched him climb out and walk to the fence and gaze at what he knew was his brother's handiwork. Some birds had fluttered out the gate or into the safety of the henhouse. At least half were dead or badly wounded, flopping around with broken wings, broken backs, fluid running from a torn eye. It was a battlefield of feathers and carcasses, with one bird still on two feet, the spent but victorious killer cock, his black coat gleaming with blood.

For a silent minute dad surveyed this carnage. His teeth pressed together until the jaw muscles stood out like flat rocks inside his cheeks. Then he turned toward Anderson, sitting on the woodpile about twenty feet away with his face in his hands. Dad walked over to the chopping block, freed the hand axe and stood there until Anderson raised his head. Seeing the axe, he swallowed what he probably figured was going to be his final swallow.

Dad turned away and walked to the chicken pen and kicked open the gate and kicked leghorn carcasses out of the way. When he had the battle-weary rooster cornered, he grabbed it behind the neck in a grip so sudden and tight, the bird looked paralyzed. Squeezing it at arm's length, he brought it back to the block. This seemed to revive the bird, whose squirming life-fear, in turn, revived Anderson. Cold sober now, his face filled with pleading, he looked up and said, "Don't do it, Dudley."

The hand axe rose, and Anderson said it again. "Please don't do it. That rooster cost me fifty dollars."

"FIFTY DOLLARS!" my father shouted. "That's damn near half your pension check!"

"That's what I'm trying to tell you."

The axe fell with such force, the blade sank two inches into the wood, while the black head went one way, and the rest of the bird went the other.

They watched it run in circles, with blood spurting from the open neck, until the life was spent and it fell over into the dirt.

Quietly my father said, "I want you to go get that bird and pluck it."

Tears were streaming down Anderson's face, tears of relief that he himself was still alive. He said, "Pluck it?"

"I want you to pull out every last feather, and that includes the real small ones underneath the wings and inside the legs."

"What for?"

"We're gonna eat that bird for dinner tonight. If it cost fifty dollars, we might as well get some use out of it."

"I tried to bargain that fella down, Dudley. I swear I did. But he just wouldn't listen. Fifty was his bottom offer."

Disgusted, my father stepped back into the pen, where he began to clean up the mess, salvage what he could. He sent me out to round up the strays. Anderson went to work on the rooster. About an hour later he presented it to my mother, who had come home from an afternoon's shopping to find her dinner menu slightly revised. She had cooked a lot of chickens, but never a fighting cock. She decided to boil it, and she let it boil for a long time, hoping for some kind of stew.

Late that night, when we sat down to supper, we discovered that boiling only made it tougher. In death as in life that bird was solid muscle. Though narrow strips of flesh could eventually be torn from the bone, they were unchewable. Several minutes of silent struggle passed before anyone dared to mention this.

With a hopeful grin Anderson said, "It's not that bad."

"I suppose I could have tried roasting it," my mother said.

"It's not that bad at all," Anderson went on, "considering the life this bird has led."

He winked at me and then at my sister, and we would have laughed, were it not for the cloud hanging over the table, which was the great cloud of my father's disappointment in the brother who had gone too far. Anderson knew this, even as he tried one more time to get a rise out of him.

"Fact a the matter is, what we're lookin at here is a fifty-dollar dinner. Now I know you ain't never had a dinner that was that expensive, Dudley. I'd say we're eatin mighty high on the hog tonight!"

Dad nodded. "I guess you're right, Andy. We'd have to drive clear to San Francisco to get a dinner that cost this much."

Anderson's laugh burst out, raucous and full of phlegm. He pounded on the table. "You kids hear what your daddy just said? We'd have to drive clear to San Francisco!"

His laugh filled the kitchen and went on for a long time, but all it drew from dad was a thin smile, a painfully courteous smile for the brother who had finally pushed him past his limit.

Years later, we would all be able to laugh about that day, dad too, the way he laughed about the time Andy's foot got stuck behind his neck. I see now that Anderson had always been the one to do this for him, in a way no one else could—rile him, stir him, tickle his funnybone. But this time forgiveness was still a long way off. And it turned out to be the last night Anderson sat at our table.

As time went by, news would trickle our way, from other relatives who had taken him in, or invented reasons not to. For a while, as I heard the stories others had to tell, I thought dad had been too gullible, the way he had let Andy talk him into things year after year, then steal his clothes and his time and his trust. It's clear to me now that dad loved him more and had put up with his antics longer than anyone else had been able to.

I don't know what passed between them, in private, before he left, but he was gone the next morning, heading back to Texas, the dark uncle, the dangerous uncle, the uncle you never forget.

Water Witch
Louis Owens
Salinas Valley

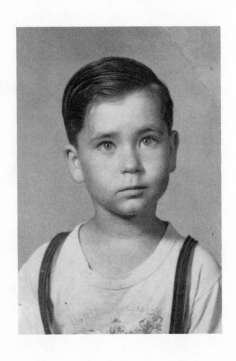

For a while, when I was very young, my father was a water witch. He took us with him sometimes, my older brother and me, and we walked those burned-up central California ranches, wherever there was a low spot that a crop-and-cattle desperate rancher could associate with a dream of wetness. The dusty windmills with their tin blades like pale flowers would be turning tiredly or just creaking windward now and then, and the ranch dogs—always long-haired, brown and black with friendly eyes—would sweep their tails around from a respectful distance. The ranches, scattered near places like Creston, Pozo, San Miguel, and San Ardo, stretched across burnt gold hills, the little ranch houses bent into themselves beneath a few dried up cottonwoods or sycamores, some white oaks if the rancher's grandfather had settled early enough to choose his spot. Usually there would be kids, three or four ranging from diapers to hotrod pickups, and like the friendly ranch dogs they'd keep their distance. The cattle would hang close to the fences, eyeing the house and gray barn. In the sky, red-tailed hawks wheeled against a washed-out sun while ground squirrels whistled warnings from the grain stubble.

He'd walk, steps measured as if the earth demanded measure, the willow fork held in both hands before him pointed at the ground like some kind of offering. We'd follow a few yards behind with measured paces. And nearly always the wand would finally tremble, dip and dance toward the dead wild oats, and he would stop to drive a stick into the ground or pile a few rock-dry clods in a cairn.

83

A displaced Mississippi Choctaw, half-breed, squat and reddish, blind in one eye, he'd spit tobacco juice at the stick or cairn and turn back toward the house, feeling maybe the stirring of Yazoo mud from the river of his birth as if the water he never merely discovered, but drew all that way from a darker, damper world. Within a few days he'd be back with his boss and they'd drill a well at the spot he'd marked. Not once did the water fail, but always it was hidden and secret, for that was the way of water in our part of California.

When I think now of growing up in that country, the southern end of the Salinas Valley, a single mountain range from the ocean, I remember first the great hidden water, the Salinas River which ran out of the Santa Lucias and disappeared where the coastal mountains bent inland near San Luis Obispo. Dammed at its headwaters into a large reservoir where we caught bluegill and catfish, the river never had a chance. Past the spillway gorge, it sank into itself and became the largest subterranean river on the continent, a half-mile-wide swath of brush and sand and cottonwoods with a current you could feel down there beneath your feet when you hunted the river bottom, as if a water witch yourself, you swayed at every step toward the stream below.

We lived first in withdrawn canyons in the Santa Lucias, miles up dirt roads into the creases of the Coast Range where we kids squirmed through buck brush and plotted long hunts to the ocean. But there were no trails and the manzanita would turn us back with what we thought must be the scent of the sea in our nostrils. Rattlesnakes, bears and mountain lions lived back there. And stories of mythic wild boars drifted down from ranches to the north. In the spring the hills would shine with new grass and the dry creeks would run for a few brief weeks. We'd hike across a ridge to ride wild horses belonging to a man who never knew that the kids rode them. In summer the grasses burned brown and the clumps of live oaks on the hillsides formed dark places in the distance.

Later we lived down in the valley on the caving banks of the river. At six and eight years we had hunted with slingshots in the mountains, but at ten and twelve we owned rifles, .22s, and we stalked the dry river brush for quail and cottontails and the little brush rabbits that, like the pack rats, were everywhere. Now and then a deer would break ahead of us, crashing thickets like the bear himself. Great horned owls lived there and called in drumming voices, vague warnings of death somewhere. From the river bottom we pinged .22 slugs off new farm equipment gliding past on the flatcars of the Southern Pacific.

Once in a while, we'd return to Mississippi, as if my father's mixed blood sought a balance never found. Seven kids, a dog or two, canvas water bags swaying from fender and radiator, we drove into what I remember as the darkness of the Natchez Trace. In our two-room Mississippi cabin, daddy longlegs crawled across the tar papered walls, and cotton fields surged close on three sides. Across the rutted road through a tangle of tree, brush, and vine, fragrant of rot and death, was the Yazoo River, a thick current cutting us off from the swamps that boomed and cracked all night from the other shore.

From the Yazoo we must have learned to feel water as a presence, a constant, a secret source of both dream and nightmare, perhaps as my father's Choctaw ancestors had. I remember it as I remember night. Always we'd return to California after a few months, as much as a year. And it would be an emergence, for the Salinas was a daylight world of hot, white sand and bone-dry brush, where in the fall, red and gold leaves covered the sand, and frost made silver lines from earth to sky. Here, death and decay seemed unrelated things. And here, I imagined the water as a clear, cold stream through white sand beneath my feet.

Only in the winter did the Salinas change. When the rains came pounding down out of the Coast Range, the river would rise from its bed to become a half-mile-wide terror, sweeping away chicken coops and misplaced barns; whatever had crept too near. Tricked each year into death, steelhead trout would dash upstream from the ocean, and almost immediately the flooding river would recede to a thin stream at the heart of the dry bed, then a few pools marked by the tracks of coons, then only sand again and the tails and bones of big fish.

When I think of growing up in California, I think always of the river. It seemed then that all life referred to the one hundred and twenty miles of sand and brush that twisted its way northward, an upside-down, backwards river that emptied into the Pacific near Monterey, a place I didn't see till I was grown. As teenagers, my brother and I bought our own rifles, a .30-.30 and an ought-six, and we followed our father into the Coast Range after deer and wild boar. We acquired shotguns and walked the high coastal ridges for bandtail pigeon. We drove to fish the headwaters of the Nacimiento and San Antonio rivers. And from every ridge top we saw, if not the river itself, then the long, slow course of the valley it had carved, the Salinas. Far across were the rolling Gabilan Mountains, more hawk hills than mountains, and on the valley bottom, ranches made squares of green and gold with flashing windmills and tin roofs.

After school and during summers we worked on the ranches, hoeing sugar beets, building fences, bucking hay, working cattle (dehorning, castrating, branding, ear-clipping, innoculating, all in what must have seemed a single horrific moment for the bawling calf). We'd cross the river to drive at dawn through the dry country watching the clumps of live oak separate from the graying hillsides. Moving shadows would become deer that drifted from dark to dark. Years later, coming home from another state, I would time my drive so that I reached that country at daybreak to watch the oaks rise out of night and to smell the damp dead grasses.

Snaking its way down through our little town was a creek. Dipping out of the Coast Range, sliding past chicken farms and country stores, it pooled in long, shadowed clefts beneath the shoulders of hills and dug its own miniature canyon as it passed by the high school, beneath U.S. 101, around the flanks of the county hospital and on to the river where it gathered in a final welling before sinking into the sand. Enroute it picked up the sweat and stink of a small town, the flotsam and jetsam of stunted aspirations, and along its course in tree shadow and root tangle, under cutbank and log, it hid small, dark trout we caught with hook and handline. From the creek came also steelhead trapped by a vanished river, and great blimp-bellied suckers which hunkered close to the bottom, even a single outraged bull-head which I returned to its solitary pool. At the place where the chicken-processing plant disgorged a yellow stream into the creek, the trout grew fat and sluggish, easily caught. We learned every shading and wrinkle of the creek, not knowing then that it was on the edge already, its years num-bered. I more than anyone, fisher of tainted trout, kept what I thought of as a pact with the dying creek: as long as the water flows and the grass grows.

Up on Pine Mountain, not so much looming as leaning over the town of my younger years, a well-kept cemetery casts a wide shadow. From this cemetery, one fine summer evening, a local youth exhumed his grand-mother to drive about town with her draped across the hood of his car, an act so shocking no punishment could be brought to bear. Later, when I asked him why, he looked at me in wonder. "Didn't you ever want to do that?" he asked. That fall, after a bitter football loss, members of the high-school letterman's club kidnapped a bus full of rooters from a rival school, holding them briefly at gunpoint with threats of execution. The summer before, an acquaintance of mine had stolen a small plane and dive-bombed the town's hamburger stand with empty beer bottles. The town laughed. Later, he caught a Greyhound bus to Oregon, bought a shotgun in a small town, and killed himself. It was that kind of place also. Stagnant between Coast Range and river, the town, too, had subterranean currents, a hot-in-summer, cold-in-winter kind of submerged violence that rippled the sur-face again and again. Desires to exhume and punish grew strong. Escape was just around a corner.

Behind the cemetery, deep in a wrinkle of the mountain, was an older burial ground, the town's original graveyard, tumbled and hidden in long grasses and falling oaks. Parting the gray oat stalks to read the ancient stone, I felt back then as astonished as a Japanese soldier must have when he first heard the words of a Navajo code talker. Here was a language that pricked through time, millenia perhaps, with painful familiarity but one that remained inexorably remote.

A year ago, I drove back to the house nine of us had lived in on the banks of the river. The house was gone, and behind the empty lot the river had changed. Where there had been a wilderness of brush and cottonwoods was now only a wide, empty channel gleaming like bone. Alfalfa fields swept coolly up from the opposite bank toward a modern ranch house. "Flood control" someone in the new Denny's restaurant told me later that afternoon. "Cleaned her out clear to San Miguel," he said.

Central Valley

Going in Naked
Richard Dokey
Stockton

There were no suburbs when I was a boy. There was just a town, and you went over a railroad track, a road or a canal and there was the country.

I lived in the country.

Stockton was a small place among smaller places strung up and down the Central Valley, and it had no pretensions, as it does now, of being a big place. Growing up, ten miles out of town on the 99 among farms and fields, I thought San Francisco was a thousand miles away because I always fell asleep in the car coming home from there. My world has been shrinking ever since, and now everyplace is just next door.

There was no television when I was a boy. There were no stereos or computers or digital phones. There were not even any electric ranges, dishwashers or garbage disposals. No central air or heat. No frozen food. Our Wedgewood gas stove had two miniature black manhole covers you lifted off with a wire handle to burn paper. I stood above a floor grate in the hallway near the bathroom door in the winter and held my Levis and cords over the furnace so the heat would warm them before I put them on. My mother dried clothes there across a red kitchen chair.

We had a fireplace and the wood was stacked in the shed out back. A man named Jay brought a truckload of mill ends from a lumberyard each year and we had two metal baskets on the hearth, one for the blocks and another for the logs. A fire was always going. Sometimes, when it got truly cold, my mother would leave the oven door open in the kitchen and turn up the blue flame. I put my hands inside the oven to get them warm.

Having nothing electronic to do, my brother Jack and I became self-reliant. We made up everything. When it wasn't fishing or hunting or swimming or bike riding or fort building, it was popping tennis balls against my parents' bedroom wall or building model planes out of balsa wood or reading our collection of Big Little Books with the pictures up in the corner that moved when you thumbed the pages or watching the rain sheet down from the shingled roof or playing on the swings at school.

It was a big brick grammar school and the teachers were women and we played football and baseball and soccer and shot marbles in a circle on the blacktop under the oaks or laid out a course of small holes in the clay dirt and worked our way up and down through them, taking turns. We rode in circles on the merry-go-round, and I liked riding on it by myself. I held onto the metal wheel and ran it around and around as fast as I could and then jumped onto the bar and climbed down into the metal tray where all the spokes came together. I lay down there, my head hanging over the edge, and watched the whole world spin. Or I pumped myself up as high as I could in the swing until the steel legs began to lift and then got it up truly high and allowed myself to fly out of the seat at just the apex and drop like a stone into the sand below. Or I went headfirst down the slide that had the steel shiny from the pants and dresses over all the years, or a bunch of us would gang up, locking our legs around each other, and go down like a huge centipede.

The teachers didn't supervise us much and sometimes we fought out on the playground or climbed over the chain link fence into the wheat fields beyond. We played hide and seek and sang, "All you, all you outs in free," and made up a game about throwing a volleyball over the brick shed where the principal parked her car.

Jack and I built go-cycles. We took the wheels off a couple pair of old roller skates and fastened them to yard-long planks of scrap wood, two wheels in front, two in back. Then on one end we nailed a lug box up at right angles and fixed a board across that for a handle. When the traffic was clear on the 99, we skimmed the go-cycles along the macadam surface. My father made us a couple pairs of stilts and we hopped around the backyard, racing and falling to the grass.

When the Barnum and Bailey Circus came to town, we got up early and my father drove us to the depot where they were unloading the animals. I liked to watch the elephants with their great thick walking and how, later, they used their rope skin trunks to lift the long poles and help set up the tents in the vacant lot. All the circus people pitched in and there was much noise and dust and then that night we went to see the real show, three rings going and the clowns with baggy pants and polka-dot suspenders and red bulb noses and people spinning through the air being caught and horses running around and around with beautiful women standing on them and tigers jumping through burning hoops. There was nothing like the circus.

Sometimes I would sleep over at Harold Parrish's house. He lived on a farm on Lower Sacramento Road and we built forts in the hay bales in the barn or went horseback riding or made slingshots out of tree branches and old inner tubes and shot at tin cans or blackbirds. In the summer I rode on the yellow Cat while he plowed the fields. I went to sleep listening to the cattle lowing out in the pasture, and in the morning his mother gave us oatmeal with raisins and oven-baked bread.

Or I would hang out at Slim's Market, which was a block up the 99. Slim kept his ice cream in a metal floor box next to the register. The box had three lids with black rubber handles, and when you opened it, ice cream air came out. The ice cream was in cardboard barrels and there were chocolate, strawberry and vanilla and sometimes maplenut, which was my favorite. The Popsicles and Eskimo Pies were stacked along one side and Slim didn't want you to eat ice cream and read comic books at the same time, so I would sit on the floor next to the rack and read Superman or Captain Marvel and then buy my ice cream for a nickel a scoop and walk home.

Slim was always generous with his ice cream and lived behind the store and trusted everyone, and one day he was in back so I stole a five cent bag of Planters Peanuts, went out under a telephone pole and ate them. I could not sleep that night and the next day I went back to the store and, when he was looking the other way, I put one of my nickels onto the register. Then I sat down and read comic books.

*   *   *

Our house had a basement. Actually, it wasn't a basement, it was a cellar, a cubicle ten-by-eight. The house sat up on pillars and you could see the underpinnings of the flooring where unspeakable creatures lived. There were a couple of light bulbs. A cot was on one side and on the other, above a wooden cabinet, where my mother stored the crocks of green and black olives she put up and the canned waxed peppers, beets, cucumbers, string beans, tomatoes from the garden, the apricot, peach and grape preserves and all the fruit from the trees out back and my father kept his pickled catfish and horseradish, Jack and I built our model airplanes and kites.

It was the only cool place in the summer, and often I'd go down there and close the cellar door, which was just above the ground, and absorb the cool insouciance of concrete and earth.

The house was a wood frame structure with two bedrooms and one tiny bath whose screened window looked out onto the backyard. There was a porcelain tub in the bathroom. The tub got too small for me quite soon, but I didn't know what a shower was and took my first one after a P.E. class in high school when I was thirteen.

There were lots of windows in the house and in the summer they were always open. I liked that better than having the swamp cooler on. It sat on a wooden platform that stood outside my parents' bedroom window. My father built the cooler out of a fruit box and cut up potato sacks. He rigged a hose to drop water across the sacks and put a small fan into the box. The fan blew air through the wet sacking into the house. On the truly hot days it was as humid as a jungle.

When it really stoked up in the late afternoon, we set the kitchen table out on the lawn behind the house. Mom laid out the oilcloth and we carried all the food outside and swatted flies away as we ate the corn and tomatoes, the fried chicken and biscuits and drank the lemonade from the glass pitcher decorated with yellow flowers. There was a porch swing out back too, and I rode it or lay down or ate watermelon, spitting the seeds into the lawn and throwing the rinds into the Podesta's walnut orchard next door.

Jack and I were always hungry. We consumed a small loaf of white Langendorf bread and a half gallon of milk between us every time we sat down. There were always home-baked pies and cookies and cake. My mother made everything from scratch. All the soft drinks were regular, straight stuff, and my father mixed his whiskey with Coke before dinner. He called it a Coke High, and the refrigerator an icebox, and he played the harmonica and was a damned good cook.

I liked lying on a blanket on the lawn at dusk on a summer evening and watching the light fade from the sky. All the stars came out from behind a dark tissue, and when the moon was up, the air was filled with a pale luminosity against which the nightbirds formed darting silhouettes. The traffic on the 99 lessened and Jack and I could guess what car was coming by the sound of the engine. "That's a Chevy." "No, that's a Ford." And you could hear a big semi a long way off and then the growl going by opposite the house and then the distance of it bound for Sacramento.

Later, near sleep, I would watch the headlights of the cars move along my bedroom wall. The lights appeared when the car was far off. They traveled slowly at first, illuminating the rose-flowered wallpaper above my window. Then they hurried a bit, turning the corner and moving along the south wall until, with a quick brightness, they disappeared into the dark above my brother's bed.

I loved the wide and solitary night as well as the day, and I loved the lights that moved along my bedroom wall. They were as constant and unchanging as the beating of my heart.

My father always had a garden and I hated working there. He had been raised on a farm in Michigan and there were farms all around us but my father was a printer now and I saw no reason for hoeing and weeding and watering vegetables when we could go down to Slim's Market and buy all we wanted.

But I did love the corn picked fresh from the stalk and the sweet white onions pulled from the ground and popped into my mouth like candy. I loved the smell of tomatoes warm on the vine and the way eggplant looked in the sunlight. So my father made me work there and it was a good thing, after all, because I learned that often we must do things we don't like to have the fruit of that which we enjoy.

We had a Royal Anne cherry tree behind the house and my father added booze and made Maraschino cherries. He made beer and fermented it in two large crocks in the cellar. He kept a worm bed too. It was under one of the faucets out back that we used to irrigate the garden. We dumped coffee grounds on the bed and the dirt was always rich and damp. You could put a shovel down anytime and in a couple of turns find all the red worms you wanted for a day of fishing out in the delta.

We were always out there, seated along a levee with bobbers floating in the earth-brown water, and my father threw the perch and catfish into a metal bucket to keep them alive. We cleaned them at home and I was always bothered by the catfish because if one of those spines went into you, you'd feel it for days, and they always had a way of going into you.

My father cooked the perch and catfish and even the trout we caught up on the Mokelumne in the Sierra by dumping them into a paper lunch bag of flour, salt and pepper and then laying them on a greased pan. My brother and I still cook them that way, only now we do our fishing in Montana.

There were sheds for rabbits and chickens and turkeys. The rabbits were slaughtered and hung up to drain. My father had driven two nails through a board and then fastened the board to the shed wall. He pegged both feet of a rabbit to a nail, made a cut around the feet and then pulled the skin away all in one piece right over the head, and the blood dripped along the grey boards and puddled on the concrete walk. Later the hides were nailed to the clapboard walls. There was a chopping block for chickens and when the ax came down in one quick stroke, they flopped in an idiotic, pointless way, spraying blood everywhere, until the bodies realized the heads were off.

We plucked the chickens by dumping them into boiling water, holding them in our laps and then stripping them. There was a kid down the highway named Alvin who, when he went swimming, had hair that smelled that way too, just like wet chicken feathers out of a boiling pot.

My father even decided once that he wanted to raise chickens professionally to make a little extra money. It was the true farm blood coming out. So he bought some brooders and chicks. The brooders were aluminum, pie-shaped things with light bulbs and the bulbs had to burn all night to keep the chicks warm. I liked to pet the tiny yellow bodies in winter when they huddled together. It was okay for a while and my father sold some of the chickens when they got big to a couple of restaurants in town and to a few friends. Then the pullets started pecking each other and some died and then some from the cold or disease and my father couldn't watch them all the time because he had to work and my mother was handling Jack and me anyway, so they started really dying and my father said to hell with it and sold the fryers and the brooders. And then Jack and I used the sheds to play in.

That was when the famous BB gun affair happened.

We got matching Red Ryders that year and went out plinking fence posts and apples and a stray cat or two. Then I let Jack have one for the heck of it one afternoon just to see what it would be like. After all, I was bigger by seventeen months. He wouldn't dare do anything. So he yelled, cursed me and, tearing for the house, shouted his cry of revenge.

I hid beneath one of the roosting shelves in the sheds, huddled back in the far corner where he couldn't see me.

In a few moments I saw his legs come into the shed. His feet walked around a bit. I held my breath. The legs stopped on the concrete pad just where I was hiding. Then I saw his face appear, bent over to leer at me.

"No, Jack, no," I pleaded.

But he pointed the Red Ryder at me and carefully let me have it in the shoulder.

And so we were even.

There was a rail that ran the length of the sheds and was fixed to the interior roof. A wooden platform the size of a small mattress was suspended from this rail on wheels. It was originally meant to make it easy to move sacks of feed through the sheds, but Jack and I used the platform like a skateboard, racing up and back, riding on one knee and pumping with the other foot. Or we took turns pushing each other and got the thing up to speed and let go. We could glide the whole distance that way.

One day a crop duster crashed into Podesta's walnut orchard next door. We ran over to look. The plane was nose down in the earth and the pilot was okay and a lot of people stood around and watched the plane just stuck there tail up. The pilot stood too and we all looked, as though something wondrous and exciting were about to happen. Nobody seemed to realize that it already had. That was the day I lost my brown leather wallet with my dollar bills, while running under the walnut trees toward the fallen plane.

We had a dog. Actually, there were several dogs, but they all disappeared or were killed on the highway, so there was only one dog really, Tippy, a blue-tongued chow. My parents got him when I was three.

Tippy was a smart dog. He slept under the concrete washtub on the back porch and roamed freely about the countryside. We took him on all the camping trips into the Sierras. My father nailed a wooden handle at right angles to the bottom edge of the screen door, and he got in that way whenever he felt like it.

One day he went over to Podesta's and killed two dozen chickens. Podesta wanted to shoot him so my father offered to pay for the chickens, but Podesta wouldn't take the money because the dog was only a puppy. My father beat Tippy with the dead chickens and even tied a dead chicken around his neck, but it didn't do any good. On another day our turkeys got out and Tippy killed them all and we had to stay up late plucking feathers and my father sold the turkeys to a restaurant in town, and then Tippy stopped being a puppy and the massacres ended.

Then he got hit out on the highway by a big semi and we thought he was done. His hind end was crooked. He crawled under the tub on the back porch, dragging his back legs, and my father couldn't shoot him so he went to Mr. Krupke, a German neighbor, and asked him to do it. I was crying and so was my brother. Mr. Krupke said he would do it and came over with his shotgun but when he saw Tippy, he said, "Just keep him warm, he will be all right," and went away. My father put blankets around him and Tippy lay under the tub for three weeks. Jack and I placed saucers of water near his head and scraps from the table and he finally got better. After that he always crossed the highway like a person, looking both ways, and he sat on his haunches out front waiting for Jack and me to get out of school, and when he saw us coming along the highway, he ran to meet us. Tippy lived to be seventeen and died of the things all dogs die of, one day in the shade under the gas tank of my car when I was home from Berkeley for the weekend. He didn't recognize me.

Hoboes came to our house. There was a regular parade of them. They were everywhere in the thirties and early forties and it was okay. Nobody ever got robbed or hurt by a hobo.

They marked our mailbox because my mother was a soft touch. Maybe it was that she was from a family of twelve kids and oranges at Christmas were a big deal.

The hoboes came to the back door, two or three a week, asking, "Ma'am, could you please spare some coffee and a bite to eat?" and my mother would fix a sandwich, sometimes with a cookie or a piece of fruit. I watched the man standing there outside the screen door waiting. He was usually dressed in a dirty shirt and scruffy brown pants and shoes that looked like feet. His bundle rested on the ground. He mopped his brow and there was a red line where his hat stopped. He waited with a patience that seemed almost tranquil. There was no place he had to go and he was in no hurry to get there. Sometimes my mother told me to give the man the food she had wrapped in waxed paper. I did but thought there was something I might catch if the man's fingers touched mine. It was hard to look into a hobo's eyes.

Sometimes a hobo would rake leaves or work a little for the food but my mother never made one work. Nobody ever asked for money. Some of them wanted to sleep in the sheds out back but my father said no because all the hoboes smoked and he was afraid the sheds would catch fire. One Thanksgiving a hobo came to the door just as we were having dinner and my father filled a plate and took it out to him.

But what they wanted most of all was coffee, and it's been a long time and there are no hoboes anymore, but I think now that I did catch something from those wandering men who owned nothing and went alone through the valley of my childhood.

*   *   *

When I wanted to go anywhere as a kid, it was usually on my bike, a red Schwinn with balloon tires. My parents gave matching ones to my brother and me one joyous Christmas morning. The night before we had gone to bed with no inkling of what the dawn would bring. Usually my mother kept the gifts in the hall closet because Jack and I were adept at peeling back the wrappings and checking out the boxes and oddly shaped bundles as they appeared beneath the tree in those days before Christmas. So we scouted the closet, Jack stationed to watch as I noiselessly pried away at the gifts.

But my father outfoxed us. He had taken the bikes next door to Ross and Isa's, and so there they were, shining behind the tree on Christmas morning. That bike was the finest gift I had ever received.

I rode it everywhere, miles from home, carrying my trunks, a towel around my neck to go swimming, or I borrowed my brother's over-and-under 4-10 to shoot pheasant or quail or duck or just birds, or I went up Hammer Lane to watch the airplanes take off and land at Orange's Airport, and I even rode it into town.

There were open fields all around and I liked riding alone up a road with no white line. There was one particular place, where a dirt lane went off along the S.P. railroad tracks. That was prime hunting territory. Rabbits and squirrels as well as quail and pheasant. I prowled through the brush and grass. There were no sounds except those I made. No houses to worry about. No people. Just me and the over-and-under 4-10, hunting through the wilderness of childhood. Most of the time I didn't care if I shot anything. It was just the idea that I was there and I had that 4-10 and I could take the life of any flying or hopping creature that came my way. It gave me a sense of humility and respect for life. So after a while I didn't want to kill anything. I was only hunting myself anyway.

My father had an old white Hudson coupe, and that's the car I learned to drive in. One day he said, "Here, take the keys and go on up the back road."

I had sat in his lap plenty of times holding the wheel and steering. And Jack and I had ridden on the fenders, the wind whipping our hair. It was no big deal, I thought.

I got in behind the wheel and started the car. I could barely see over the dash to the rutted path that was an extension of our gravel driveway. The path went in a straight line between Podesta's walnut orchard to the south and our land to the north and past a field where we flew our kites. Then it connected to a paved road a quarter of a mile away.

I drove with courage and no skill. The Hudson ducked to left and right and I oversteered to compensate, trying to manage all those things, clutch, brake, wheel and shift knob. I was helped by the field grass that grew down the center and both sides of the path. When I strayed too far, it let me know.

When I got to the gravel road, I drove up to Morada Lane and turned around. I had conquered the world and knew that the two wheels of my red Schwinn would no longer be enough to satisfy my wanderlust.

I hitchhiked into town a lot or took the Greyhound. All I had to do was stand by the 99 when one came along, wave and it would stop in a pillow of dust, enormous black tires coming toward me at eye level. The door hissed open and away I went.

There was no problem hitchhiking. It was an honorable way to travel. I rode often with strangers.

One time I was walking along the 99, my back to traffic, the way you do while resting from the rigors of lifting your thumb. Cars and trucks flew by, blowing my shirt and pants.

Then I felt a violent thud against the backs of my legs, and my knees buckled. I looked up to see a flatbed truck hurrying by filled with watermelons and this sonofabitch in a white T-shirt riding on the watermelons and laughing. He had been just a bit off. Another half second and he would have caught me in the small of the back. As it was, there were red pulp and seeds all over my legs, so I had to go home and change my pants.

The only time I've ever been lost was on that Schwinn bike. I had gone up Morada Lane into territory I had never before explored. I came into an intersection, staring about at the strange trees and the strange houses. When I looked down, I could not remember which way I had come. All the roads were the same, and even at that age I knew that if I went off down one, I might be going in the opposite direction from home. So I walked tentatively up to a front door and knocked. It was the most embarrassing thing to tell the man who answered that I was lost. "What's your name?" he asked. I told him and I guess he looked in the phone book because in a few minutes my father appeared, loaded the Schwinn into the trunk of the car and drove me home.

I have since wandered about Europe with no itinerary and only a single bag on my shoulder, knowing not where I would spend the night, unafraid because I knew that when I asked myself the question, "Where am I?" I could answer exactly. "I'm in Spain."

*   *   *

There were floods when I was a boy. There are photographs of me standing on Ashley Lane, my back to a field filled with brown water. My look is that of a refugee child waiting by the road out of a town that the enemy has been bombarding.

There were no dams then and a couple of times Bear Creek overflowed and the water came down the 99 and filled our cellar. We drove the cars through it and it made little wakes around the tires and I would open the car door and listen and put my hand down into the water. We couldn't use the gas furnace for a while or the stove and so my father had to break out the Coleman camp stove to cook dinner. He bought boots for us because even after the water left, the ground was muddy and we could slip off the boots before we entered the back porch. Luckily the water stayed out of the house, but Podesta's walnut orchard was a lake. We took the water out of the cellar with buckets and on the concrete floor were dozens of red worms.

There were peat dust storms. The winds came up in the spring and early summer when the farmers plowed out in the delta. The dust lifted and formed an immense cotton ball of fine dirt that rolled toward the southeast. It was as though a desert had emptied into the sky. The ball came on covering everything and when it hit town, the dust pushed under the doorsills, where it fluttered in the wind currents making little heaps and taking on the shapes of cracks and holes. My mother shut up the house, but it leaked through the windowsills anyway and covered the tables and chairs. She hosed off the windows so we could see. The traffic stopped on the 99 sometimes, it was so thick. The dust got into the corners of your eyes. You blew your nose and there was dust in your handkerchief. You wiped the sweat and there was dust, and when you took your shirt off, dust was under your arms and along the back of your neck. In the middle of the day the sky was black and sometimes the sun shone red through a piece of it, like the end of the world.

The tule fog appeared usually around the first week in November. It was a vapory, gray fog and you could see the droplets hanging in the air. Sometimes the fog, as it still does, hung on for weeks, and after a while you forgot there was a sky or sun. You forgot there were clouds or birds. There were ducks, though, or geese, flying through the mist, trailing plaintive, mournful cries, like the tails of kites.

I always liked the fog. It was deep and mysterious and seemed to shed the earth, like a bright skin, and leave only my little world of school and home. Everything else went away, but I and all that was mine remained, covered by a blanket.

Later, when I was in high school and staying out, I drove home late at night, the window down and my head into the swirling gray air, trying to see that one white line ahead beneath my headlights.

The Second Great War came through my boyhood. Truck convoys went by our house along the 99. I didn't know what war was but I liked watching the long strings of olive drab vehicles go by, driven by men who wore clothes that were the same color. There were big trucks with what appeared to be tents in back, like Conestoga wagons, and the tents were filled with men dressed in olive drab. Some of the trucks pulled cannons with big black tires and the line of them went on so long, each vehicle evenly spaced from the others, that I was always disappointed when the last one vanished from view and there were only automobiles. Sometimes a train would go by on the S.P. railroad tracks while I was hunting for rabbits, and I saw army tanks with great steel treads. The tanks were green too.

Then there were the B-17s, like huge swarms of petrified birds that glided overhead. A hundred or more would come, low, engines a cataract of noise. I liked the B-17s more than the trucks. It was as though the sky had become a tapestry of gleaming metal, painted in odd, curling designs. When they were gone the silence was deafening.

Sometimes when I went into town to see movies, they would have the *Eyes and Ears of the World News* and there would be those tanks and cannon bucking and making smoke and the B-17s, like stone birds, releasing strings of sausage black droppings that went down to the earth and made splashes of dust.

One summer morning at 2 A.M., a munitions truck loaded with bombs, shells and cartridges blew up on the highway just north of the school. The truck was headed for Sharpe's Depot in Stockton.

Isa Martin ran down the stairs of her house "naked as a jaybird," Ross said later, and the whole neighborhood was under artillery attack.

Shells fell everywhere, some into our backyard. The truck burned and continued to lay down a barrage against a corner of the San Joaquin Valley. Grass fires started. The truck driver ran up and down the highway waving his arms. Then the police came and kept people away and the firemen came and the fires were put out. My father picked up a couple of shells that had dropped behind the house and kept them for souvenirs.

And that was my war.

*   *   *

There was an irrigation canal across the 99 where I lived. It was a deep, earthen canal. The water was an emerald green. Along the banks were cattails and reeds. Tall oaks hung over the sides.

I learned to swim in that canal. My father held me under the chest and I dog-paddled in a circle around him. I felt elated and was all confidence. After a few circles I looked around. My father was standing in the shallow water near the bank. I went down like a rock, blubbered up and made for the shore.

I've learned many things since then in the same way.

My father and Ross Martin constructed a wooden platform that extended over the surface of the water. It was on pilings and a ladder went down into the water. We dove from this platform and the ladder made it easy to get out. But it wasn't very high, and so Jack and I built another platform just large enough for one person to stand on twelve feet up in the oak tree. We nailed scrap boards for rungs up the side of the tree.

Standing on that platform, the water like a slick green wall below me, I dreamt of performances. I was a parachutist dropping from a burning plane, an aerialist in a circus. I fell, stunned, through the hot valley air, and cut through the surface like a knife. When I came up, I spit water and my hair was plastered back and I laughed.

We built a raft, too, and kept it tied to the tree. We poled the raft up the canal to the bridge that crossed over to the school. We dove from the raft, gliding beneath it like sharks looking for prey. There weren't any reeds or cattails that way so it was easy going. We tied a rope to a limb of the oak tree and flung ourselves out, dropping as close to the other bank as we could.

The water level in the canal fluctuated as the farmers around us used it. We adapted, discovering the technique of using our bodies as a plane and bridging up just as we entered the surface. We got so we could dive from the high platform even when the water was only three feet deep. No one ever stuck his head into the peatbog bottom.

I took excursions alone down the reed-infested part of the canal, swimming with the current, diving beneath the surface when the cattails were thick, weaving my way like a crocodile. Sometimes I was scared. There were water snakes, and though they couldn't hurt you, a snake was a snake. Swimming back against the current was tough but I always made it.

The gang played water tag along the banks of the canal and had mud fights. Green tufts of grass whose roots were congested with mud made great weapons. We hurtled them at each other and dove beneath the surface to avoid revenge.

Sometimes the whole family would walk over to swim, and my father would go in naked and lie on his back and sing, "Toot toot, I'm a steamboat." I was embarrassed by that. My mother always wore a suit.

An old man lost a pair of false teeth one afternoon while swimming in our hole. I wasn't there but I heard about it and believed it, of course. People dove all afternoon looking for the teeth until someone stepped on them. For a time after that I was a little hesitant about allowing my feet to touch the muddy bottom of the ditch.

At night sometimes my father would lead my brother and me across the highway and we would hold the flashlight while he speared frogs among the reeds. He dropped the frogs into a bucket of tap water and cleaned them at home and my mother fixed them for dinner. They tasted like chicken.

I saw my first naked girl in the canal. It was always a good thing to swim naked with friends, and we often did, and one afternoon we saw this girl, who looked to be in early high school, and two male companions climb through the barbed wire to our spot and disappear. My friends and I waited and then followed.

The two guys were already in the water. And there she was, naked, getting ready to go in. She sat on the bank and looked at us and I saw the dark, triangular place that was like mine, and yet not like mine at all. There was nothing there, it seemed, but I knew that wasn't so. Something quite marvelous was there, and that's why it wasn't like mine.

Nobody said a word and the boys in the water smiled weakly. The girl didn't smile or say anything and after a while we went away.

We often played in the holes the big turbine pumps cut into the earth while irrigating the fields. The Jorys across the highway had the best one. You could stand up to your chest in the center of it and the water was white and you could barely endure it. It was fine to flop down under the summer sun after coming out of the water and get so hot that you started to sweat and then jump into the hole and have that white water strike you all at once. For one instant there was absolutely no thought in your head.

We were always in water as kids. When it wasn't the canal or a pump hole, it was a swimming pool owned by one of the wealthy families up Morada or Hildreth Lane. The Browns asked us to sand their pool each summer, but that was all right because it was a fine pool and they had an old trolley car for a bathhouse with a hole that you could see through to the girls' side. When pools were not available and we didn't feel like going across to the canal, we ran through sprinklers. I liked to lie on the grass in the sunlight, put my head on my arms and let the water come down over me.

Generally we'd put on our bathing suits in the morning and go swimming until noon, then come home for lunch—you had to rest an hour after eating before returning, to avoid cramps, my mother always insisted. We'd slide back home in the afternoon for a snack, homemade hermit cookies maybe and fresh squeezed lemonade, and then swimming again, day after endless summer day.

My father used to pull our suits down in front of company to show the contrast of our white butts to the rest of our bodies.

*   *   *

When the 99 was just a two lane road running the length of California, flocks of sheep went along it in front our house in the early summer. The sheepdog cut across our lawn to keep them away but sometimes they got into the grass, stopping momentarily to graze. The cars backed up along the highway but there wasn't much traffic then so it didn't matter. And, anyway, there was no reason to hurry. The sheep were only going up the highway a piece to be sheared. Then the shepherd's shack went by and this man with a stick, who whistled at the dog, and the sheep moved along and I ran out to touch a few of the rough, corrugated hides. A week or two later they came back the other way, looking naked and thin.

They moved our house two times when more people came and the traffic got heavier. The two walnut trees out front went down that first time and the house went up on blocks and was shoved back to the new foundation. They dug us a new cellar and helped with the new lawn. Huge yellow dirt wagons and earth movers went back and forth all day in front of the house.

We built sails for our bikes and let the wind carry us miles down the un-opened roadway. We could do this on Saturday and Sunday, after dark when the men weren't working, but we had to be careful at night because the materials left on the roadway were a hazard to wind-sailing bikes. The thrill of flying effortlessly at high speed more than compensated for the hard pump back with the sail furled over the handlebars. They made the 99 three lanes then and that was before I went to grammar school.

Then there were more people and the house went up on blocks again before I left the eighth grade and the highway was four lanes now and called a freeway and most of the front yard was gone and we were back against the sheds. We lost the big cherry tree and a weeping willow that time. I almost got killed one afternoon crossing the freeway to go swimming.

My boyhood was a time of non–interference. There were no truant officers or police—except for Homer Raleigh, who rode for the highway patrol and stopped at the house once in a while to visit with my parents and let Jack and me sit on the black leather seat of his motorcycle. No one attacked anyone or took anyone away in a car and you found them later maybe in a ditch or hidden in some deserted field. The doors to the house were never locked, except when we went for a long time to the mountains, and nobody ever robbed us or stole anything.

I did what I wanted and all my mother needed to know was where I was going in case she had to get hold of me and the only advice my father ever gave me was to keep my pants zipped when I went off to college.

There was danger when I was a boy, but we didn't know it because when we were ready to do anything, we did it, and whatever happened, that's what happened and so we learned. Life was not a warning about what might occur if we weren't careful.

There was an automobile accident one evening in front of the house and the people were carried in from the 99 bleeding and they lay bleeding on the front lawn and my mother brought clean towels and called the ambulance, and then Lupe and Cornelia were killed when their father lost control of his pickup one afternoon and they were thrown out on the highway and Lupe was decapitated. A boy named Elmer, everybody said, was screwing his sister and that seemed believable because at school his face was always puffy and red and he smelled funny, but he never hurt anyone.

It was the tail end of The Great Depression and then The Second Great War and Franklin Delano Roosevelt was the only president I ever knew, and I ran home one day from school because Mr. Roosevelt was dead, they said so on *The Standard Hour,* and in all the suffering and loss and the despair of those years, there was, growing up in the valley of California, the experience of something that was maybe the end of a beginning; when airplanes always had propellers and cars had running boards and there was only the radio, and the motion picture theaters had two features and a couple of cartoons and a serial and the *Movietone News* and previews of coming attractions. All this, and the fact that I grew up in the country, meant that I learned independence at an early age, tempered only indifferently by an idle pleasure that technology might afford.

Then Isa and Ross next door got a television when I was in the eighth grade and invited us over sometimes on Saturday night to watch the black and white screen, and one day my father bought a television because he wanted to follow the Friday night fights.

And boyhood was over.

The Quiet Girl
Maxine Hong Kingston
Stockton

One afternoon in the sixth grade (that year I was arrogant with talk, not knowing there were going to be high-school dances and college seminars to set me back), I and my little sister and the quiet girl and her big sister stayed late after school for some reason. The cement was cooling, and the tetherball poles made shadows across the gravel. The hooks at the rope ends were clinking against the poles. We shouldn't have been so late; there was laundry work to do and Chinese school to get to by 5:00. The last time we had stayed late, my mother had phoned the police and told them we had been kidnapped by bandits. The radio stations broadcast our descriptions. I had to get home before she did that again. But sometimes if you loitered long enough in the schoolyard, the other children would have gone home and you could play with the equipment before the office took it away. We were chasing one another through the playground and in and out of the basement, where the playroom and lavatory were. During air raid drills (it was during the Korean War, which you knew about because every day the front page of the newspaper printed a map of Korea with the top part red and going up and down like a window shade), we curled up in this basement. Now everyone was gone. The playroom was army green and had nothing in it but a long trough with drinking spigots in rows. Pipes across the ceiling led to the drinking fountains and to the toilets in the next room. When someone flushed you could hear the water and other matter, which the children named, running inside the big pipe above the drinking spigots. There was one playroom for girls next to the girls' lavatory and one playroom for boys next to the boys' lavatory. The stalls were open and the toilets had no lids, by which we knew that ghosts have no sense of shame or privacy.

Inside the playroom the lightbulbs in cages had already been turned off. Daylight came in x-patterns, through the caging at the windows. I looked out and, seeing no one in the schoolyard, ran outside to climb the fire escape upside down, hanging on to the metal stairs with fingers and toes.

I did a flip off the fire escape and ran across the schoolyard. The day was a great eye, and it was not paying much attention to me now. I could disappear with the sun; I could turn quickly sideways and slip into a different world. It seemed I could run faster at this time, and by evening I would be able to fly. As the afternoon wore on we could run into the forbidden places—the boys' big yard, the boys' playroom. We could go into the boys' lavatory and look at the urinals. The only time during school hours I had crossed the boys' yard was when a flatbed truck with a giant thing covered with canvas and tied down with ropes had parked across the street. The children had told one another that it was a gorilla in captivity; we couldn't decide whether the sign said "Trail of the Gorilla" or "Trial of the Gorilla." The thing was as big as a house. The teachers couldn't stop us from hysterically rushing to the fence and clinging to the wire mesh. Now I ran across the boys' yard clear to the Cyclone fence and thought about the hair that I had seen sticking out of the canvas. It was going to be summer soon, so you could feel that freedom coming on too.

I ran back into the girls' yard, and there was the quiet sister all by herself. I ran past her, and she followed me into the girls' lavatory. My footsteps rang hard against the cement and the tile because of the taps I had nailed into my shoes. Her footsteps were soft, padding after me. There was no one in the lavatory but the two of us. I ran all around the rows of twenty-five open stalls to make sure of that. No sisters. I think we must have been playing hide-and-go-seek. She was not good at hiding by herself and usually followed her sister; they'd hide in the same place. They must have gotten separated. In this growing twilight, a child could hide and never be found.

I stopped abruptly in front of the sinks, and she came running toward me before she could stop herself, so that she almost collided with me. I walked closer. She backed away, puzzlement, then alarm in her eyes.

"You're going to talk," I said, my voice steady and normal, as it is when talking to the familiar, the weak, and the small. "I am going to make you talk, you sissy-girl." She stopped backing away and stood fixed.

I looked into her face so I could hate it close up. She wore black bangs, and her cheeks were pink and white. She was baby-soft. I thought that I could put my thumb on her nose and push it bonelessly in, indent her face. I could poke dimples into her cheeks. I could work her face around like dough. She stood still, and I did not want to look at her face anymore; I hated fragility. I walked around her, looked her up and down the way the Mexican and Negro girls did when they fought, so tough. I hated her weak neck, the way it did not support her head but let it droop; her head would fall backward. I stared at the curve of her nape. I wished I was able to see what my own neck looked like from the back side. I hoped it did not look like hers; I wanted a stout neck. I grew my hair long to hide it in case it was a flower-stem neck. I walked around to the front of her to hate her face some more.

I reached up and took the fatty part of her cheek, not dough, but meat, between my thumb and finger. This close, and I saw no pores. "Talk," I said. "Are you going to talk?" Her skin was fleshy, like squid out of which the glassy blades of bones had been pulled. I wanted tough skin, hard brown skin. I had callused my hands; I had scratched dirt to blacken the nails, which I cut straight across to make stubby fingers. I gave her face a squeeze. "Talk." When I let go, the pink rushed back into my white thumb-print on her skin. I walked around to her side. "Talk!" I shouted into the side of her head. Her straight hair hung, the same all these years, no ringlets or braid or permanents. I squeezed her other cheek. "Are you? Huh? Are you going to talk?" She tried to shake her head, but I had hold of her face. She had no muscles to jerk away. Her skin seemed to stretch. I let go in horror. What if it came away in my hand? "No, huh?" I said, rubbing the touch of her off my fingers. "Say 'No,' then," I said. I gave her another pinch and a twist. "Say 'No.'" She shook her head, her straight hair turning with her head, not swinging side to side like the pretty girls'. She was so neat. Her neatness bothered me. I hated the way she folded the wax paper from her lunch; she did not wad her brown paper bag and her school papers. I hated her clothes—the blue pastel cardigan, the white blouse with the collar that lay flat over the cardigan, the homemade flat, cotton skirt she wore when everybody else was wearing flared skirts. I hated pastels; I would wear black always. I squeezed again, harder, even though her cheek had a weak rubbery feeling I did not like. I squeezed one cheek, then the other, back and forth until the tears ran out of her eyes as if I had pulled them out. "Stop crying," I said, but although she habitually followed me around, she did not obey. Her eyes dripped; her nose dripped. She wiped her eyes with her papery fingers. The skin on her hands and arms seemed powdery dry, like tracing paper, onion paper. I hated her fingers. I could snap them like breadsticks. I pushed her hands down. "Say 'Hi,'" I said. "'Hi.' Like that. Say your name. Go ahead. Say it. Or are you stupid? You're so stupid, you don't know your own name, is that it? When I say, 'What's your name?' you just blurt it out, OK? What's your name?" Last year the whole class had laughed at a boy who couldn't fill out a form be- cause he didn't know his father's name. The teacher sighed, exasperated, and was very sarcastic, "Don't you notice things? What does your mother

call him?" she said. The class laughed at how dumb he was not to notice
things. "She calls him father to me," he said. Even we laughed although we
knew that his mother did not call his father by name, and a son does not
know his father's name. We laughed and were relieved that our parents had
had the foresight to tell us some names we could give the teachers. "If
you're not stupid," I said to the quiet girl, "what's your name?" She shook
her head, and some hair caught in the tears; wet black hair stuck to the side
of the pink and white face. I reached up (she was taller than I) and took a
strand of hair. I pulled it. "Well, then, let's honk your hair," I said. "Honk.
Honk." Then I pulled the other side—"ho-o-n-nk"—a long pull "ho-o-n-
n-nk" a longer pull. I could see her little white ears, like white cutworms
curled underneath the hair. "Talk!" I yelled into each cutworm.

I looked right at her. "I know you talk," I said. "I've heard you." Her
eyebrows flew up. Something in those black eyes was startled, and I pursued it. "I was walking past your house when you didn't know I was there.
I heard you yell in English and in Chinese. You weren't just talking. You
were shouting. I hear your shout. You were saying, 'Where are you?' Say
that again. Go ahead, just the way you did at home." I yanked harder on the
hair but steadily, not jerking. I did not want to pull it out. "Go ahead. Say,
'Where are you?' Say it loud enough for your sister to come. Call her. Make
her come help you. Call her name. I'll stop if she comes. So call. Go
ahead."

She shook her head, her mouth curved down, crying. I could see her tiny
white teeth, baby teeth. I wanted to grow big, strong yellow teeth. "You do
have a tongue," I said. "So use it." I pulled the hair at her temples, pulled
the tears out of her eyes. "Say, 'Ow,'" I said. "Just 'Ow.' Say, 'Let go.' Go
ahead. Say it. I'll honk you again if you don't say, 'Let me alone.' Say, 'Leave
me alone,' and I'll let you go. I will. I'll let go if you say it. You can stop this
anytime you want to, you know. All you have to do is tell me to stop. Just
say, 'Stop.' You're just asking for it, aren't you? You're just asking for another honk. Well then, I'll have to give you another honk. Say, 'Stop.'" But
she didn't. I had to pull again and again.

Sounds did come out of her mouth, sobs, chokes, noises that were almost words. Snot ran out of her nose. She tried to wipe it on her hands, but
there was too much of it. She used her sleeve. "You're disgusting," I told
her. "Look at you, snot streaming down your nose, and you won't say a
word to stop it. You're such a nothing." I moved behind her and pulled the
hair growing out of her weak neck. I let go. I stood silent for a long time.
Then I screamed, "Talk!" I would scare the words out of her. If she had had
little bound feet, the toes twisted under the balls, I would have jumped up
and landed on them—crunch!—stomped on them with my iron shoes. She
cried, sobbing aloud. "Cry, 'Mamma.' Say, 'Stop it.'"

I put my finger on her pointed chin. "I don't like you. I don't like the weak little toots you make on your flute. Wheeze. Wheeze. I don't like the way you don't swing at the ball. I don't like the way you're the last one chosen. I don't like the way you can't make a fist for tetherball. Why don't you make a fist? Come on. Get tough. Come on. Throw fists." I pushed at her long hands; they swung limply at her sides. Her fingers were so long, I thought maybe they had an extra joint. They couldn't possibly make fists like other people's. "Make a fist," I said. "Come on. Just fold those fingers up; fingers on the inside, thumbs on the outside. Say something. Honk me back. You're so tall, and you let me pick on you.

"Would you like a hanky? I can't get you one with embroidery on it or crocheting along the edges, but I'll get you some toilet paper if you tell me to. Go head. Ask me. I'll get it for you if you ask." She did not stop crying. "Why don't you scream, 'Help'?" I suggested. "Say, 'Help,' Go ahead. Like this." I screamed not too loudly. My voice hit the tile and rang it as if I had thrown a rock at it. The stalls opened wider and the toilets wider and darker. Shadows leaned at angles I had not seen before. It was very late. Maybe a janitor had locked me in with this girl for the night. Her black eyes blinked and stared, blinked and stared. I felt dizzy from hunger. We had been in this lavatory together forever. My mother would call the police again if I didn't bring my sister home soon. "I'll let you go if you say just one word," I said. "You can even say 'a' or 'the,' and I'll let you go. Come on. Please." She didn't shake her head anymore, only cried steadily, so much water coming out of her. I could see the two duct holes where the tears welled out. Quarts of tears but no words. I grabbed her by the shoulder. I could feel bones. The light was coming in queerly through the frosted glass with the chicken wire embedded in it. Her crying was like an animal's—a seal's—and it echoed around the basement. "Do you want to stay here tonight?" I asked. "Your mother is wondering what happened to her baby. You wouldn't want to have her mad at you. You'd better say something." I shook her shoulder. I pulled her hair again. I squeezed her face. "Come on! Talk! Talk! Talk!" She didn't seem to feel it anymore when I pulled her hair. "There's nobody here but you and me. This isn't a class-room or a playground or a crowd. I'm just one person. You can talk in front of a person. Don't make me pull harder and harder until you talk." But her hair seemed to stretch; she did not say a word. "I'm going to pull harder. Don't make me pull anymore, or your hair will come out and you're going to be bald. Do you want to be bald? You don't want to be bald, do you?"

Far away, coming from the edge of town, I heard whistles blow. The cannery was changing shifts, letting out the afternoon people, and still we were here at school. It was a sad sound—work done. The air was lonelier after the sound died.

"Why won't you talk?" I started to cry. What if I couldn't stop, and everyone would want to know what happened? "Now look what you've done," I scolded. "You're going to pay for this. I want to know why. And you're going to tell me why. You don't see I'm trying to help you out, do you? Do you want to be like this, dumb (do you know dumb means?), your whole life? Don't you ever want to be a cheerleader? Or a pom-pom girl? What are you going to do for a living? Yeah, you're going to have to work because you can't be a housewife. Somebody has to marry you before you can become a housewife. And you, you are a plant. Do you know that? That's all you are if you don't talk. If you don't talk, you can't have a personality. You'll have no personality and no hair. You've got to let people know you have a personality and a brain. You think somebody is going to take care of you all your stupid life? You think you'll always have your big sister? You think somebody's going to marry you, is that it? Well, you're not the type that gets dates, let alone gets married. Nobody's going to notice you. And you have to talk for interviews, speak right up in front of the boss. Don't you know that? You're so dumb. Why do I waste my time on you?" Sniffling and snorting, I couldn't stop crying and talking at the same time. I kept wiping my nose on my arm, my sweater lost somewhere (probably not worn because my mother said to wear a sweater). It seemed as if I had spent my life in that basement, doing the worst thing I had yet done to another person. "I'm doing this for your own good," I said. "Don't you dare tell anyone I've been bad to you. Talk. Please talk."

I was getting dizzy from the air I was gulping. Her sobs and my sobs were bouncing wildly off the tile, sometimes together, sometimes alternating. "I don't understand why you won't say a word," I cried, clenching my teeth. My knees were shaking, and I hung on to her hair to stand up. Another time I'd stayed too late, I had had to walk around two Negro kids who were bonking each other's head on concrete. I went back later to see if the concrete had cracks in it. "Look. I'll give you something if you talk. I'll give you my pencil box. I'll buy you some candy. OK? What do you want? Tell me. Just say it, and I'll give it to you. Just say, 'Yes,' or, 'OK,' or, 'Baby Ruth.'" But she didn't want anything.

I had stopped pinching her cheek because I did not like the feel of her skin. I would go crazy if it came away in my hands. "I skinned her," I would have to confess.

Suddenly I heard footsteps hurrying through the basement, and her sister ran into the lavatory calling her name. "Oh, there you are," I said. "We've been waiting for you. I was only trying to teach her to talk. She wouldn't cooperate, though." Her sister went into one of the stalls and got handfuls of toilet paper and wiped her off. Then we found my sister, and walked home together. "Your family really ought to force her to speak," I advised all the way home. "You mustn't pamper her."

Chowchilla Summertime, 1956

Frank A. Cross, Jr.
Chowchilla

It is summertime in my memories of my eleventh year. I'm walking home along a country road, cracked blacktop and bermuda grass encroaching, narrowing the lanes. In the distance, to the east, I see our neighbor's huge, dark eucalyptus trees, shading the old farmhouse from the 106 degree afternoon. I'm walking home from rafting on Berenda Slough with my friend John. We built the raft from old power poles and fence blanks nailed together. We'd dive from it into the mossy water to swim with the frogs and pollywogs. The banks were overgrown with bamboo cane and cottonwood trees and we'd pretend we were explorers from an earlier time, rafting down an uncharted river, observing the wildlife and plants.

Along the road I hear the shrill warning of a nesting killdeer. As I come closer to the nest, she leaves it and runs ahead of me flopping along as if she had a broken wing, leading me away. These courageous little birds would even try to lead a tractor away from their nests they often made in cotton rows.

I turn the corner and take in the view of our farm to the south. Large trees shade the house and shop and farther back stands the big dairy barn and corrals. Most of the barns around Chowchilla at that time seemed to be made from the same blueprints. There was a high center section used for hay storage, and on each side, with a slightly lower roof of the same pitch as the upper, were the feeding and milking parlors. There was a small milk house connected to the north side of the barn with a breezeway. The milk house was lined with cement about half way up the walls and used to cool and store milk until the truck came to pick up the ten-gallon milk cans.

I walk in the yard and head straight for the barn where my dad and the hay buckers are stacking bales up to the rafters. They had backed the bob-tail truck, with its seven high load of bales, right up against the stack already begun in the barn. They were dragging bales off the top of the load and on up the stair-step stack they'd made. Hay dust danced in shafts of sunlight coming through knot holes and between siding planks. Dad handed me a pair of long-handled hay hooks and told me to help out the other end of the hundred-and-twenty-pound bale he was dragging up the rafters. Hay stacking in the barn in summer was killing work that made field hauling seem easy.

Hauling hay was an art. You either ran the job or it ran you. All kinds of old flatbed trucks were needed for the job. The truck driver and hay bucker would change jobs after each load to get a rest. The truck driver would drive down a line of bales in the alfalfa field in such a way that each bale would be centered in the chute of the drag chain, hay load hitched to the left side of the truck. The bale would then be hooked by the chain and dragged up the ramp to the top of the loader and pushed onto a small deck where the hay bucker would snag it with his hay hook and bring that bale rolling off onto the stack. The art was to keep up the momentum of the bale to put it where you wanted it on the interlocking stack with a minimum of lifting and dragging.

After we finished unloading the hay truck, Dad and I walked over to the shop to service up the John Deere Model D. Dad was going to disc the barley stubble for a few hours in the cool of the evening. These old John Deere tractors were often called "Johnny Poppers" because of the distinctive bark of the two-cylinder exhaust. The horizontal engine had a six and three-quarter-inch cylinder bore and a seven-inch piston stroke. It had a cross-mounted crankshaft with a big flywheel on the left side and a belt pulley on the right. The engine was started by turning over the flywheel by hand! First, the carburetor was drained of the "stove oil" fuel from its previous run. Then the carburetor was filled with gasoline from a small tank mounted behind the main fuel tank. Next, petcocks on the sides of the cylinders were opened to reduce the compression. The throttle was opened about half and the choke was pulled full on. Then the big flywheel was gripped by its rim and turned until a piston came up on compression. Then the operator, with as much strength as he could muster, snapped the piston over top dead center and if conditions were right, the engine would be off and running. Otherwise, he kept on turning and yanking on that flywheel until it did start or he found the reason why not or he gave out from exhaustion. After the engine ran for a time on gasoline to heat up, it was switched over to the cheaper "stove oil" which would vaporize and burn after going through the hot manifold. I could hear Dad's Model D from miles away when it was pulling hard: PLOCK! PLOCK! PLOCK!

The next morning I awoke to the crying of the mourning doves and a still air promising a very hot day. I looked east to the dark peaks and valleys of the Sierras, misty under the just risen sun. I long to spend the day swimming in Bass Lake up in those mountains, but Dad has other plans for me. After breakfast he sharpens two cotton hoes and hands me one. Soon we're out walking the furrows in the cotton field, whacking down and digging out pigweed, careless weed, water grass and the dreaded Johnsongrass. Johnsongrass, if not controlled, can infest and choke out large areas of a cotton field. It grows in large clumps six feet tall and sends out rhizomes underground to infest an ever widening area. We cut down the clumps of grass and dug out as much of the rhizomes as we could find; but it only took an inch-long rhizome segment to start a new plant growing. We kept our field relatively free of Johnsongrass, but it was a battle every year with this alien.

By noon it was 106 degrees again and after lunch, Dad said I could go over to John's place and swim in the slough; but to be sure and be back by three o'clock to help stack more hay in the barn. As I was walking to John's I saw a hen pheasant leading her brood of tiny chicks across the road. Like fuzzy brown-and-yellow Ping-pong balls, the chicks scurry along behind and beside the hen. She leads them down into the bar ditch and up through the weeds of the fencerow. She leads them along, hunting and pecking, showing the chicks the way to survive in their hostile world of cars, cats, dogs, hawks, coyotes and hunters in November. The chicks were growing and learning every day and some would survive to raise their own chicks next year.

Guggenheim's Water Tower, Fresno, 1921

William Saroyan

Fresno

The tank was at the top of a timber derrick among the Santa Fe Railroad tracks, at the end of San Benito Avenue. The timber was old and rickety. The ladder rungs had been nailed to the frame long ago. The nails had rusted, and some were loose. In one place, midway, a rung was missing. The climber going up had to put some muscle into it, and coming down he had to see that he didn't slip. The water tanks had had a sign saying that it was against the law to climb the tower, but somebody had sensibly removed the sign.

One summer I climbed the tower a couple of times a week, once to drop a cat, which landed on its feet, bounced, and ran away at full speed. I was never mean to animals, and on this occasion I was more stupid than mean. I really believed the cat would not be injured in the fall. Perhaps it wasn't. All the same I have always felt a little guilty about having dropped the cat. And ashamed.

The railroad tracks and the eucalyptus trees among the tracks, in the Jungle, where the hoboes rested and cooked their stew and smoked cigarettes and talked, black and white alike, but never immigrants, never people who came to America to make good, the railroad tracks had cat packs, old toms, females, and half-grown young cats, all lean, all tough, all dirty. The cat I had taken up with me and had dropped from the top of the tower was one of these—a cat which had been trusting, unlike most of the others in the pack, which were suspicious of human beings, and afraid of them. This cat considered me a friend, and there it was—I betrayed the cat. I dropped it to hard ground from a height of at least a hundred feet.

And I had to be clever to do it, for the cat clung to my arm, and spoke, not piteously but rather bravely, as if to say, "You're not going to do something stupid, are you?"

I had to turn quickly and let the cat go. Even while it was tumbling head over heels and the boys who were with me, watching, cheered and laughed, I thought, "Please spare the poor animal, and I will never do such a stupid thing again."

I was thrilled when the cat struck the hard ground *lightly,* feet first and bounced so swiftly that it was almost as if it had not in fact a real impact with the ground, and then raced away. The escape and survival of the cat thrilled me deeply, because it made my mischief something less than a criminal act upon life.

The climbing to the top of the tower, then walking around the tank and looking around at the whole small town in all directions, and the climbing down, required concentration and care. It was all very definitely dangerous. Why did I do it, then?

Because I believed in my ability to do it. After having done it, I actually was able to feel I had accomplished something of some importance to me.

Being Mean

Gary Soto

Fresno

W e were terrible kids, I think. My brother, sister and I felt a general meanness begin to surface from our tiny souls while living on Braly Street, which was in the middle of industrial Fresno. Across the street was Coleman Pickles, while on the right of us a junkyard that dealt in metals—aluminum, iron, sheet metal, and copper stripped from refrigerators. Down the street was Sun-Maid Raisin, where a concrete tower rose above the scraggly sycamores that lined Braly Street. Many of our family members worked at Sun-Maid: Grandfather and Grandmother, Father, three uncles, an aunt, and even a dog whose job was to accompany my grandfather, a security guard, on patrol. Then there was Challenge Milk, a printing job, and the 7-Up Bottling Company where we stole sodas. Down the alley was a broom factory and Western Book Distributor, a place where our future step-father worked at packing books into cardboard boxes, something he would do for fifteen years before the company left town for Oregon.

This was 1957. My brother Rick was six, I was five, and Debra was four. Although we looked healthy, clean in the morning, and polite as only Mexicans can be polite, we had a streak of orneriness that we imagined to be normal play. That summer—and the summer previous—we played with the Molinas who lived down the alley from us right across from the broom factory and its brutal "whack" of straw being tied into brooms. There were eight children on the block, ranging from twelve down to one, so there was much to do: wrestle, eat raw bacon, jump from the couch, sword fight with rolled-up newspapers, steal from neighbors, kick chickens, throw rocks at passing cars. . . . While we played in the house, Mrs. Molina just watched us run around, a baby in her arms crying like a small piece of machinery turning at great speed. Now and then she would warn us with a smile, "Now you kids, you're going to hurt yourselves." We ignored her and went on pushing one another from an opened window, yelling wildly when we hit the ground that, in our imagination, was a rough sea of snub-nosed sharks ready to snack on our skinny legs.

What we learned from the Molinas was how to have fun, and what we taught them was how to fight. It seemed that Sotos were inherently violent. I remember, for instance, watching my aunts go at one another in my grandmother's backyard, while the men looked on with beers in their hands and mumbled to one another, perhaps noting the beauty of a right jab or a left uppercut. Another time the police arrived late at night in search of our Uncle Leonard who had gotten into a fight at a neighborhood bar. Shortly thereafter, I recall driving with my mother to see him at what she said was a "soldier's camp." She had a sack of goods with her, and after speaking softly to a uniformed man we were permitted to enter. It was lunchtime and he sat on a felled log laughing with other men. When he saw us coming, he laughed even harder.

In turn, I was edged with meanness; and more often than not the object of my attacks was Rick. If upset, I chased him with rocks, pans, a hammer, whatever lay around in the yard. Once, when he kicked over a row of beans I had planted, I chased him down the alley with a bottle until, in range, I hurled it at him. The bottle hit him in the thigh and, to my surprise, showered open with blood. Screaming, his mouth open wide enough to saucer a hat inside, he hobbled home while I stood there, only slightly worried at the seriousness of his wound and the spanking that would follow. I shouted that he had better never kick over my beans. And he didn't.

I was also hurt by others who were equally as mean; I'm thinking particularly of an Okie kid who yelled that we were dirty Mexicans. Perhaps so, but why bring it up? I looked at my feet and was embarrassed, then mad. With a bottle I approached him slowly in spite of my brother's warnings that the kid was bigger and older. When I threw the bottle and missed, he swung his stick and my nose exploded blood for several feet. Frightened, though not crying, I ran home with Rick and Debra following behind, and dabbed at my face with toilet paper, poked mercurochrome at the gash that bubbled, and then lay on the couch, swallowing blood as I slowly grew faint and sleepy. Rick and Debra stayed with me for a while, then got up to go outside to play.

Rick and I and the Molinas all enjoyed looking for trouble and often went to extremes to try to get into fights. One day we found ourselves staring at some new kids on the street—three of them about our age—and when they looked over their picket fence to see who we were, I thought one of them sneered, so I called him a name. They cussed at us, and that provocation was enough to send Rick to beat on one of them. Rick entered their yard and was swiftly caught in a whirlwind of punches. Furious as a bee, I ran to fight the kid who had humbled my bigger brother, but was punched in the stomach, which knocked the breath out of me so I couldn't tell anyone how much it had hurt. The Molinas grew scared and took off, while Rick and I, slightly roughed up but sure that we had the guts to give them a good working over, walked slowly home trying to figure out how to do it. A small flame lit my brain, and I suggested that we stuff a couple of cats into potato sacks and beat the kids with them. An even smaller light flared in my brother's brain. "Yeah, that'll get them," he said, happy that we were going to get even. We called to our cat, Boots, and found another unfortunate cat that was strolling nonchalantly down our alley. I called "kittykittykitty," and it came, purring. I carried it back to our yard where Rick had already stuffed Boots into a sack, which was bumping about on the ground. Seeing this, the cat stiffened in my arms and I had trouble working the cat into the sack, for it had spread its feet and opened its claws. But once inside, the cat grew calm, resigning itself to fate, and meowed only once or twice. For good measure I threw a bottle into my sack, and the two of us—or, to be fair, the four of us—went down the alley in search of the new kids.

We looked for them, even calling them names at their back porch, but they failed to show themselves. Rick and I agreed that they were scared, so in a way we were victors. Being mean, we kicked over their garbage cans and ran home where we fought one another with the sacks, the cats all along whining and screaming to get out.

Perhaps the most enjoyable summer day was when Rick, Debra and I decided to burn down our house. Earlier in the summer we had watched a television program on fire prevention at our grandmother's house, only three houses down from us on Sarah Street. The three of us sat transfixed in front of the gray light of our family's first TV. We sat on the couch with a bowl of grapes, and when the program ended the bowl was still in Rick's lap, untouched. TV was that powerful.

Just after that program Rick and I set fire to our first box, in which we imagined were many people scurrying to get out. We hovered over the fire, and our eyes grew wild. Later, we got very good at burning shoe boxes. We crayoned windows, cut doors on the sides, and dropped ants into the boxes, imagining they were people wanting very badly to live. Once the fire got going, I wailed like a siren and Rick flicked water from a coffee can at the building leaping with flames. More often than not, it burned to ash and the ants shriveled to nothing—though a few would limp away, wiser by vision of death.

But we grew bored with the shoe boxes. We wanted something more exciting and daring, so Rick suggested that we brighten our lives with a house fire. "Yeah," Debra and I cried, jumping up and down, and proceeded to toss crumpled newspaper behind the doors, under the table, and in the middle of the living room. Rick struck a match, and we stood back laughing as the flames jumped wildly about and the newspaper collapsed into parachutes of ash that floated to the ceiling. Once the fire got started we dragged in the garden hose and sprayed the house, the three of us laughing for the love of good times. We were in a frenzy to build fires and put them out with the hose. I looked at Rick and his eyes were wide with pleasure, his crazed laughter like the mad scientists of the movies we would see in the coming years. Debra was bouncing up and down on the couch, a toy baby in her arms, and she was smiling her tiny teeth at the fire. I ran outside flapping my arms because I wanted to also burn the chinaberry that stood near our bedroom window. Just as I was ready to set a match to a balled newspaper I intended to hurl into the branches, our grandmother came walking slowly down the alley to check on us. (It was her responsibility to watch us during the day because our father was working at Sun-Maid Raisin and our mother peeling potatoes at Reddi-Spud.) Grandma stopped at the gate and stared at me as if she knew what we were up to, and I stared back so I could make a quick break if she should lunge at me. Finally she asked, "How are you, honey?" I stared at my dirty legs, then up to her: "OK. I'm just playing." With the balled newspaper in my hand, I pointed to the house and told her that Rick and Debra were inside coloring. She said to behave myself, gave me a stick of gum, and started back to her house.

When I went back inside Rick and Debra were playing war with cherry tomatoes. Debra was behind the table on which the telephone rested, while Rick crouched behind a chair making the sounds of bombs falling.

"Rick," I called because I wanted to tell him that Grandma had come to see how we were doing, but he threw a tomato and it splashed my T-shirt like a bullet wound. I feigned being shot and fell to the floor. He rolled from behind the chair to hide behind a door. "Are you dead?" he asked. I lifted my head and responded: "Only a little bit."

Laughing, we hurled tomatoes at one another, and some of them hit their mark—an ear, a shoulder, a grinning face—while others skidded across the floor or became pasted to the wall. "You Jap," Debra screamed as she cocked her hand to throw, to which I screamed, "You damn German!" We fought until the tomatoes were gone. Breathing hard, we looked at the mess we had created, and then at each other, slightly concerned at what it might mean. Rick and I tried to clean up with a broom while Debra lay exhausted on the couch, thumb in her mouth and making a smacking sound. I can't recall falling asleep but that's what happened, because I awoke later to Rick crying in the kitchen. Our mother had come home to an ash-darkened living room, a puddled kitchen, and tomato-stained walls. She yelled and spanked Rick, after which she dragged him to the stove where she heated a fork over a burner and threatened to burn his wrists. "Now are you going to play with fire?" she screamed. I peeked into the kitchen and her mouth puckered into a dried fruit as Rick cried that she was hurting him, that he was sorry, that he would never do it again. Tears leaped from his face as he tried to wiggle free. She threw the fork into the sink, then let him go. She turned to me and yelled: "And you too, *Chango!*" She started after me, but I ran out the front door into the alley where I hid behind a stack of boards. I stayed there until my breathing calmed and my fear disappeared like an ash picked up by the wind. I got up and, knowing that I couldn't return home immediately, I went to the Molinas. Just as I turned into their yard I caught sight of two of them climbing, hand over hand, along the telephone wires that stretched from above the back porch to the pole itself. A few of the younger Molinas looked on from an opened window, readying for their turn, as the radio blared behind them. I threw a rock at the two hanging from the wires, and they laughed that I missed. The other kids laughed. Their mother, with a baby in her arms, came out to the back porch, laughed, and told us God was watching and for us to behave ourselves.

My First Kill
Art Cuelho
Riverdale

On the day after my twelfth birthday I left the shop at the Wheatville farm with my .22 automatic rifle and a pocket full of shiny new hollow point shells. I was almost tempted to stop in the old harvester junkyard out back to take potshots at some rusty tin cans, but I remembered what my dad had told me about making every bullet count. When I was a frog jump higher than a cream can, I used to lift up the dark funny-smelling railroad ties and spear the blue-bellied lizards with the sharpened ends of surveyor sticks. The lizard tails always amazed me when they fell off into my fingers. I was too old for that kind of child's play now. I looked down at the new rifle in my hand and knew something had changed. The game would be bigger than English sparrows this time. And more important, my dad would want to know exactly how the morning went. Later I'd have to look straight into his eyes and measure up to everything that happened during the hunt.

I walked beside an irrigation ditch towards the slough. A ditch plow had recently cut with its steel blade both sides of the levee into shiny slices. I looked at the dry earth where the cleat marks of the D-7 Cat made its path. I saw the rank green water grass had dried to a dull color in the sun. One side of the dirt road above the ditch bank was infested with napweed. The blooms of the flowers were purple and could be seen from a great distance across the fields of the valley. My dad had sprayed the ground with weed killer where the plants grew in patches. Nothing would grow in that spot for three years afterwards; and then the growth was stunted. The

129

neighboring farmer never tried to control the spread of the napweed on his land and the wind each year blew new seeds into the fields. The grain companies would dock you so much a ton on the price of barley if they found napweed and the entire crop for that year would have to be recleaned.

The slough was about a mile from the Wheatville shop. Halfway there, Dave, a fieldhand, pulled up beside me in an old, dusty Ford pickup. He stopped and asked if I wanted a ride.

"I better not risk it," I said. "I might see something along here."

"You never can tell," Dave said. "Are you hunting anything special?"

"Anything I can eat. The boss said if it ain't good enough to put on our supper table to forget it. He already warned me about shooting owls. They catch field mice. You know how he hates it when they tear into sacks of seed barley. And sandhill cranes. They're a no–no too. He said he'd skin me alive if I killed anything just for the hell of it."

"If you cut through this barley stubble you might see something just before you get to those clumps of old willow trees," Dave said. "There's a patch of wild red clover there."

"You mean where Gene used to turn his hogs loose?"

Dave nodded and pointed with his finger.

"Where'd you get the rifle?"

"The boss gave it to me. She's brand new. Ain't even fired it yet. I got it for my birthday. She's a real honey."

"Automatic?"

"Yeah. Holds a bunch of bullets. You put 'em right in here." I pointed to a narrow opening at the top of the magazine tube. "No jack is gonna get away from me."

"You like rabbit meat?" Dave asked.

"Never had any that I know of," I said.

"Well, kill a young one."

"How can I tell if they're too old?"

"That's easy. The old ones wear bifocals like me," Dave said laughing.

"You set me up for that one."

"I guess I did at that."

There was a short silence between Dave and me and a dust devil kicked up in the barley stubble and hurled a spiral of loose straw from the harvester beds high into the air.

"I guess I better get back to my hunting now."

"Good luck."

"I'll probably need it," I said to Dave.

Then I crossed the stubble field. My hightop shoes cracked against the dry barley stalks. I took steps twice my normal stride. I was thinking of the red clover and the jack rabbits and I kept checking to see if my rifle was on safe. When I pushed it on fire there was a red spot on the safety. My heart beat faster every time I saw the crimson slot flash before my eyes.

I stopped at the edge of the wild clover. I looked closely at the ground all around me. The clover had little red flowers at the tops of the green stems. A slight westside breeze ruffled over them. I could hear the sound of the wings of the honeybees as they gathered their nectar. There were several white bee boxes across the slough bank near the old abandoned homestead windmill. I wanted to make sure not to fire in that direction. When I was five years old I got into a yellow jacket nest at my first cousin's in Lemoore and they stung me around the eyes so bad that I could not see for a week.

Not long after I stepped into the clover patch a jack rabbit jumped out in front of me. I raised my rifle and pulled the trigger. I had forgotten to take off the safety. I still managed to get off six rapid-fire shots. Dust kicked up all around the jack when he got up on the levee road. He quickly scrambled back into the cover of the clover and was gone. I realized what dad had told me now. "Speed is not the most important thing to hunting, son. It's the calculated reflex that counts. Accurateness takes a kind of cool patience and skill. You jump the gun and it's all over. Anybody can pull the trigger fast, but not everyone can hit the mark. You can't always depend on luck to be on your side. And it's not good to waste shells. I still feel a little guilty about not making every shot count. I remember when I couldn't afford a box of .22 shorts. I'd go out with two bullets a day that my father gave me and I had to bring in something for supper. It made me a good shot. I learned to pass up the hard ones. I knew we'd get stew without meat if I didn't make my kill."

I kicked the evidence of the empty metal cartridges off the levee road. I did not want dad to see how many times I'd fired my rifle while standing in one spot. I had a bad case of rabbit fever alright. I didn't even use my open sights. I barrel-shot that jack.

I reloaded the .22 automatic and combed the entire bank of clover thoroughly. The rabbit must have slipped through to the field on the other side of the slough. I did see several ground squirrels but they popped down in their holes before I had a chance to shoot. My dad shot at them all the time with his .22 rifle and had made them very gun-shy. When the farm pickups came along the banks of the slough they ran for the safety of their network of holes.

I walked down under some willows and sat down. I was thirsty from the long walk in the valley sun. I took my army surplus canteen off my belt and took several big swigs of water. I decided to wait in the shade a while until I felt rested. Maybe if I stood in one spot the animals and birds would come down to drink from the slough and I could get the drop on them. I reached my hand down to my Levi pantlegs and pulled the cockleburs off and flicked them on the adobe ground near a stretch of headed out foxtail grass. The heat from the sun had made me lazy. I laid my new rifle down beside me. It was all shiny from the oil I had rubbed into it. The night before, dad said I was going to wear the stock out by rubbing it so much with the oil rag. The pride I had for my rifle was all swelled up inside of me. It made me feel good and I patted the automatic and put one of my hands on the stock. I laid down flat on my back and looked up at the willow leaves. The light filtered through and reflected off the green blades and hit the ripples of the slough water that washed up on the bank below my feet. I shaded my eyes with my straw hat. It was the lapping of the water and the good feeling of the rifle beside me that helped me to doze off underneath the tree.

While I was asleep two cock pheasants came out on the opposite bank of the slough. The younger cock did not have the full brilliance of his feathers yet. He was smaller and it was the first time he had the privilege to fight for the right to mate with the hens. The hens were waiting at the edge of the cotton rows.

It was the battle cries of the cocks that had aroused me from my nap on the slough bank. I saw them squared off on each other and I reached for my rifle. My first impulse was to shoot before they had a chance to run away. If I hadn't forgotten about the safety again I would have fired at them without thinking. By the time I flicked the safety on red something made me hesitate. The drama of the fight had momentarily distracted me. The older cock pheasant had the young one backing up and he spurred him under the wing. He had drawn blood. I could see the younger cock looked badly wounded. The old cock had full confidence in himself now. He strutted bravely before the hens. He was going in for the kill as he had done so many times before. The young cock was faking the extent of his injury to make the older one more sure of himself. When the old cock came after him he came dauntlessly straight ahead, and the younger pheasant drove a spur deep into his breast. The old cock fell over on his side. He shivered violently on the ground and in a few seconds he died. The young pheasant stood up on his legs and flapped his wings in triumph and cried out to his harem of hens.

I lifted up my .22 rifle and took careful aim. I rested the barrel on my knee and pulled off the trigger slowly. The young cock toppled over on impact from the bullet and the hens scattered back into the mouths of the cotton rows.

Two dead pheasants. I was jumping up and down with excitement. The quarter of a mile walk to get around to the opposite slough bank where the game birds were seemed like forever to me.

When I got up close and saw the bloody spurs above their feet I realized I had done something wrong. I began to see how the younger cock fought so bravely against the stronger one. It reminded me of Howard Davis, the school bully, who tried to take my girlfriend away. I, too, had to fight against great odds to win the love of Maria. For almost a week I had worn the shiner on my right eye like a badge of honor.

Even when the young cock was almost sure to lose he still never tried to run and escape the heat of battle. I didn't give him a Chinaman's chance. He didn't even make a break for it when I plugged him.

I wondered about the five or six hens that had disappeared quickly in the cotton rows when I fired my .22. There was nothing I could do now. The damage had been done. I had to take them back to the Wheatville shop for dad to thoroughly inspect. I would have to fake my sense of excitement and make up some story how I got the older one. I gave up on the heroic idea of telling dad that I got two in one shot. I decided I had to shoot the older pheasant. The spur wound from the young cock wasn't big enough and without a bullet hole I couldn't prove I had shot it. The last thing on this earth that I wanted to do was to make dad suspicious of my hunting ability. So I propped the old cock up against the slough bank and all the fun of the hunt had gone out of me. After I aimed I shut my eyes so I wouldn't have to see the bullet go in. When I opened my eyes I saw the new blood rush out on his brilliant chest feathers. I knew now that it was the blood and not the bullet that I was trying to hide from my vision. The sight of the blood had taken all the thrill out of the hunt for me.

When I sat down on the ground and notched my rifle stock with my scout knife I felt guilty about the second notch for the older pheasant and ashamed of the first for the young cock. But what made me hurt inside more than anything else was having to fake the thrill of the hunt for dad.

I picked up my birthday rifle and the blood on my hand left a stain on the new stock. I immediately tried to rub it out, but the mark only went in deeper and deeper the harder I wiped at the dark blood.

Splitting Extraversion
Michael Blaine
Exeter

I decided to go to Church because school was rotten and I didn't feel good around anyone anymore. I could barely sleep because I was so afraid of Hell. I decided to go to confession, even though I was really afraid because I hadn't been for a long time and I knew that since Exeter had such a small church and I used to be an altar boy that the priest would recognize my voice. In a way it was good to go to confession only once a year because then you didn't have to count your sins anymore, because when I was about to make my first confession a nun told us that if you had done something wrong more than fifty times you could just say that you had done it most of the time. I decided to go right before mass so the priest wouldn't have time to think about me after I confessed.

"Bless me father, for I have sinned. It has been about a year since my last confession, and these are my sins. . . . I talked back to my mother . . . most of the time."

"Uh-huh."

"I wished mean things against others . . . most of the time. . . . I didn't go to church most of the time."

"Uh-huh."

"I didn't say my prayers . . . most of the time."

"Go on."

"I had impure thoughts most of the time. I fought with my brother—"

"Where do you usually have them?"

"I don't know, Father. Different places."

135

"Well, do you talk with other guys?"

"A little, I guess, Father."

"After school? At recess?"

"Not much. I just have them on my own."

"Do you read magazines?"

"Yes, Father."

"What kind?"

"*Life.* And I used to read *The Junior Scholastic* at school."

"Well, those don't seem so bad. Do you read pornography?"

"No, Father."

"Are there things to keep you busy?"

"Yes, Father."

"Okay. For your penance say ten Hail Marys and ten Our Fathers and make a good Act of Contrition. And remember, idle hands are the devil's workshop."

"But Father, I have a couple more sins to tell you."

"That's okay. Mass is about to begin and your intention forgives you everything. Now say an Act of Contrition and I'll pray with you."

"Thank you, Father."

"Take care, Mike."

We prayed and he shut the sliding door, and the next person would know not to talk until he heard the door on his side slide open and saw the dim light from the bulb in the priest's chamber. I was relieved and noticed that my hand was dry when I turned the knob of the door. I went to the altar and said my penance and my whole body lightened because I knew I was clean and not guilty for anything I'd done anymore. I finally felt like I didn't have anything wrong with me, and even though English masses bored me, because you knew what the words meant and they were kind of corny, I was looking forward to communion. I didn't usually look forward to it like I did confession because communion seemed like an added-on sacrament that's supposed to help you not sin so much in the future, and confession took all the sins of your whole life away so it seemed like the biggest sacrament to me, but I was hoping that this communion would be different. My knees started to hurt before the sermon even began, and I had to keep telling myself that I didn't mind the pain but really liked it, because it put me closer to God. But the sermon was really boring and I had trouble paying attention and kept shifting back and forth in my seat and even though I tried not to, I passed gas, and I started really worrying about passing gas in church because church was God's house and He was there, so I had gotten gas in His Spirit, and I kept saying I was sorry to Jesus but I could taste the gas in my mouth so I was afraid I had made the word "Jesus" dirty, so I'd just think His name inside and look at Him on the cross above the priest. I couldn't see why they put him in a loincloth and I noticed how impressive his pectorals were, and then I felt really guilty for having such a bad thought, so I decided to stare at the floor and try to stop thinking. I spent the rest of the mass worrying about whether or not I'd committed a mortal sin and decided that maybe I had and that I'd better not go to communion because that would have been a really bad mortal sin, a lot worse than anything I might have already done wrong, but I knew that a lot of people had seen me go to confession and the priest had even recognized me, so I'd be pretty embarrassed if I'd already committed a mortal sin. I started hating everything in church and I couldn't understand why God would make you go to mass and go through so many temptations if He was really good. Everything in the building started looking ugly and the bells didn't seem holy and neither did the wine and even when the big host was raised all I could think was that it was something that was supposed to make you feel better and not so dirty. I got sick to my stomach thinking about how everything in the church looked like a bunch of objects and that all along I'd been learning to pretend that everything in the world was a bunch of objects and I was supposed to treat people like objects because they were going to treat me like an object and I'd been hiding this from myself for a long time. I couldn't remember when I decided, but probably I was really young and afraid because I knew people were treating me in certain ways, but I couldn't figure out the exact ways and they kept changing. My parents treated me like lots of people. Sometimes my mom would treat me like I was the head of the family and my dad was the baby, and my dad sometimes couldn't recognize me when he was drunk and called me Brian and called my brother Mike. I was always tall and older guys used to push me around a lot when I was young because I was so tall and at some time I knew I had to forget a lot about how I was treated, even though that meant I would have to change myself and go on changing myself and forgetting how I'd changed. I had to act like I was the thing people wanted me to be and I had to forget that by doing this I was treating everyone else like objects that never changed, at least for the time I was with them, and were pure or nobody would ever forgive me, and if I didn't forget about what I'd done I'd never forgive myself.

I hated the mass and Jesus, and when I got in line to receive communion I decided I wasn't going to follow the rules. When you get the host you're supposed to swallow it as fast as you can so it stays a whole circle, or if you can't do that, you're supposed to let it melt, but I was so angry that I bit down hard about ten times, crushing His legs and arms and biting off His head and grinding down His feet, until Jesus was split into so many pieces that no one could ever put Him back together again.

The Horned Toad
Gerald Haslam
Oildale

"*Expectoran su sangre!*" exclaimed Great-grandma when I showed her the small horned toad I had removed from my breast pocket. I turned toward my mother, who translated: "They spit blood."

"*De los ojos,*" Grandma added. "From their eyes," mother explained, herself uncomfortable in the presence of the small beast.

I grinned, "Awwwwww."

But my Great-grandmother did not smile. "*Son muy toxicos,*" she nodded with finality. Mother moved back an involuntary step, her hands suddenly busy at her breast. "Put that thing down," she ordered.

"His name's John," I said.

"Put John down and not in your pocket, either," my mother nearly shouted. "Those things are very poisonous. Didn't you understand what Grandma said?"

I shook my head.

"Well . . ." mother looked from one of us to the other—spanning four generations of California, standing three feet apart—and said, "of course you didn't. Please take him back where you got him, and be careful. We'll all feel better when you do." The tone of her voice told me that the discussion had ended, so I released the little reptile where I'd captured him.

During those years in Oildale, the mid-1940s, I needed only to walk across the street to find a patch of virgin desert. Neighborhood kids called it simply "the vacant lot," less than an acre without houses or sidewalks.

Not that we were desperate for desert then, since we could walk into its scorched skin a mere half-mile west, north, and east. To the south, incongruously, flowed the icy Kern River, fresh from the Sierras and surrounded by riparian forest.

Ours was rich soil formed by that same Kern River as it ground Sierra granite and turned it into coarse sand, then carried it down into the valley and deposited it over millenia along its many changes of channels. The ants that built miniature volcanoes on the vacant lot left piles of tiny stones with telltale markings of black on white. Deeper than ants could dig were pools of petroleum that led to many fortunes and lured men like my father from Texas. The dry hills to the east and north sprouted forests of wooden derricks.

Despite the abundance of open land, plus the constant lure of the river where desolation and verdancy met, most kids relied on the vacant lot as their primary playground. Even with its bullheads and stinging insects, we played everything from football to kick-the-can on it. The lot actually resembled my father's head, bare in the middle but full of growth around the edges: weeds, stickers, cactuses, and a few bushes. We played our games on its sandy center, and conducted such sports as ant fights and lizard hunts on its brushy periphery.

That spring, when I discovered the lone horned toad near the back of the lot, had been rough on my family. Earlier, there had been quiet, unpleasant tension between Mom and Daddy. He was a silent man, little given to emotional displays. It was difficult for him to show affection and I guess the openness of Mom's family made him uneasy. Daddy had no kin in California and rarely mentioned any in Texas. He couldn't seem to understand my mother's large, intimate family, their constant noisy concern for one another, and I think he was a little jealous of the time she gave everyone, maybe even me.

I heard her talking on the phone to my various aunts and uncles, usually in Spanish. Even though I couldn't understand—Daddy had warned her not to teach me that foreign tongue because it would hurt me in school, and she'd complied—I could sense the stress. I had been afraid they were going to divorce, since she only used Spanish to hide things from me. I'd confronted her with my suspicion, but she comforted me, saying, no, that was not the problem. They were merely deciding when it would be our turn to care for Grandma. I didn't really understand, although I was relieved.

I later learned that my Great-grandmother—whom we simply called "Grandma"—had been moving from house to house within the family, trying to find a place she'd accept. She hated the city, and most of the aunts and uncles lived in Los Angeles. Our house in Oildale was much closer to the open country where she'd dwelled all her life. She had wanted to come to our place right away because she had raised my mother from a baby when my own grandmother died. But the old lady seemed unimpressed with Daddy, whom she called *"ese gringo."*

In truth, we had more room, and my dad made more money in the oil patch than almost anyone else in the family. Since my mother was the closest to Grandma, our place was the logical one for her, but Ese Gringo didn't see it that way, I guess, at least not at first. Finally, after much debate, he relented.

In any case, one windy afternoon, my Uncle Manuel and Aunt Toni drove up and deposited four-and-a-half feet of bewigged, bejeweled Spanish spitfire: a square, pale face topped by a tightly-curled black wig that hid a bald head—her hair having been lost to typhoid nearly sixty years before—her small white hands veined with rivers of blue. She walked with a prancing bounce that made her appear half her age, and she barked orders in Spanish from the moment she emerged from Manuel and Toni's car. Later, just before they left, I heard Uncle Manuel tell my dad, "Good luck, Charlie. That old lady's dynamite." Daddy only grunted.

She had been with us only two days when I tried to impress her with my horned toad. In fact, nothing I did seemed to impress her, and she referred to me as *el malcriado,* causing my mother to shake her head. Mom explained to me that Grandma was just old and lonely for Grandpa and uncomfortable in town. Mom told me that Grandma had lived over half a century in the country, away from the noise, away from clutter, away from people. She refused to accompany my mother on shopping trips, or anywhere else. She even refused to climb into a car, and I wondered how Uncle Manuel had managed to load her up in order to bring her to us.

She disliked sidewalks and roads, dancing across them when she had to, then appearing to wipe her feet on earth or grass. Things too civilized simply did not pleased her. A brother of hers had been killed in the great San Francisco earthquake and that had been the end of her tolerance of cities. Until my Great-grandfather died, they lived on a small rancho near Arroyo Cantua, north of Coalinga. Grandpa, who had come north from Sonora as a youth to work as a *vaquero,* had bred horses and cattle, and cowboyed for other ranchers, scraping together enough of a living to raise eleven children.

He had been, until the time of his death, a lean, dark-skinned man with wide shoulders, a large nose, and a sweeping handlebar mustache that was white when I knew him. His Indian blood darkened all his progeny so that not even I was as fair-skinned as my Great-grandmother, Ese Gringo for a father or not.

As it turned out, I didn't really understand very much about Grandma at all. She was old, of course, yet in many ways my parents treated her as though she were younger than me, walking her to the bathroom at night and bringing her presents from the store. In other ways—drinking wine at dinner, for example—she was granted adult privileges. Even Daddy didn't drink wine except on special occasions. After Grandma moved in, though, he began to occasionally join her for a glass, sometimes even sitting with her on the porch for a premeal sip.

She held court on our front porch, often gazing toward the desert hills east of us or across the street at kids playing on the lot. Occasionally, she would rise, cross the yard and sidewalk and street, skip over them, sometimes stumbling on the curb, and wipe her feet on the lot's sandy soil, then she would slowly circle the boundary between the open middle and the brushy sides, searching for something, it appeared. I never figured out what.

One afternoon I returned from school and saw Grandma perched on the porch as usual, so I started to walk around the house to avoid her sharp, mostly incomprehensible, tongue. She had already spotted me. *"Venga aquí!"* she ordered, and I understood.

I approached the porch and noticed that Grandma was vigorously chewing something. She held a small white bag in one hand. Saying *"Qué deseas tomar?"* she withdrew a large orange gumdrop from the bag and began slowly chewing it in her toothless mouth, smacking loudly as she did so. I stood below her for a moment trying to remember the word for candy. Then it came to me: *"Dulce,"* I said.

Still chewing, Grandma replied, *"Mande?"*

Knowing she wanted a complete sentence, I again struggled, then came up with *"Deseo dulce."*

She measured me for a moment, before answering in nearly perfect English, "Oh, so you wan' some candy. Go to the store an' buy some."

I don't know if it was the shock of hearing her speak English for the first time, or the way she had denied me a piece of candy, but I suddenly felt tears warm my cheeks and I sprinted into the house and found Mom, who stood at the kitchen sink. "Grandma just talked English," I burst between light sobs.

"What's wrong?" she asked as she reached out to stroke my head.

"Grandma can talk English," I repeated.

"Of course she can," Mom answered. "What's wrong?"

I wasn't sure what was wrong, but after considering, I told Mom that Grandma had teased me. No sooner had I said that than the old woman appeared at the door and hiked her skirt. Attached to one of her petticoats by safety pins were several small tobacco sacks, the white cloth kind that closed with yellow drawstrings. She carefully unhooked one and opened it, withdrawing a dollar, then handed the money to me. *"Para su dulce,"* she said. Then, to my mother, she asked, "Why does he bawl like a motherless calf?"

"It's nothing," Mother replied.

"Do not weep, little one," the old lady comforted me, "Jesus and the Virgin love you." She smiled and patted my head. To my mother she said as though just realizing it, "Your baby?"

Somehow that day changed everything. I wasn't afraid of my great-grandmother any longer and, once I began spending time with her on the porch, I realized that my father had also begun directing increased attention to the old woman. Almost every evening Ese Gringo was sharing wine with Grandma. They talked out there, but I never did hear a real two-way conversation between them. Usually Grandma rattled on and Daddy nodded. She'd chuckle and pat his hand and he might grin, even grunt a word or two, before she'd begin talking again. Once I saw my mother standing by the front window watching them together, a smile playing across her face.

No more did I sneak around the house to avoid Grandma after school. Instead, she waited for me and discussed my efforts in class gravely, telling mother that I was a bright boy, *"muy inteligente,"* and that I should be sent to the nuns who would train me. I would make a fine priest. When Ese Gringo heard that, he smiled and said, "He'd make a fair-to-middlin' Holy Roller preacher, too." Even Mom had to chuckle, and my great-grandmother shook her finger at Ese Gringo. "Oh you debil, Sharlie!" she cackled.

Frequently, I would accompany Grandma to the lot where she would explain that no fodder could grow there. Poor pasture or not, the lot was at least unpaved, and Grandma greeted even the tiniest new cactus or flowering weed with joy. "Look how beautiful," she would croon. "In all this ugliness, it lives." Oildale was my home and it didn't look especially ugly to me, so I could only grin and wonder.

Because she liked the lot and things that grew there, I showed her the horned toad when I captured it a second time. I was determined to keep it, although I did not discuss my plans with anyone. I also wanted to hear more about the bloody eyes, so I thrust the small animal nearly into her face one afternoon. She did not flinch. *"Ola señor sangre de ojos,"* she said with a mischievous grin. *"Qué tal?"* It took me a moment to catch on.

"You were kidding before," I accused.

"Of course," she acknowledged, still grinning.

"But why?"

"Because the little beast belongs with his own kind in his own place, not in your pocket. Give him his freedom, my son."

I had other plans for the horned toad, but I was clever enough not to cross Grandma. "Yes, Ma'am," I replied. That night I placed the reptile in a flower bed cornered by a brick wall Ese Gringo had built the previous summer. It was a spot rich with insects for the toad to eat, and the little wall, only a foot high, must have seemed massive to so squat an animal.

Nonetheless, the next morning when I searched for the horned toad it was gone. I had no time to explore the yard for it, so I trudged off to school, my belly troubled. How could it have escaped? Classes meant little to me that day. I thought only of my lost pet—I had changed his name to Juan, the same as my Great-grandfather—and where I might find him.

I shortened my conversation with Grandma that afternoon so I could search for Juan. "What do you seek?" the old woman asked me as I poked through flower beds beneath the porch. "Praying mantises," I improvised, and she merely nodded, surveying me. But I had eyes only for my lost pet, and I continued pushing through branches and brushing aside leaves. No luck.

Finally, I gave in and turned toward the lot. I found my horned toad nearly across the street, crushed. It had been heading for the miniature desert and had almost made it when an automobile's tire had run over it. One notion immediately swept me: if I had left it on its lot, it would still be alive. I stood rooted there in the street, tears slicking my cheeks, and a car honked its horn as it passed, the driver shouting at me.

Grandma joined me, and stroked my back. "The poor little beast," was all she said, then she bent slowly and scooped up what remained of the horned toad and led me out of the street. "We must return him to his own place," she explained, and we trooped, my eyes still clouded, toward the back of the vacant lot. Carefully, I dug a hole with a piece of wood. Grandma placed Juan in it and covered him. We said an Our Father and a Hail Mary, then Grandma walked me back to the house. "Your little Juan is safe with God, my son," she comforted. We kept the horned toad's death a secret, and we visited his small grave frequently.

Grandma fell just before school ended and summer vacation began. As was her habit, she had walked alone to the vacant lot but this time, on her way back, she tripped over the curb and broke her hip. That following week, when Daddy brought her home from the hospital, she seemed to have shrunken. She sat hunched in a wheelchair on the porch, gazing with faded eyes toward the hills or at the lot, speaking rarely. She still sipped wine every evening with Daddy and even I could tell how concerned he was about her. It got to where he'd look in on her before leaving for work every morning and again at night before turning in. And if Daddy was home, Grandma always wanted him to push her chair when she needed moving, calling, "Sharlie!" until he arrived.

I was tugged from sleep on the night she died by voices drumming through the walls into darkness. I couldn't understand them, but was immediately frightened by the uncommon sounds of words in the night. I struggled from bed and walked into the living room just as Daddy closed the front door and a car pulled away.

Mom was sobbing softly on the couch and Daddy walked to her, stroked her head, then noticed me. "Come here, son," he gently ordered.

I walked to him and, uncharacteristically, he put an arm around me. "What's wrong?" I asked, near tears myself. Mom looked up, but before she could speak, Daddy said, "Grandma died." Then he sighed heavily and stood there with his arms around his weeping wife and son.

The next day my Uncle Manuel and Uncle Arnulfo, plus Aunt Chintia, arrived and over food they discussed with my mother where Grandma should be interred. They argued that it would be too expensive to transport her body home and, besides, they could more easily visit her grave if she was buried in Bakersfield. "They have such a nice, manicured grounds at Greenlawn," Aunt Chintia pointed out. Just when it seemed they had agreed, I could remain silent no longer. "But Grandma has to go home," I burst. "She has to! It's the only thing she really wanted. We can't leave her in the city."

Uncle Arnulfo, who was on the edge, snapped to Mother that I belonged with the other children, not interrupting adult conversation. Mom quietly agreed, but I refused. My father walked into the room then. "What's wrong?" he asked.

"They're gong to bury Grandma in Bakersfield, Daddy. Don't let 'em, please."

"Well, son . . ."

"When my horny toad got killed and she helped me to bury it, she said we had to return him to his place."

"Your horny toad?" Mother asked.

"He got squished and me and Grandma buried him in the lot. She said we had to take him back to his place. Honest she did."

No one spoke for a moment, then my father, Ese Gringo, who stood against the sink, responded: "That's right . . ." he paused, then added, "We'll bury her." I saw a weary smile cross my mother's face. "If she wanted to go back to the ranch then that's where we have to take her," Daddy said.

I hugged him and he, right in front of everyone, hugged back.

No one argued. It seemed, suddenly, as though they had all wanted to do exactly what I had begged for. Grown-ups baffled me. Late that week the entire family, hundreds it seemed, gathered at the little Catholic church in Coalinga for mass, then drove out to Arroyo Cantua and buried Grandma next to Grandpa. She rests there today.

My mother, father, and I drove back to Oildale that afternoon across the scorching westside desert, through sand and tumbleweeds and heat shivers. Quiet and sad, we knew we had done our best. Mom, who usually sat next to the door in the front seat, snuggled close to Daddy, and I heard her whisper to him, "Thank you, Charlie," as she kissed his cheek.

Daddy squeezed her, hesitated as if to clear his throat, then answered, "When you're family, you take care of your own."

Breaking One Hundred
William Rintoul
Taft

I walked across the Yellow Rose Golf Course, carrying the golf bag slung by the padded strap. The clubs made a satisfying thumping sound, muffled by the cardboard reinforced sides of the bag. There were four irons and one wood. I had paid Mr. Barclay ten dollars, which was almost all the money I had. I'd had a moment's hesitation when I learned the clubs had belonged to Mr. Barclay's wife, whom he called Pidge. However, nothing on the clubs said they were women's clubs, unless the bag might give it away. The bag had been light green once with darker green trim in padded seams, but there were worn places now, as if the bag had been dragged across rough surfaces. I had decided it looked battered enough to hide its previous ownership.

I headed toward the caretaker's shack, heedless of heat. The afternoon sun soared in a dusty sky, taunting the grassless surface of the golf course, which responded with a mirage of distant water.

"Golf?" my mother had said incredulously. "In July?"

Now that I was about to play for the first time, the Yellow Rose Golf Course looked different. I had only been on the course once before. It was a nine-hole course beside County Road on the edge of my hometown of Taft. Taft was a small oil town in the southern San Joaquin Valley, which was a part of California the All-Year Club did not tell tourists about. It had been summer then, too. I had taken a shortcut across the course, carrying a paper bag full of pop bottles I'd collected for the nickel deposit. The ground had looked like someone had dragged a bulldozer's blade across it.

There was no grass or evidence there ever had been any, only sparse clumps of drying weeds and few enough of them. The ground glittered in the sun, reflecting light with blinding intensity. The greens were made of oil sand, brown and redolent with the tarry smell of crude oil. Two wooden derricks rose out of the desolate landscape. I'd felt like a trespasser. I had not ventured on the course again. Neither then nor in other times when I had passed by the course had I seen anyone playing golf. I had supposed, to the extent I had given the matter any thought, that the Yellow Rose Golf Course was one more casualty of the depression.

Now the course suddenly looked interesting. It was an adversary. The two wooden derricks that stood starkly over idle wells were obvious obstacles. Sagebrush could be a problem in fields on two sides of the course. Chase a ball out there and I might flush out a rattlesnake. There were houses on the other two sides. Drive a ball into one of them and I might break a window. Well, they'd have a hard time collecting from me, considering the flatness of my wallet. What if I drove the ball into Brother Bob's? I shuddered. The ramshackle frame buildings stood apart. In front, there was a stand like ones from which farmers sold fruit along the roadside. The stand offered a surface on which people might leave boxes of discarded clothes, or whatever else they wanted to give away, without having to talk to, or look into the eyes of, Brother Bob or the rheumy-eyed men who loitered in the shade of the chinaberry trees in the back, where religious services were held. I tried to put the thought of Brother Bob's Free Relief Mission out of my mind.

I looked about the golf course, assessing the nine holes. Each would be a challenge. It would not be like a boxing match where you tried to knock out your opponent. This was a game of skill, a gentleman's game, Cortez had called it, where it was one person against the course, the hazards and the distance. Cortez had said the trick for a beginner was to break one hundred.

The first time the subject of golf had come up had been a few months before, one late afternoon of one of those January days when the tule fog carries the cold right through your clothes and you wonder why you ever complained about heat in summer. I'd just gotten home from high school, where I was a sophomore, and was circling the canvas bag I'd hung from the limb of the cottonwood tree in the backyard, moving in and out, punching with both hands, jabbing with my left, crossing with my right, moving on my toes over thoroughly beat-down ground. The bag responded crazily, lurching to the rhythm of blows, absorbing the jabs in the recesses of the rags I'd packed tightly into it, dancing back under the impact of harder rights, always swinging back into range, held by the supporting rope from getting away.

I'd heard the gate open with the complaining sound of dry metal hinges.

I'd seen Cortez enter the yard. The heavy black jacket my father had loaned him was drawn up around his throat. His face looked dusty, his eyes rimmed with red from the cold. He didn't look like he had any of his usual clever or humorous remarks to make. It had been his first day on the Indian mound.

"It didn't come," I'd said, saving Cortez the trouble of asking whether there had been a reply to the inquiry he had made to the state asking to have his three years of teaching school in Arizona accepted in place of the one year of practice teaching required for a credential in California. "Did you find anything?"

Cortez shook his head. "Some of the others found a few arrowheads and beads." Cortez, who at twenty-five was eleven years older than I, was an uncle on the O'Connell side, which was my mother's side. He had moved in with us in the fall after coming to California to look for work. The job on the Indian mound at the foot of San Cayetano Hills eight miles out of town wasn't exactly what he had in mind, but, like my father said, when half the country's out of work, who can be choosy? It was a government project that was supposed to last three or four months. They were going to dig up the mound to find out more about the Indians who used to live in the San Joaquin Valley. Technically, Cortez wasn't qualified. The newspaper had said the only ones they would consider were men who had been unemployed for some time and had families, in effect, the hard cases, the ones whose pockets were empty and whose kids were hungry. Spiritually, Cortez qualified. It had been almost two years since he had worked steady, teaching in Arizona. Though he was not married and did not have any kids, you wouldn't have found a man with less in his pockets. He was so broke, in fact, he had had to give up smoking. My mother, who had taken him in without complaint and certainly would not see him starve, was not about to give him money for cigarettes, especially since she didn't feel smoking was a good example for him to set.

Standing by the canvas bag, Cortez had raised his hands in a mock square-off, clenched his fists and executed a fancy shuffle more like a ballroom dance than the footwork you need to defend yourself in the ring. He moved in and out without throwing a blow. "Boxing's crude," he said. "It's for vulgarians."

I'd grinned. We had gone through this before. Cortez did his best to make boxing sound like a ridiculous sport, peopled by dim-witted sluggers who, however amiable, could not speak correctly, had few brains and those scrambled, and fewer abilities. It was hardly my description of Jimmy Braddock, whom they called the Cinderella Man. He had been on relief and was supposed to be washed up, but he had fought his way back, winning one fight with a broken right hand. The first thing he did when he got his first good purse was pay back all the money they gave him on relief. He was going to fight Max Baer for the heavyweight championship, even though everyone said he didn't have a chance. I had concluded Cortez wouldn't come right out and say not to do something. He tried to make it sound so ridiculous you wouldn't do it. I supposed that was the school-teacher surfacing.

"Why don't you take up something gentlemanly?" Cortez had said.

I'd gone on punching the bag.

"Something you might like," Cortez had said. "Golf. I've only played once or twice myself, but I understand it's a game of skill. It's for gentle-men. It's not crude like boxing."

The thought of Cortez made me feel depressed. It would not have been so hard having Cortez leave, even under the circumstances, if he had gotten something better than what he was doing, like if he had shipped out on a freighter or gotten a job working high in the air on one of those dams or bridges the newsreels showed the government building. But the only place he'd been able to get on was up north with the railroad, working in a gang that broke out cement that fog and rain washed out of cement dust in the air and caused to harden between the rails of the spur line that went to a big cement plant in the Buena Vista Mountains out of San Francisco. It was not much of a job, Cortez had written.

The caretaker's stand was a wooden shack no larger than the watchman's shack by the railroad crossing in Bakersfield. The opening from which an at-tendant might have looked out was shuttered. A chinaberry tree partially shaded the shack. It was the only tree on the course. The shadow from its umbrellalike branches fell across a thermometer that hung on a nail driven into the two-by-four that framed the shuttered opening. Eat at the Shamrock Cafe, the advertisement on top said. The thermometer read 107 degrees.

On a narrow wooden counter, I saw a Voseco notebook, held open by a rock. At the top of the page someone had written in ink, July 17. Below the date was space for those who played to sign their names. The page was blank. A pencil hung on a string from the edge of the counter. Following the string I came to a horizontal slit in the side of the shack above which nearly obliterated letters said, Pay Here. Twenty-five cents. I found a quar-ter in my pocket and dropped it through the slot. I listened for a clink against other coins. I heard no sound. After signing beneath the day's date, I thumbed back through the pages. There was a date at the top of each page. Each page was empty. I leafed back to the first page without finding a single name. Uneasy, I turned the notebook back to the page on which I had signed, replaced the rock and put the pencil in the fold of the book. I looked at houses on the sides of the course. Was the caretaker watching from one of those houses, not showing himself but looking out through a curtained window, waiting to apprehend anyone who did not pay? The houses suddenly looked ominous.

A small box by the shuttered window held scorecards and several stub pencils. On the scorecard, one column listed the number of each hole and opposite it, the par. Par for the nine holes totaled thirty-six. Twice around the course would be eighteen holes, equivalent to play on a regular course. Par would be seventy-two. That was for people who had played. The first step would be to break one hundred. I shouldered the golf bag and walked with rising anticipation to the first tee.

A small slab of roughly finished concrete offered a place to stand opposite a square of tar from which a splintered tee protruded. I unzipped the pouch on the golf bag and examined the three balls inside, selecting the one with the fewest scars. I rummaged through the pouch until I found an undamaged tee. In the search, I discovered a lady's filmy handkerchief, which I jammed down to the bottom of the pouch. I zippered the pouch, laid the bag to one side, forced the tee into the tar and balanced the ball on top. I selected the wood driver. Taking a position opposite the ball, I looked at the green in the distance, brought the club up over my shoulder, reminded myself to follow through as Mr. Barclay had said to do and swung. The club connected solidly, lifting the ball in a gentle arc, in a straight line, always in sight, falling to strike the hard surface of the course, roll forward and stop no more than twenty yards from the brown patch that was the first green. Pleased, I shouldered the bag and walked toward the ball, scarcely noticing the mirage that kept its distance in front of me.

Dirt had been banked to form a barrier around the green, enclosing it inside a levee three feet high, open in front in a line with where the ball lay. I chose the seven iron, meaning to lift the ball onto the green. I swung, sending the ball flying over the green and out of sight beyond. I angrily returned the club to the bag. I found the ball only yards short of the oiled road that separated the course from sagebrush. Two strokes later, I was on the oil sand green. A wooden pole marked the cup. The pole was topped with a rough-cut piece of rug. I picked up the ball, drew a line to mark where it lay, then took the pole out of the cup and pulled the rug moplike over the green to smooth a path through oil sand to the cup. I pulled the mop over the cup, almost filling it. I scooped out oil sand, scattering it over the green. The sand gritted against my fingers. The odor of crude oil hung heavy in simmering air. I put down the ball, took the putter from the bag and two strokes later, holed out. I hurried off the green to escape heat that burned through the soles of my tennis shoes. On the scorecard, I wrote in the blank space after par three my score, which was five. Mentally I multiplied five by nine and the result by two. Ninety. At this rate, I easily would break one hundred.

According to the marker, the second hole was a short one, only one hundred and twenty-five yards. Par three. I drove with the wood. The ball rose sharply, veered and landed far to the side of the green. I took two shots, the last with the putter, to get on the green, three more to hole out. Disgusted, I wrote six by the par three.

The third hole was another short one. One hundred and thirty-five yards. Par three. I made it in five strokes. I hurried off the green. There was a makeshift drinking fountain beside the fourth tee, consisting of one-inch pipe that rose waist high through a larger pipe about six inches in diameter. Coarse sand and gravel filled the space between the two pipes. A valve handle protruded on a stem from the inner pipe. I gripped the valve, meaning to open it and allow water to bubble up and fall back to wet the insulating sand and gravel. I quickly released my grip. Metal burned my fingers. I used the handkerchief from the pouch to shield my fingers while I held the valve open, allowing water to run until sand and gravel would absorb no more. I drank sparingly. Water was hot, the sun blistering. My forehead felt greasy with sweat.

The fourth hole paralleled the oiled road. It was a longer hole. Two hundred yards. Par four. To the left was an abandoned sumphole beside the first of the two wooden derricks. I teed up, mindful of the trap. I used the wood, slicing the ball to the right, across the road and into sagebrush. While I was looking for it, I heard a sudden whirring sound. Frightened, I stood still, mindful that a rattlesnake will try to get away. I saw grasshoppers rising, and realized they had made the sound. I found the ball, swung with the two iron and lifted the ball back onto the course and into the sumphole. I found the ball in a crevice among blocks of parched, cracking earth and hardened, clay-like residue that reminded me of a picture in one of the books at school of drought in Africa. I placed the ball on a chunk of sunbaked clay and lifted it with the five iron over the embankment. I putted onto the green, smoothed a path to the cup and holed out, taking six strokes.

The fifth hole was hardly more than one hundred yards, with no traps, par three. The hole paralleled the street on which frame houses fronted. Some houses looked empty. Most were run down. There were few trees, fewer lawns. I looked apprehensively at the houses, weighing them as hazards. Wavy lines of water danced on the street. I selected the five iron, teed up, drove and sent the ball hooking toward the caretaker's shack. I debated resting in the shade of the chinaberry tree. I decided against it. I would need all the time I had to play eighteen holes. There was no mop at the green. I putted against an uneven surface. It took six strokes to hole out. I had an uneasy feeling I was not doing well.

The sixth hole was longer, paralleling the road. There was a car in front of one house. At another, a garden hose sprayed a fan of water over a small lawn. The water sparkled in the sun. I debated walking through the spray. The hose was inside the fence. I would have to open the gate. I surveyed the hole, two hundred yards away. Furrowed levees lay between the tee and green. I selected the seven iron, no longer trusting the wood. I lifted the ball over furrows, landing within easy reach of the green. Two more strokes and I was on. I smoothed the green, heedless of oil sand that fell into the cup. I decided to leave that for someone else. A residue of sand still gritted hot in pores of my hands. I ringed the cup. Angrily, I putted without lining up the shot. I missed. It took two more strokes to get in. Seven when I should have had an easy five.

The seventh hole was the longest of the course, more than four hundred yards, the only hole along the County Road side. The pole that marked the green looked disjointed in watery mirage. The green was set deeper into the course in apparent recognition of traffic on the road. It would be one thing to hit a parked car on the intersecting street I had just paralleled, another to drive the ball into a moving car on County Road. Midway down the road were the decaying buildings of Brother Bob's Free Relief Mission. I weighed the chances of driving a ball into the shacks. If that happened, Brother Bob could consider the ball a donation. Teeing up, I drove the ball straight, getting a good one hundred and fifty yards with the two iron. The clubs felt heavy. The strap chafed. My feet burned. I used the two iron to blast the ball down the course, the runner-up to get on, the putter to hole out. Six strokes. Seven holes down, two to go. There was a drinking fountain by the green identical to the one on the fourth tee. Using my shirttail to protect my hand, I opened the valve, letting water fall back to soak the dry sand and gravel. I rinsed my mouth and spit out the first hot mouthful, then drank sparingly.

The eighth hole was a short one, paralleling the north side of the course. Teeing up, I drove with the two iron. The ball flew over the green, dropping out of sight. Par three, the scorecard said. I found the ball three feet from the cup on the first green. I drove with the seven iron, sending up a brown cloud of oil sand. I smoothed the divot. Four strokes later I holed out. I wrote six beside par three.

The ninth hole paralleled the first, taking me back to the caretaker's shack. The only hazard was the second wooden derrick. Oil tarred the floorboards and hardened on the ground beneath. The walking beam was idle. I drove. The ball flew into the derrick, struck timber, rebounded wildly, ricocheting off to the seventh fairway. It took five strokes to hole out. In the shade of the chinaberry tree, I added my score. Fifty-four. It was hot, even in the shade. I looked at the thermometer, which was in full shade. The mercury stood at one hundred and nine. Impulsively, I took the thermometer from the nail and placed it on the ground in the sun. I sat, resting my back against the trunk of the tree. I was thirsty. My head felt hot. The mop on the pole on the first green floated in a sea of rolling waves. In the distance, dust rose on the horizon. I wiped my forehead. I dried my hand on my pants, staining the pants with oil sand. At this rate, I would not break one hundred.

I wondered if Cortez ever got a chance to play tennis any more. That was his game, bounding around the court in clean white tennis clothes, enthusi-astically hitting the ball, enjoying the motion and the crisp sound of the ball striking the strings, acting on those spring days like he had been set free from the drudgery of the mound, the tedious digging and screening, the constant dust and the decaying, loosely-woven fabric and yellowing bones that came up from the burials. One thing for sure, Cortez wouldn't be out on the court laughing and joking with anyone as pretty as Katie Gehringer, whose long hair brushed silkily against her neck every time she swung her racquet. I wondered if Cortez wrote to Katie. Or Katie wrote to Cortez. My mother wondered the same thing. I had heard her talking with my fa-ther, who said all he wondered was what in God's name ever possessed Cortez. My mother had been enigmatic about one bit of information my father had brought home two days before. My father said he had heard that Kathryn Gehringer had given Rafton Bonnard notice. She was quitting her job at the supervisor's road district office, where she had worked for almost four years. The job as secretary was a good one, by town standards. My mother had said she wondered if Katie knew what she was doing. I won-dered if what Katie was doing had anything to do with what I had seen at the library. I'd seen Katie at the table by the newspaper rack where I went to look at the sports sections of the out-of-town papers to see if there was anything about Jimmy Braddock. I had never seen Katie there before. She was looking at the *San Francisco Chronicle.* She had seemed startled. Even as I spoke, she had folded the newspaper as if she did not want me to see what she was looking at. It was the classified section where they advertised things like jobs and places to live. She had asked if I was enjoying vacation, and I had said I was, as I knew that was what I was expected to say, even though there wasn't anything to do around town. Neither of us had men-tioned Cortez. After I went to the seven-day shelf, she had resumed look-ing at the same part of the newspaper.

I looked at the first tee and remembered my drive. Had it been the only straight one? I could get distance with the wood, but what good was dis-tance when the ball curved to the right or left? I suddenly thought of an al-ternative. Why not use the putter to drive? At least the ball would go reasonably straight. Why not settle for less distance, but get it in a straight line? The surface of the course was as hard as if it had been paved. The ball would roll. Taking the putter, I walked eagerly to the tee. I teed up, raised the putter and swung as hard as I could. The ball shot out, rolling along the ground in a straight line toward the hole. It did not stop until it had gone almost one hundred yards. I shouldered the bag and hurried to the ball. I hit again with the putter, driving almost to the green. A third stroke and I was on. One more and I had holed out. I excitedly wrote four in the space for the score. I had shaved off one stroke. I carried the clubs to the second tee. Again I drove with the putter. Again the ball rolled straight. I made the hole in five. Why hadn't I thought of this before? Instead of strokes to knock off my score, I would be well on my way to breaking one hundred. Now there was not any margin. I had to make each shot count. I shaved another stroke on the third hole. I stopped by the drinking fountain. The water I had run the first time around had soaked in, leaving sand dry on top. Shielding my fingers with my shirttail, I opened the valve, letting water run. It was not as hot as before. I rinsed my mouth, spit out lukewarm water, then drank, stopping before I had drank as much as I would have liked, mindful of cramps if you drink too much on a hot day. The sun seemed unusually high. The afternoon seemed hotter. I wondered why they had not planted trees.

On the fourth hole, I holed out with four strokes, two less than before. I was back in the game. I had an outside chance. I carried the clubs to the caretaker's shack and propped the bag there, taking only the putter. I felt like resting. There was not time. I looked at the thermometer on the ground. The thin red column of mercury had flooded the bubble at the top opposite 125 degrees, which was the highest the thermometer read. Mindful that whoever owned the thermometer might not like this kind of usage, I returned the thermometer to the nail in the shade. My shorts beneath my pants felt like they had been soaked in water. They were beginning to bunch, making it uncomfortable to walk. My socks felt wet. My eyes burned. I closed them. They burned even more.

At the fifth tee where the hole paralleled houses along the street, I saw a woman in a rocking chair looking at me from the porch of the third house down. A man stood in front of another house, watching. There was a man in a porch swing at another house, looking in my direction. I confidently teed up. I struck the ground, scarcely hitting the ball, which trickled off only a few yards. Dismayed, I hurried to the ball, telling myself to calm down. I did not have strokes to spare. If those people thought I would blow it, they had another think coming. I swung carefully, sending the ball down the fairway. Four strokes later I holed out. I was still in the running.

On the sixth tee, the tar into which I pushed the tee was softer than before, like the sun was melting it. I was careful not to touch the surface. Heat traveled through the soles of my shoes and up my ankles, where sweat trickled down my legs to challenge it. I noticed more people watching. I swung. The ball rolled straight. I shouldered the putter, careful not to touch the metal head, grateful for the rubber grip on the handle. I walked slowly toward the green. Walking was an effort. My face burned. My body felt damp. The shorts jockeyed up my legs, cutting at my crotch. I looked at the fan of water in the yard across the street. The water looked more inviting than before. I wondered if whoever lived there would mind if I walked through the water. I looked at the green ahead and kept walking toward it, wiping my forehead to keep sweat out of my eyes. It seemed to take forever to get on, longer to get in. Nine strokes. I quickly walked off the green to get away from the hot oil sand. I added scores for the first six holes of the second nine. Thirty-two. If I was going to break one hundred, I had to make the last three holes without unnecessary strokes.

There seemed to be more people watching. On one porch, an old woman stared at me, shapeless in a print dress and withered as sagebrush struggling to survive without water. On another porch, there was a heavy man in coveralls, wiping his forehead with a handkerchief. Had any of them played golf? Did they know what it was like trying to break one hundred?

I stood on the seventh tee. The hole was the longest of all. The mop that marked the green was barely visible over dancing water. The derrick loomed to the side, waiting to catch the crooked drive and ricochet the ball. A car passed on County Road. The driver slowed to look. I bent to tee up. When I stood, my head felt light. I blinked and shook my head to clear it. I raised the putter, looked at the distant green and swung. I connected solidly, sending the ball down the fairway dangerously close to the road. I walked toward the ball. My legs were rubbery. They felt removed, like they belonged to someone else. They were burning, though my body felt cooler when I moved than when I stood still. My face felt hot. My clothes were like wrinkled wet towels wrapped around my body. I walked for what seemed a long time. The ball still seemed far away. I rubbed sweat from my face. I looked at the sky. The sun was riding high, hardly dipping. The ground burned. I felt shaky. I looked at the houses. They seemed far away. Even Brother Bob's Free Relief Mission seemed distant, though I had walked toward it. I felt like I had shrunk and what had seemed a reasonable walk the first time around had become an impossible distance. I shook. I steadied myself with the putter. My stomach felt like I was going to be sick.

The enormity of the situation dawned. I had wanted to break one hundred, but what was the point? What would that prove? The course was a parody of a golf course. There wasn't any grass, like there should have been. Only one tree. Not even a water trap. Nor a sand trap. The whole thing was a fraud. A fake. It wasn't a fair test. It wasn't what anyone could have in mind when they said golf was a gentleman's game. It was a poor equivalent. I debated putting the putter back in the bag, taking the bag and going home. Why not see if Mr. Barclay would give back my money? Tell him I had decided not to play golf. Tell him my mother objected, or my father, that they demanded I get my money back. Get rid of the clubs and be done with golf. The sun beat down, unchallenged by clouds. I angrily debated leaving the ball where it lay, letting it be an object lesson to anyone crazy enough to go out on the Yellow Rose Golf Course. The distant green mocked me. The wooden derrick cast a lengthening shadow, daring me. I wished I had never seen the course, never bought the clubs, never come out to play, never listened to Cortez. I wiped off sweat. Why hadn't Cortez shipped out on a freighter or gotten a job high in the air?

I recalled the Sunday morning in the kitchen. I had come downstairs worried. There had been no sign of Cortez in the screened-in sleeping porch upstairs. No sign anyone had slept in his bed. I had looked out the window. There was no sign of Cortez's ancient Chevrolet. Downstairs, I had known immediately something was wrong. Cortez had been at the stove, heating water for coffee. He had not looked up. His face looked puffed, his eyes bloodshot. My mother was at the sink rinsing dishes. She scarcely had spoken. Her eyes looked red. My father had not been anywhere around. I had thought maybe he was working in his vegetable garden, but I had not seen him there. I had not seen him, in fact, until late that evening. Even as I had known something was wrong, I had known that I did not dare ask. I had said good morning. Cortez had looked up. His eyes were so red I wondered if he had been crying. He had not said a word, going back to watching the water on the stove. There had been no Sunday dinner that day with all of us together around the table. I had known of one of the events of the previous day. I had been there when the official-looking envelope arrived, returning Cortez's letters of recommendation and advising him he could not be considered qualified to teach in California. It would only be later that I would learn of other events: the disappearance of the bottle from my father's trunk, the afternoon at Frankheimer's beer garden where the fan dancer was outraging the town's gossips, the wild ride uptown that night shouting at loitering men that drinks would be on Cortez O'Connell at Frankheimer's, the cops-and-robbers chase by the constable with red light blinking through alleys and across vacant lots, the too-sharp turn that laid the Chevy on its side and pitched Cortez into the oleanders by the library and, finally, the early morning call from the jail. If I lived to be an old man, I would never forget the look in Cortez's eyes that Sunday morning. I had not known grown-ups could look so anguished, or so completely without hope. He looked like he had given up.

I walked toward the ball. If the sun meant to make me stop, to beat down so hard I would quit, it would have to get hotter than it was. If the people on the porches thought they were going to see me fall on my face, they would be a long time watching before they saw that happen, and a lot longer before they saw me stay down. I looked across County Road and saw a man watching from Brother Bob's. He was a figure like those in the illustrated Bible some relative had given us. The Bible sat unread on the bookshelf, but I had looked at the pictures. The men in the pictures had beards and wore flowing robes and looked crazy. I stared without flinching at the man, then looked at the ball, brought the putter up and swung, sending the ball rolling past the wooden derrick. On the green, oil sand scorched my feet. I took my time, mopping a path to the hole, lining up the putt, carefully hitting the ball. I put the ball in the hole with three more strokes. Without losing pace, I teed off for the eighth hole. I wished for a drink of cold water. I drove into the sun, hit again, putted. I made the hole in four.

The ninth green seemed farther away than the first time. My legs were exhausted. I felt dizzy. I was not afraid. I was going to finish. I made the hole in four. I added the score. Ninety-nine. I had broken one hundred. In the shade of the chinaberry tree, I drew a deep breath, careful to do so slowly for fear I might scorch my lungs. Sweat broke out when I stopped moving, running down my face. My clothes hung like damp rags. My socks bunched, hurting my toes. I shouldered the clubs. I started for home, catercorner on the way that would lead past the biblical figure who watched from Brother Bob's, past people on porches. I did not know what they expected. I had bought the clubs. I had set out to play golf, and I had played. I would have to write Cortez. He would be glad to hear I had taken up golf.

Southern California

Ojai, 1959
Valerie Hobbs
Ojai

What I remember most about those days, more vividly than anything senses can summon up second-hand, is what immortality felt like. Not the illusion of immortality, that shadow dance we do with our minds to get from one day to the next, but the real thing. The absolute certainty that one is bigger and far more important than one really is. That wacky narcissism of the gods, and of teenagers. Dying was something somebody else did, usually at the end of a long life, someone like my grandmother who lived across the continent, whose memory I could formally grieve and then lay to rest.

We lived in our senses then, no better proof that we would last forever.

Ojai was, still is, a small dusty town twenty miles inland from the California everybody knows, the California of postcards. We got there by mistake, a wrong turn off the freeway. "A happy accident," my mother said, already in love with the pseudo-Spanish arches. The restaurant would have to be there or nowhere. All we owned was packed in the car, a gull gray '49 Plymouth, or in the plywood box roped to the top. "California or Bust" the box announced in bright orange letters across one side, Allan's idea. He was ten. Crossing the country was a 3000-mile adventure for him. For me, it was an agony I slept through. Indiana was a cornfield, Utah had some mountains. All the rest was gas stops and cheap motels.

From the shade beneath the arches, we surveyed our new home. Drugstore, pool parlor, tack shop, city hall, gas station with a single pump. One hundred and three in the shade, the drugstore thermometer read. A dry heat, my mother said. There was no one on the streets. Inside the drug-store, a girl about my age sat at the soda fountain twirling her right foot and the straw in her coke. Like Gatsby's Daisy, she was dressed all in white—shoes, sundress, white ribbon trailing the length of her silver-blond ponytail. Her skin was the honeyed gold of Sunday morning waffles, her lips and fingernails a perfectly executed, perfectly matched, bright crimson. I hated Ojai from that moment.

Until school began that fall, I read trash novels or walked the back streets kicking dust through my sandals, crying. But soon the tears stopped, and I became as dry and parsimonious as the landscape. Meanwhile, my parents invented a restaurant out of bolts of red-and-white checkered fabric, mis-matched tables from the Salvation Army, assorted travel posters, and Allan found half a dozen friends with names like Luis and Hector, all brothers and cousins with dark, laughing eyes. Congratulations all around. Treach-ery, my heart said.

At Nordhoff High, I was the one in dyed-to-match gray, a shadow who could slide into back-row seats while every head was turned away. Anonym-ity ended one sixth-period American History class when I was asked to read from the textbook. "Louder, please," Mr. Milroy called, as I fumbled my way through the first few sentences of a passage as long as my trembling arm.

"General Sherman," I began again. "Alawng with fawty of his ablest commandiz . . ." The room grew suddenly still, ominously quiet. As in waiting. As in snakes in the sun. Not a paper rustled. Not a foot skimmed the floor. Then a snort, an exploded giggle, whispers traveling at the speed of light. Head down, hair shielding my flaming face, I fought with Sher-man to the sea and finished the passage. As I fled down the hall to the girls' room, twin hearts beat in my ears. Dumb shit dumb shit dumb shit.

"So where ya from?" She was putting on mascara, touching the tiny brush to the tips of her lashes, giving each lash individual attention. I wasn't sure she had spoken to me, but there was no one else in the room. Just me and what *Seventeen* would have put on a cover and called the quin-tessential California girl. Wide-set mischievous green eyes, blond pageboy kissing the curve of tanned half-bare shoulders. I thought for a minute she might be the drugstore girl, but her lipstick was a soft pink, her nails buffed to a natural gloss and I couldn't be sure.

"New Jersey," I said. "Plainfield."

"Well, Jersey," she said, slinging her purse over her shoulder and gather-ing up her books. "You'd better do something about that hair."

I watched the door close behind her and turned, as if ordered, toward the the mirror. Red-rimmed eyes of indeterminate color, freckle-spattered nose, chipped front tooth, failed dull brown pageboy. I knew right then that I wasn't going to make it. I would never be one of them. The way they walked, the things they said. They were different from eastern kids. Slicker, cleverer. They knew things I would never know. Always a step behind, I would be lost forever in the labyrinth of a language, an entire way of life, created long before I came along, in girls' rooms where California girls spawn.

And then William came along. The way all the best and the worst things happen. Not by dreaming or planning, the way things happen in fiction, but by accident, the way it is in real life.

William David Warren III. Heir apparent in a fine, old California family with no apparent, or little apparent anything to be heir to. William David Warren II, decorated for bravery, had been killed in Korea, leaving Will's mother, a woman I worshiped and detested by turns, to rear three sons on a meager military pension and the living demands of memory. She was more than equal to the task. Certain things were taken for granted. Like the fact that Will, as his father before him, would attend West Point where he had been enrolled shortly after birth. When he himself passed on, hopefully at the culmination of a long and successful military career, he would be buried with the requisite twenty-one gun honors in the family plot at Arlington.

Will accepted all this gracefully, thoughtfully but without pride. He accepted it with what I would have called wisdom, had I been able to identify what was then for me and for those I emulated a word in another language. Will was wise and decent and grown-up. But I had only the vaguest sense of who he really was. From the night I first saw him in the restaurant, I thought he was something straight out of the movies, a gunslinger.

To my father's delighted surprise, The Welsh Kitchen became one of those little-known places everybody knew about. Father cooked, mother waited on tables, Allan ran errands and emptied the trash. When need overcame my snobbishness, I waited on tables too, terrified always that the Student Body President or the Head Cheerleader would wander in for dinner or, worse, would reserve the entire dining room for the Awards Banquet. But the customers were generally people whose children, like the Warrens', attended local private schools.

They presented themselves for the first time, Mrs. Warren in vintage silk, on a harrowing, overbooked Saturday evening. My father, who had a winning way with people, women particularly, met them at the door. Mrs. Warren listened patiently to his explanations, then dispensed a tight but courteous smile and drew her boys around her. You knew by the way they stood that they could outwait floods, and other natural or even unnatural disasters. Even the youngest Warren had that maddening, gracious, old-world patience. And then my father saw, slung beneath the eldest son's right hip, a worn leather holster and a silver Colt 45. Something in the boy's eyes must have told my father, who would not have known a Colt from a dime store facsimile, that he was in the presence of the real thing.

"You'll have to check that," my father said.

"I can't do that, sir," the boy said.

Table by table, the dining room filled with the soft patter of pretended conversation, trailing half-sentences. Heads leaned ever so slightly toward the scene at the door. California drama of the old west, or what was left of it.

Then Mrs. Warren leaned toward Will and he leaned toward her and, very briefly, they exchanged words no one else could hear. Pleasant words, as far as I could tell, reasonable words. While Mrs. Warren and the younger sons dined, Will, at military parade rest, waited outside.

I asked him once why he always carried the gun, but I don't think he knew the answer. He only smiled and shook his head sorrowfully, as if lamenting that someone so intimately connected with him would need to ask. I had known him for nearly a year by then. After that night in the restaurant, I had to know him, impelled by that same headlong curiosity that drove me so often in the opposite direction to be among my high-school friends. I wanted to do everything you didn't get to do in the east—ride a horse, drive a battered Army jeep, shoot the oo's out of Coors cans.

And then one day, in the middle of nothing memorable, one of those wonderful youthful days when you call yourself bored, he said that we were intimate. I was surprised, embarrassed. Intimacy was a crimson word splashed across the cover of *True Confessions*. But for him, whatever we did, perhaps living itself, was intimate.

One lazy summer afternoon we rode, as we often did, for miles along the dry creek bed that ran the length of the adjoining ranch. Securing the horses, we began a zigzag climb that brought us eventually to the summit just beneath the flat stone expanse of Hurricane Deck. The Warrens' small ranch, and the extended range to which it was appended like a poor relative, stretched out below us. Beyond lay the town and my parents' restaurant, an embarrassment with tentacles firmly affixed to my heart. There, too, were the friends who made up my weekday life and from whom I escaped with thin excuses, like an errant wife, to be with Will on the weekend.

Will stood with the toes of his boots just over the edge of a flat boulder looking down through a thousand feet of space, thumbs hooked into his belt loops, Stetson low on his forehead, for him an unaffected posture. He was not a tall boy. He was not the kind of boy whose existence my town friends recognized. Years earlier, a case of acne had raged, like wicked summer fire, across his face, etching lines that made him look older than he was and a little sad. His back was straight and broad, his plaid western shirt tapering neatly into a wide well-worn leather belt.

He stood looking at his toes for a while, then began removing his clothes, shucking his boots, stepping out of his jeans, dropping his plaid shirt and jockey shorts all in a single, smooth motion. Then, beginning with the top button of my blouse, he undressed me too.

There was nothing frantic in this, no heavy breathing, the silly backseat rustling I knew. Pressed against each other on that warm, flat rock, we kissed with a cherished and familiar tenderness, like ancient lovers. When Will rolled away and lay on his back, his erection looked to me like some exotic plant, a sunseeking mushroom. Overhead, hawks traced wide looping circles in the sky. In the quiet, you could hear their wings play the air. Sharp-eyed lizards shot fast across exposed rock into the protecting red-veined fingers of manzanita.

We watched the birds, named clouds, and after a while, curled into each other and innocent we slept.

Will's maternal grandfather subsidized Will's education at the most prestigious local private school, and his mother made sure the money was well spent. Will and I rarely saw each other during the week. That was when I lived my other life.

Cars were the center of that life. Fast cars, cars with candy apple paint jobs, chrome headers, oversized cams, slick rear tires on which you could slide sideways into the street, then squeal your way through a block and a half of city street, laying rubber down in long smoking strips. The particularly adept could complete the maneuver with two fingers of the left hand, right wrapped possessively around a cold Oly or the back of a girlfriend's neck. To be seen riding with the owner of one of these cars was to have reached a state of social grace; driving one was the ultimate power fix.

At the hub of this collection of men and machines was Jerry whose fingers, it was said, had infallible mechanical wisdom. He could diagnose auto illness by ear, and then operate with the skill of a fine surgeon. Whenever girls wanted to find their boyfriends, they'd just drive over to Jerry's and there they'd be like so many bees crawling all over each other under the hood of someone's car.

Jerry had an engaging smile, a wide open, ready for anything smile that people, particularly girls, fell into without watching where they were going. Or so it was with me. Jerry had a son and a divorce before he could vote. But instead of setting him off-limits, his past gave him a tragic glamour. Poor Jerry was heartbroken, the story went. Susan was "such a bitch." Whenever he had the baby for the day, he would hang around the Frostee where any number of girls would fawn over them both, finally leaving Jerry free to talk engines while they baby-sat.

I had an old red Ford then that I'd gotten in a roundabout way. A number of starving artists, actors on welfare, assorted reputable, even formerly famous but impoverished townspeople had taken immediately to my parents' restaurant; the food was excellent and abundant, prices were low. Many of the local populace, like members of a large and avaricious family, ate there every night. Some ran a tab and paid at the end of the month;

some ran out of money, in which case if they were respectable. some sort of bargain would be struck. And so it was, that in exchange for an agreement to pay the movie theatre owners' dinner tab, I inherited his second car. I paid for it more or less diligently out of my tips.

Ten years old, the Ford ran on high-grade faith and daily quarts of oil. Then one day, unwilling to go that extra lap, it stopped dead, smoking and hissing at the entrance of Saint Thomas Aquinas. With help from an amused priest on his way to work, I pushed the car into an adjoining parking lot and walked to the Frostee to call my father. Father, whose skills were exclusively culinary, said he'd do what he could, which sank my heart. Without my car, I was nothing. Powerless. I hung up the telephone and, as if I had put him there, which was still my delusion in those days, there was Jerry. It took him less than five minutes to start the car; another two, maybe three to suck up my fickle heart. Will was "sweet," I told myself, a damning epithet; Jerry was fire in the veins, supercharged.

Behind the wheel of the Ford, I could see only Jerry's long jean-clad legs, the pull of the soft, worn fabric as he leaned across the fender into the engine adjusting this, tightening that. Then he stood, winked at me, and with a devastating casualness born of accumulated experience with cars and foolish girls, dropped the hood. That, that precise action, all of it, I created, or thought I created, and what followed as well. The exact way he leaned down, that intimate look in his eyes.

"Well, little lady," he said. "You're on wheels again."

The smell of Beechnut and aftershave drifted through the car.

"You owe me one," he said, chucking my chin. "Just a little one."

In my rearview mirror I watched him slide away to his Chevy. Driving off, he was still smiling. Not at me, but at some joke all his own. In my mind, I was already in the seat beside him.

Jerry played me on a long line. One moment attentive, electrically tuned-in, the next moment he would literally disappear. This looked to my fond heart like magic, not faithlessness. Meanwhile, Will drew closer. He began counting the days we could spend together before he left for West Point.

Will had made reservations months in advance for our last night together at a restaurant just outside town. In what was then a bold venture, all the tables had been placed within the gardens, among thick stands of bamboo, roses, fragrant herbs. From a small bowed bridge, you could watch fat carp turning circles in the stream. Will named a slim, spotty one for himself and a quicksilver gray one for me. "And here come the kids," he laughed as a half dozen young fish swam into view. "Susie, Sandy . . ." Then, in the serious, slow way he had, he asked if I minded that our first son already had his name picked out. "William David Warren, The Fourth," he said. "Poor kid." Through a refracting film of tears, I watched the brightly colored fish become water through which an unseen hand spun colored ink.

*   *   *

On the subject of sex, my mother was quite clear. Not about the mechanics of it, which was all that interested me, but about all the peripherals; when and where it should be done and by whom. It was not to be done by me. Whenever I came in from a date, she would look at me, simply look, and I could see that she knew immediately whether I had returned in the same solid state in which she had created me. "You know, men don't fall for that riding horses stuff," she said. Once, in an attempt to convey the male perspective, she made the mistake of consulting my father. "A stiff one has no conscience," he said, Groucho Marxing his eyebrows.

Their admonitions were no match for Jerry, who came on like a well-tuned engine, humming, filling me up until I became the humming too. He was in me almost before I knew it. "Don't worry," he breathed as I cried. "I pulled out in time." The rain on the car roof spat and danced. "You're my girl," he said. His words ran over me like a memory of something I once wanted more than life. The leather seat was cold. I wanted to be home in my bed caught up in a strange dream. I got out of Jerry's car a block from the restaurant and crept around to the back porch where I sat until dawn, knees to chin, wrapped in my father's old sweater.

I stopped writing to Will, but his letters continued. For a while, they were the same as always. He was enjoying army life more than he expected to. He was studying or playing sports every minute of the day, but at lights-out, he said, he whispered across the distance to me. Did I hear? He couldn't wait until semester break when he could see me again. When I didn't answer, he began to sound puzzled. "Are you okay?" he asked. When he began sounding frantic, I stopped reading his letters. I did not see myself as cruel. I had simply become someone else, someone he would not have written to had he known who she really was.

Still, I remembered the date of his return and stayed at home, half hoping he'd drop by and that, somehow, everything would be the way it was before, intact. But Jerry came over instead. We hung around the darkened dining room getting on each other's nerves.

"What's the matter with you?"

"Nothing. What's the matter with you?"

"Nothing."

And then I heard the jeep. It had an unmistakable miss in the engine every third stroke that my heart took up like an old song. We watched Will climb out of the jeep and amble up to the front door. He had the beginning traces of a smile on his face, the kind of smile a fond husband might allow himself returning home after a hard day's work.

"You know this guy?" Jerry said.

I opened the door before Will could knock, and his presence, the outdoors and the rightness of him hit me like something solid in the chest.

Then Jerry was beside me, one hand at the back of my neck, the other extended. "I'm Jerry," he said.

Will hesitated, looked at me, then took Jerry's hand.

"Come in," I said faintly, but I knew he wouldn't.

"No, I . . . I just came to say hello. It's okay," he said, as if to himself and then maybe to me. "It's okay."

Then he turned, adjusted his Stetson, and walked slowly back to his jeep.

"Where'dja know that shitkicker from?" said Jerry.

The next morning when I awoke, my father was sitting on my bed, head down as if he were sleeping sitting up, or maybe praying.

"Daddy?"

"Will had an accident, honey," he said. "With the gun."

I leapt up and he caught me, taking my screams into his chest.

No one who knew Will, knew what kind of boy he was, believed the rumors that licked their way across town toward the Warren ranch. Even those I called my friends wanted to call it a suicide. There was a story in that. Romance. No one remembers a simple mistake, not even a tragic one. Will had gone to visit his grandmother that afternoon and when he didn't arrive, she called his mother who went out looking for him. Halfway to Los Angeles, along a stretch of untouched country, the last there was, she found the jeep parked on the side of the freeway. She found the gun on the floor. The county coroner located the small hole in Will's femoral artery through which his life spilled, it was said, in less than eight minutes.

Will and I lived in that old jeep. Talking, planning. Driving, just like my town friends, to have the feeling of control over where we were going. Sometimes, who knew why, Will would reach for his gun and aim it out the window, at a jackrabbit only he could see loping across an open field. If you knew him intimately, you didn't worry about it. You knew he only shot bullets into Coors cans, not into living things. Still, it would have taken time to remember that and to understand. Until then, as if spun out into thin space, you handled it all as well as you could.

The Warrens were at their finest on the day of the memorial service. Like the soldier she was, Mrs. Warren stood caliber straight, shaking hands, accepting condolences. As I moved toward her in the line, I became more and more hysterical until I was babbling, "I'm sorry, I'm sorry."

She held me up with her two thin hands and said, "It couldn't be helped, my dear. You musn't go on so."

His brothers looked on me with well-bred scorn.

Many times in the years that followed, during school breaks and holidays, I hiked along the periphery of the Warren ranch, climbing up to the flat rocks below Hurricane Deck. In the beginning it was easy to cry, to do penance. Afterwards, castigating myself for traces of impatience, I began to write. "Loved and Lost," I scribbled across the top of the page and turned all my maudlin tears to ink. I did not realize how much time had passed until the day I thought I saw Will leading his Appaloosa along the edge of a newly plowed field and realized it was the youngest brother, all grown-up. In that time, on each visit to what I called "our spot," I would draw into me the requisite amount of pain, the ache that was beginning, in the natural course of things and in spite of my fond suffering, to fade. You had no control over anything, I wrote. Things just happened. They were out of your hands.

Flat Serve
Christopher Buckley
Santa Barbara

It was not divorce, nor business partners who stole him blind, nor the fortunes in real estate he should easily have made, nor the fact that he just missed fame as a singer with a big band; it was surfing—surfing broke my father's heart. . . .

I was given my first tennis racket at age two and by four I was dragging it around between games in my father's Sunday matches on the parking lot-like court in Manning Park. This was '52 and the racket was squared-off, strung as loosely as a fish net with what they then called "cat gut." I would stand just inside the service line and hit balls lobbed toward me from across the net, and when I connected, my racket would slingshot the ball toward the blue, from where it finally sank to bounce high off the chicken wire fence. The racket was cheap and built for an adult; the grip was too thick, and so I often took a swing with both hands and was always quickly corrected on my form. And when I was caught smashing acorns on the cement picnic table with it, I received my first lecture on the correct use and care of rackets.

I was soon learning a proper forehand, and when I was able to remember to get to the courts after school, that is as early as six years old, my father began to hold forth on the moral imperative of a flat, power serve—Big Bill Tilden hit it that way, first *and* second serve, and so would I. He praised Pancho Gonzales as well—a cannonball first server—but couldn't for the life of him figure out why Gonzales put spin on the second ball. And as far as I could tell there was something equally corrupt in a slice backhand; it was for "dinks" and "pushers" I soon learned. Don Budge was the master of the backhand drive and my father proclaimed the absolute virtue of a flat, one-handed stroke. Rosewall with his slice, Segura with his two-handed chip, why Budge would have killed them both! This was a matter of character and I was going to have it.

Lucky for us both I had the talent that I did. The pro, Byron De Mott, said I was a *natural;* moreover at lessons, I hit the ball harder than anyone else and liked it—so my father seemed relieved, if not happy. Weekends I was religiously at the courts. All through grammar school I got off the bus at day's end and walked up the road to the country club courts. I was growing up among the rich, in a rich fashion almost. For while my father was a DJ for a local station and mother worked as a secretary for the city schools, we lived on a full acre in Montecito, the woodsy section of town flanking the foothills. My parents built our house pretty much on their own, and across the street was a wilderness of scrub oak, acacias, laurel, and eucalyptus—even the out of place palm tree by a pool or creek. I knew the trails and the borders of ferns, the maroon shade or the air stunned with sunlight atop house-sized boulders which just sat outright on the land like worn idols from a chapter heading in Bible History. I took it all simply on faith; days passed slowly as drifting clouds and were full of coveys of quail, wild peacocks, chipmunks, lizards, gliding spirals of hawks before the sandstone face of mountains. It was that simple. No choices had to be made, no judgements; there was nothing and everything to do under the sky. To be sure, there were large, private estates, manicured grounds, a fountain or two—a little old money here and there belonging to folks who had made it big in the market and then moved here to beat the Chicago winters. Most mansions were back of the trees—long drives we could never sneak all the way up without being run off by a caretaker. But it seemed people could live anywhere they wanted; I had friends whose uniform cords had as many rips in the knees as mine, yet who lived in huge homes—ranch houses, two story haciendas with fruit trees and automatic sprinklers. I'd stay over night as we would climb in the avocado trees or run down their hills—it seemed perfectly natural to always be running through all that space.

But more and more I had less time for my friends. The pro at the club struck a deal for my father. Byron thought I was a prospect and for nothing more than the love of the game and out of his good nature, he talked whoever was in charge into allowing me to hang out at the courts and play so long as my father paid for one lesson a week. I spent all my time there without having to join the club—something we never could have afforded. And while adults could kick any kid off any court, I soon saw there was a difference among equals. Most of the others, after putting in the required time at group lessons or seeing who could hit the most balls over the fence onto the fairways, spent their time racing down to the grill for hamburgers and shakes; they just signed their names on their parents' tab and came away with everything. Even when I went to pick up lunch for Byron and was encouraged to order an ice cream for myself, I never did—something in the eyes of the waiters made me feel they knew I had no business ordering or signing for anything.

Almost overnight, it seemed, I was good—though a couple of long summers hitting against the backboard had passed. In local tournaments I got to the finals where I lost to Stevey Fisk or Bendy White, boys slightly older who had had more lessons. My father dropped me off early in the mornings and came by after work, when everyone else had left. Stevey's father, Haley Fisk, was always at the club. I wondered what Haley did. When Stevey was playing, Haley coached through the fence, always trying to psyche out Stevey's opponent for him. One day when I was serving well, I almost beat Stevey, and though he had seen me play before, Haley turned back toward the court as he and Stevey headed for the grill and said,"Stick around kid, we'll make a star out of you too." For a moment I felt flattered for the attention, but soon put down and resentful. I wondered if he had been talking to my father. But my father was rarely at the club and never went to the grill; I don't think he would have talked to Haley anyway. Haley wore alligator shirts with a blue blazer and grey slacks, and cordovan loafers without socks, which I thought was very strange. He was always headed for the grill once Stevey had the match in hand, and toward the end would reappear—his face red, his thin hair white in contrast, and the sand of his voice commenting on the points. And among the women there was Bendy's mother who arrived after lunch in her white, convertible Mercedes—a large white chow stationed in the front seat with Bendy and his older brother in the back. Her hair was frosted, streaked with long lines of gold over the grey—her head seemed to match the many bracelets and necklaces which rattled about as she played doubles on the first court with Mattie De Mott—the golden blossoms of the eugenia hedge blooming, the omniscient sunlight, a whole bright world spangled in starched tennis whites. They played with a stiff gentility and displayed no desire to kill the ball, even if the ability had been there; I hated being kicked off the courts by those who couldn't play as well.

One day Byron wanted to teach me a slice serve. My father was not there and so I decided to give it a try, tossing the ball out to my right and hitting around it instead of over the top. There was a swishing "ping" sound like a dull harp being plucked, and fluff from the thick nap of the Dunlap ball suspended for a second in the air. It worked the first time, landing in the far forehand corner and abruptly jackknifing into the side fence for an ace. It was quite a trick for someone my age and I used it especially for the second serve. But I was pressured into hitting it flat for both serves when my father watched in tournaments, or when I went through a full shopping cart of practice serves after my weekly lesson. He paid for the racket, the lessons and my one set of tennis clothes. I had a Lacoste shirt and Jack Purcell shoes—the ones with the large half-dome of rubber over the toe, the heavy ones that lasted best. And while more than once I wore my high-top PF Flyers until holes in the soles made holes in my socks, while the knees of my corduroys were layered with iron-on patches, I had the gear for tennis—he just knew I would make something of myself. And at thirteen I had my photo in World Tennis for winning some tournament in Palm Springs and for him it looked like this might make up for something in the world.

That year I moved down the hill to the municipal courts; there were more and better programs for junior tennis, more competition and tournaments. But I suspected it was because Mike Koury, the pro there, gave weekend lessons for free, that I was told to ride my bike and play there instead of at the country club. Also by then, the club probably wanted us to pay up. I also think my father realized Byron had taught me the spin serve, or maybe he'd seen him hit a slice backhand, or, God forbid, his "Peruvian"—a trick shot that amazed kids and club players alike; from the forehand side he would hold the racket face like a plate, flat-up at the sky, then hit under the ball with a tremendous backspin, and the ball would hit on the other side of the net and draw back over before the opponent could reach it—definitely not stuff for future champions. I improved with Koury. He called me "bull-moose" and worked with me on the serve and volley game. There was always the pressure to win, to beat the boys from the club in tournaments, and I went through a temperamental streak, smashing a few rackets, throwing others into the podocarpus trees which lined the courts. But even when I outgrew that stage, I went through my Victor Imperial gut every two weeks; the combination of hitting the cannon-ball flat serve followed by the slicing can-openers and high-hopping American Twists was deadly for strings. Playing a power game mushed-out the wooden frames in a month, so it was a good thing I could earn my own rackets; I was able to garden around the nine courts and stadium earning a dollar an hour toward frames and strings at Koury's Pro Shop.

I began high school at a prep school in Ojai, California—a small horsey town about an hour and a half south and inland from Santa Barbara. Football was the thing there, and so I felt compelled to play in the fall and winter instead of practicing full-time for tennis. But there was as much or more pressure to conform and produce according to a standard, and so when spring came I did not go out for training with the rest of the guys in crew cuts, but rather played on the tennis team. We had good players and won the tri-valley conference. Things looked good until the summer when I drew Bob Lutz in the first round of a big tournament and there wasn't much I could do. My serve won me five games in two sets which my friends assured me was a good showing. Later that month, playing in both the Thirteens and Fifteens, Stan Smith clobbered me. But I kept things in perspective—those guys were from L.A. and already famous, especially Lutz. Overall, it still came pretty easily and I played for the Santa Barbara city team on weekend trips against Oxnard, Ventura, and Ojai, and at summer's end against the team from the L.A. Tennis Club. One year, Clayton Smith and I beat Hobson and Rombeau, two top-ranked players in the 16s, and that was really the last grand moment in tennis for me. They walked onto the courts in matching Jack Kramer creme-colored whites, carrying about six or eight rackets apiece, joking to themselves about us like we'd just fallen off the last turnip truck from Bakersfield. Clayton had a Jack Kramer jacket and we both had two rackets, though they were different makes, which showed we weren't on any "free list" from a manufacturer like ranked players. Clayton poached well and put the ball away with crisp, angle-volleys; my serve and overhead were sharp. It took three sets for us to beat them, with Hobson changing rackets every couple games as if their losing were a fault of his equipment. Santa Barbara lost the match but we felt great anyway. That was the second summer in prep school, but when my father could no longer pay the bill I was allowed to attend the local Catholic high in Santa Barbara, which was where I really wanted to be.

That was the end of the fifties and start of the sixties and next to nobody was surfing though Santa Barbara had several good spots as I would find out later. Then, only a few old guys in their thirties were in the water—on planks and "big guns" in Hawaii, or south of town at Rincon Point. They were considered beatniks and no one thought much about it. But now a lot of my friends were surfing. Those were innocent days when you could leave your board strapped to racks on top of your '59 Chevy in the school parking lot and it would still be there when you got out of class. There were good beaches with lefts and rights and a swell always running, or so it seemed, especially in early fall when school began, and September was hotter that any summer month. The last class would let out an exodus for Hope Ranch, The Pit, Hammond's Reef, or Miramar Point. I learned to surf one weekend at a place called Shark's Cove—a spot at the other end of the small bay formed by Miramar and Fernell Points. The waves had good form and a slow break that was great for learning. Soon, I had my first board—a Yater with split redwood stringers fanned-out at the tailblock; it was used, but it was classic. Then I was worrying about "grimmies"— mean little kids who couldn't surf well but who would take off in front of you on the best wave of the day, and if you yelled "coming down" to let them know you had speed and position in the wave, they bailed out and let their wrecked boards corkscrew in the soup hoping to give your board a couple of good dings in a collision.

Surfing meant social distinctions as well. It was easy acceptance as long as you really went into the water; everybody knew who the "hodads" were—those who dressed the part and drove their woodies to surf spots without ever taking their boards out of the back. And there was a dress code—white Levis, T-shirts and wool Pendleton shirts. We all wore blue tennis shoes. If you were really cool you wore Sperrys, and if you weren't, the less popular Keds. But if you were a surfer, it was blue. At the city Rec dances you would band together with other surfers mostly, but at school dances there was no need for group protection. And then there were the movies; for surfers they were the most important social event. Bruce Brown filled the vast Santa Barbara High auditorium time and again with *Surfing Hollow Days.* There was *Big Wednesday* with Ricky Gregg and Greg Knoll out-racing twenty-five foot walls at Waimea or Makaha. In those days, two-to-four foot swells ran much of the summer and we were in the water as long as there was light. For weeks at a time we were happy and unbothered in our lives.

The coach at Bishop High School was incompetent, a fact he tried to hide with a condescending manner. I went out to the first practice, hit some shots past his ears and never showed up again. He lost the best player he could get, but was smug and happy about it; he then could work the other, mostly beginning players, without too much embarassment to himself. I got a part-time job at the local grocery chain which paid for my car, a new board, and gas to go north or south looking for waves. On the Feast of the Immaculate Conception or The Feast of The Assumption, we'd load our boards in a friend's VW bus by 5:30 and be pulling off the 101 Freeway as the sun came up, determined to get Rincon to ourselves while all the public-school guys wrestled with algebra or sweated out biology. And on days I didn't want to drive that far, I hit Hope Ranch, a beach break with no rocks, where I sometimes ran into three or four friends I used to play singles or doubles with at the municipal courts. It was good to be a local and know people, then there was no fighting over the waves. We were all, in our rice-paddy baggies, civil to each other, and tried to ride the nose with that casual aplomb we'd seen Phil Edwards display in all the films. Phil was the first one to ride the Banzai Pipe Line in Hawaii, the tubes steaming in overhead and breaking on a shallow bed of coral which accounted for the shape and power. We'd all seen Edwards crank a hard left bottom-turn, crouch about a foot from the nose and come flying out of the curl with the wave spitting spume close behind. Or at Malibu, on waist-high sections, there was Phil, nonchalant as you please, riding six inches from the nose, feet parallel, both hands clasped casually behind his back. Ultimately cool. We were all "stoked" and spent hours wiping out and "pearling" off our boards in attempted imitation. My father silently gave up on pushing the tennis. Since I was paying for all my own expenses, there seemed to be nothing he could do. He just offered his half despondent look when I began loading the car with my gear.

I was in the water at every opportunity until I went away to college at a small school in northern California. I played a little on the tennis team but the captain was obsessive, a real "come-on-guys" type and the school did not furnish rackets or clothes; we were given little more than gas money and greasy sandwiches and told to drive to some state university for a match. For the rest of college I took up golf and played on the team and with friends. But during graduate school, especially in summers, I was playing tennis again—largely out of economic necessity, as I could get jobs teaching at the municipal courts and at other courts around town in the city's summer program. By summer's end I was playing even with friends who had been at it all year. But one kid I had beaten with regularity years before had become a celebrity of sorts— winning tournaments in Los Angeles and in the east. Word was he had just signed with Philadelphia for World Team Tennis. And as for me, well it was just too late though I'd get a couple rounds in local summer tournaments. My father knew this, though he hadn't seen me play since I was fourteen. Nevertheless, I was offered a job at one of the local clubs; my old pro, Mike Koury, seemed to be making the recommendations, and he put my name in based on my ability as a teacher. It was then a choice between more school and writing, or a permanent job in the sun, playing the other local pros a couple times a week, watching the station wagons pull up summer mornings and the kids pour out like myrmidons across the courts while the mothers went off for lunch on the terraces or patios beneath the blue shade of oak trees in Montecito— and saying until I'm sixty, " . . . better racket preparation Mrs. Johnson, bend the knees, follow through all the way now . . ." And even though I wasn't going to make the WCT Tour, even though Bob Lutz had just half-volleyed and spin-served his way through the best players in the world to the U.S. Pro Indoor Title and his knees would begin to give out the next year and I'd never get another shot at him, my father was truly disappointed when I turned down the job. And from that day forward, although I took my degrees, published and taught at universities, he would continue to say how surfing had ruined my career. I never saw it like that—saw it exactly the opposite in fact, satisfied as I was with all that water and air and light, satisfied as I was with myself.

Recollections of a
Valley Past
Catherine Mulholland
Northridge

F ive generations of my family have lived in the San Fernando Valley. My mother's people arrived as homesteaders in Calabasas during the 1880s and never left the Valley. My father's story is more complex. Although he lived his adult life in the Valley, he was born in Los Angeles, the oldest son of William Mulholland, the noted and controversial builder of the Owens River Aqueduct, and for many years, Chief Engineer of the Los Angeles Department of Water and Power (DWP). Although the older Mulholland never lived in the Valley—his home was in town—he bought the land which my father ranched and on which I grew up.

Born in 1923, I was taken as a newborn to the family's 640-acre ranch in the northwest valley, an area between two almost nonexistent hamlets known, respectively, as Chatsworth and Zelzah (now Northridge). Although I do not claim, as Mark Twain once did, that I increased the population of either village by one percent, I did augment my immediate family by one-third and became the first of a fourth generation to grow up in the San Fernando Valley. In later years, my mother was to say that she thought I had seen more change in the Valley in my lifetime than she and her mother had seen in theirs combined. She meant, I think, that while she and my grandmother passed most of their lives in an area that remained essentially rural, I was to be more deeply altered by the urbanization of the Valley. They remained at heart country ladies, while I did not.

But I did grow up on a ranch—on land which between 1912 and 1919, my grandfather Mulholland had bought for between 50 and 150 dollars an

179

acre, the price determined by how much hay the land would grow, dry farming being all that was feasible before the arrival of water from the Owens River. There, in 1914, Mulholland sent his son, my father, Perry Mulholland, to grow hay and beans, which he did until the end of World War I, at which time he set out orchards of citrus and walnuts. When he died in 1962, my father's forty years of work on the ranch had spanned the era of large-scale irrigated agriculture in the San Fernando Valley—finally forced out by the press of population and commercial development after World War II. When Perry Mulholland first came to the Valley, he could stand on his ranch land and see the dust from a wagon or car leaving Van Nuys, twelve and fifteen miles away. By the time he died, so many roads were paved and so many cars ran on them that he could scarcely find a spot to maneuver a tractor from one grove to another.

William Mulholland did not purchase Valley land for speculation, but with a landless Irish immigrant's dream of permanency, had hoped that each of his five children would establish homes where he, the patriarch, would end his days, blessed amidst his groves and heirs. Nor was he alone among those who desired land for their children. During this period a number of Los Angeles business and professional men bought ranching land in the Valley and sent their sons out to work it. But because both before and during the building of the Aqueduct, a powerful group of capitalists had acquired vast tracts of Valley land, leading to outcries and accusations of land grabbing and collusion with the city, my grandfather and many of his associates assiduously avoided buying land from or near those under attack. Thus, the location of my childhood home was determined in part by the land and water politics of southern California; for my grandfather cast a long shadow, not only over the city, but also over his family.

He loomed over us all and I do not remember that ever a week went by that he did not arrive at the ranch, chauffeured by either his second son, Thomas, or by his driver from the DWP (he himself never learned to drive). Often he was accompanied by his companions from the department, especially Harvey Van Norman, his closest colleague, who also owned ranch land nearby. As his arrival required that we all snap to attention, his frequent appearances must have sometimes seemed intrusive to my busy young parents, and as I grew older, I sometimes resented the call of "Come inside. Grandpa's here, and he wants to see you," which meant a reluctant breaking off of play, as my brother and I went in to greet him and answer his queries about our progress in school, which formed the chief staple of our conversation with him. In his dark suit, stiff-collared shirt, and cravat, wreathed in the smoke of his ever-present cigar, he was a given in my life, and I loved him as one loves a grandparent—respectfully and unquestioningly.

He bore about him an aura of authority, even after the disastrous failure of the St. Francis Dam in 1928, which resulted in the loss of hundreds of lives and for which he took full responsibility, saying, "I envy the dead." Even then, as he seemed to draw into himself and become at family gatherings a silent specter at the feast, he remained a powerful presence. He was gruff in manner, but once, as my eighth birthday approached, he asked me what I wanted for the occasion. I told him a bicycle. Pulling out his wad, I can still see his shaky old hand peeling off a twenty-dollar bill and handing it to me. In 1931, twenty dollars bought a very handsome bicycle! He was an intimate and unquestioned part of childhood on our ranch, while the family dinners at his home in town, with its polished mahogany staircase and wood-paneled dining room with leaded casements and painted panels of sylvan scenes, afforded glimpses of life in a metropolitan style, and opened to me, at least, vistas of a world with less isolation and, therefore, larger possibilities.

For although there were friends, relatives and workers on the ranch who provided sociability, when I think of growing up in the Valley during the 1930s, I remember solitude: the lorn sound of a train whistle disrupting the country stillness, the howl of a coyote, the solitary jackrabbit darting across my path and loping ahead as I biked to school over bumpy dirt roads. Our closest neighbors were almost a mile away and were rarely visited. School provided the mental stimulation and social life I hungered for, while my mother and other ranchers' wives arranged outings for us—picnics in Brown's Canyon, day-long treks to the beach, and most wonderful of all, swimming lessons when a municipal plunge finally opened in Reseda in the 1930s.

Occasionally, excitement interrupted the country quiet, as on an afternoon at Winnetka Avenue Grammar School when our principal, Mrs. Ethel B. Newman, visited each classroom to announce that a wild boar had been sighted in Mr. Reichart's walnut orchard and that we children were to exercise extreme caution going home. She advised that if we were to come face-to-face with the beast, we were to remain still and make no sudden move, for then it might charge us. Armed only with this information and the will to live, I left the safety of the school grounds and friends to face the unknown. Never in my life was I less inclined to loiter along the way as I set about to establish some kind of speed record pedaling those two miles home, expecting, at each turn in the road, to meet my final doom.

The Mulholland name may have overshadowed that of my mother's family, but those old Valley pioneers from whom she came were lively and compelling presences in my young life. My maternal grandmother, Katie Ijams Haas, was, at the time of my birth, a widow living in the town of Owensmouth (now Canoga Park). She and my grandfather, John Haas, were among the original purchasers of land when the town site had opened in 1912, but they were not newcomers to the area as they and their families had homesteaded land almost thirty years earlier in nearby Calabasas, and had feuded with Miguel Leonis, the overlord of Rancho El Escorpion, who tried to drive them out, claiming the government land as his own. Forming a Settlers' League, the homesteaders took him to court and won their case. The often-told stories from those days made a deep mark on me and led me finally to write *Calabasas Girls* (1976), an account of three homesteading families coping with life in that tough little frontier settlement.

Always, I was touched by the stories of the grandfather I never knew, John Haas. Of German immigrant parents who arrived in northern California in the 1850s, and who himself was born in Santa Clara County in 1867 and came to Calabasas with his father in 1888, this even-tempered man of the Old West advanced from ranch hand and cowboy to rancher, deputy sheriff and then constable in Calabasas, and finally county road-master in charge of construction of the north side of Topanga Canyon Drive, the old Topanga road, and Decker Canyon Road. According to my mother, it was a political bounty job, and "the reason we were Republicans is that when the Republicans were in office, Papa had his job." Just when it seemed that he and his family could begin to enjoy a more comfortable life in the fledgling town of Owensmouth, he was struck down senselessly. Found dead in a corral, killed by the kick of a horse as he had been dragging a bale of hay into the enclosure, the finest of horsemen was undone. My mother would always remember what the men who had found him said: that there was a perfect hoofprint outlined on his temple.

I was blessed with knowing a third grandfather, who, if not the most famous nor noblest in character, remains very dear to my heart. Isaac Clay "Judge" Ijams was my great-grandfather. (The "Judge" was an honorific he picked up when he acted as Justice of the Peace in Calabasas and later in Toluca/Lankershim—now North Hollywood.) At the time of his death in 1938 at the age of ninety-seven, the local papers described him as the Valley's oldest resident. (He had lived in the Valley for fifty-four years.) When he'd first ridden through during the terrible drought of the 1860s, he said you could ride across the entire Valley on the bones of dead sheep and cattle. An authentic frontiersman and goldseeker who made three prairie crossings in the 1850s, he was a romancer with a gift of gab, and as he grew older, none of his stories shriveled. Newspaper reporters loved to hear him spin his tales of hard times on the trail, Indian skirmishes and much else about the Old West, real or imagined. He claimed once to have founded Boise City, although nobody up in Idaho ever seems to have heard about it. Whatever the truth, he was memorable, had a love of language, and should have commanded a pulpit, stage or courtroom. If ever a man missed his true calling because of poverty and lack of opportunity, it was Grandpa Ijams, for his gifts were imaginative, not practical; verbal, not commercial.

He often tried to get things down in writing, and in 1912, a Lankershim editor asked him to write an account of his early days in southern California. What follows is a draft (original spelling and all) from one of his old ledger books:

"I came to Los Angeles Co in 1867 at that time she was scarsly on the map. her principal population being of the dark shade her chief amusements was cock fighting and hurdy gurdy dancing all of which the writer was convercent with . . . After riding horse back many hundred miles from the head of the Misury to LAngeles through Montana Utah and Arizona I first struck camp at ElMonte a damp spot where they raised corn and punkins played a game of cards that my traveling companion called crack loo 30 beans for a cent it took all day to win a sufficiency to justify the venture. I spred my blankets under the open canopy of heaven and laid down for the first time feeling safe without my gun and saddle for a pillow. The next day I visited the San Gabriel Mission. There was a small groop of Indians there but no americans I engaged the proprietor of a small store in a conversation told him I just arrived from the north he manifested an interest in entertaining me. Took me to the rear of the store and entered an inclosure surrounded by an Adoby wall it was full of birds some parrots all merily singing and orange trees in full bloom the air was fragrant with the oder. This was in January and when I contrasted it with my mountain home in Montana in 5 foot of snow it made me a true convert to California."

I don't know when I first realized that my parents did not intend that I should remain forever with them in the Valley, for the process to move me away was gradual, and the weaning program largely took the form of sending me to "better schools," which were always at some distance from the local heath. The first venture, in 1930–31, was in Hollywood at the Progressive School on Highland Avenue across from the Hollywood Bowl. Each morning for a year, a neighboring rancher's son, my brother and I were driven to an early-morning bus which we rode, along with sleepy adult commuters, into town, a trip of almost twenty miles (talk about busing!). But it was worth it. The Progressive School deserves a page in the history of private schools in southern California. With its small classes, excellent teachers and imaginative learning programs, it proved to be one of the most valuable years I ever spent in school. Moreover, the physical setting was a delight—an old Hollywood estate set against the hills with a streambed running through the grounds. (In 1987, not a jot remains; it is all a blacktopped parking lot.) We learned multiplication tables while snuggled in a treehouse built in the branches of an enormous California sycamore overhanging the wash bed. Although the school was a wonder, the daily commuting from our distant location in the Valley proved too arduous and so we resumed our attendance in the local public schools. All went well until my sixth-grade class turned rowdy and unmanageable. Teachers from town came and went, driven out by our shameful country impudence and unmanageability. I began to receive failing marks in Dependability (talking, giggling and passing notes in class). Apparently behind-the-scene conferences between my parents and teachers resulted in a decision that I should go live with my grandmother and great-grandfather in Studio City where I should attend a "better school," North Hollywood Junior High. I lasted there for one fairly miserable, lonely semester, until I began to manifest unaccountable but perturbing physical symptoms, which promptly disappeared once I was returned to my disreputable and loved schoolmates at Winnetka Avenue Grammar School.

The quest for better schools continued. After a freshman year at Canoga Park High School, I was sent to Marlborough School for Girls in Los Angeles, a really better school; but after two years, I again fell sick (no one spoke of or considered psychosomatic possibilities in those days), and was allowed to return to Canoga Park. There, in a final, glorious senior year, I bounced over dirt roads to school in a 1933 Chevy coupe with a rumble seat, which was often loaded with girlfriends in the good weather as we headed for the beach through Topanga Canyon. The times we had! Beach parties, school dances in the gym, jitterbugging at the Palladium . . . I remember those times as the halcyon days, that last moment before World War II ended the innocence of our generation. On a June night in 1940, when I stood among my classmates in the lovely old Greek amphitheatre on our school grounds (also, alas! a victim of change and long gone), I knew that soon I would be leaving the Valley to attend the University of California at Berkeley, and did not know how I could endure the parting from my comrades. But I also knew that I had to go, for by now, I had become imbued with the sense that to remain in southern California, especially the San Fernando Valley, would be to remain forever culturally inferior. As it turned out, I was gone for thirty-seven years and never thought that I would live again in southern California.

I used to keep a cartoon from *The New Yorker* over my desk, in which a New Englandish matron, gazing in bafflement at an oil portrait in a gallery, remarks to her companion: "I had no idea people from California had ancestors." The assumptions implicit in the cartoon: that to sophisticated Easterners we are a land of yahoos and Johnny-come-latelies; that although San Francisco may pass muster, southern California is something of a bad joke—or worse, a large mistake; those assumptions I came to share, as I also still clung to my identity of one who had grown up on a ranch in the San Fernando Valley. Eventually, I lived for a while in the East and experienced firsthand how deep the prejudices and ignorance ran. Once, when I was in my late twenties, I was taken by friends to a cocktail party on Cape Cod, and was introduced as a native of California to the hostess, a gracious old dame of pure Massachusetts lineage. Later, she presented me to some new arrivals.

"This is Catherine," she grandly announced; and then pausing as if to remember who, indeed, I was, she continued: "Catherine is the oldest living Californian."

No. I was never going to live again in southern California. But who foresees his own end? Or controls his destiny? My grandfather Mulholland, who dreamed of spending his final days among his children, lay a long year dying in his town home, with his family scattered, all dreams of dynasty blasted. My grandfather Haas, who, at a moment when all life's obstacles seemed behind him, found his quietus in the dirt of a corral in Calabasas. And my father? After forty years of ranching—and seeing that commerce had conquered and that agriculture in the Valley was doomed—oversaw the destruction of the groves he had planted, pulled out root and branch. And then he too was gone.

So the ranch on which my parents had lived and struggled—their life's work—the ranch from which I derived so much of my identity—vanished in the face of a growth no one could prevent, or perhaps, would even have wanted to. No. I was never going to live in the San Fernando Valley again. But for my mother's eightieth birthday, I undertook to write a story of her family in Calabasas, and in the doing of it, found another way back home, for their lives so touched me that again I was drawn to those whom I had spiritually abandoned. I knew I could not reclaim the past, certainly could not reclaim the land, but I could recall them. I could tell those who would come after that once we were here, and that we did thus and thus. And so, at long last, I came home.

Land of Boyhood
Lawrence Clark Powell
South Pasadena

I n less than thirty years I'll celebrate my California centennial. Why wait? Why not try a practice run and see how it looks from seventy? I grew up in South Pasadena on the southern side of the Raymond Hill, and I have only fond memories of a fortunate boyhood. I bear no grudge against anyone for the sorrows that have shaded my sunny life, least of all against my parents and brothers, all of whom are long since dead. I alone have been my own best enemy.

I'd rather write about the town than go there. It's now all out of proportion. The trees have grown and the houses haven't. What to my boyhood eyes were stately mansions among small trees are now just houses, dwarfed by great blue gums and tall palms. What was my earthly paradise—the blocks-square, lath-shaded Rust Nursery—long ago was lost to urban development. It was my playground, smelling of damp earth and growing things. Sunlight came through the laths in golden bars. Sometimes the Japanese gardeners would let me help water. My special friend was Sugimoto. My father said he was a wizard with plants.

Today the town is peopled with strangers. The old many-childrened families are gone—the Casses, the Fugits, the McEnirys. Boys I played and fought with are risen high or fallen low, or neither, or dead. The girls I fancied are grandmothers or greater.

Until after the second war, South Pasadena was bounded by hills and orange groves and the tracks of the Pacific Electric. I used to sell the *Evening Herald* at Oneonta Junction (the name was from the birthplace in New York of Henry E. Huntington). They cost a penny a paper. Once a passenger on a Sierra Madre car mistakenly gave me a two-and-a-half-dollar gold piece. In size and color it resembled a shiny new copper penny. By the time I realized what he had given me, the Big Red Car bearing the man was gone. I quit for the day, a wealthy independent merchant.

Those tracks along Huntington Drive were torn up after the war, as well as the ones up Fair Oaks Avenue. The world's finest interurban electrical railway system was replaced by the world's greatest gasoline-fired, smog-producing transportation system. The hills where the coyote cried are now peopled. Where I hunted the high mustard for rabbits are now streets and sidewalks, and houses that look pretty much alike. Over the first range the toyon grew. At Christmas we bunched and sold its berries from door to door as California holly. Beyond, the Arroyo Seco's spring floods were yet unchecked by the dam to be built at Devil's Gate.

Nearby was Dippy Hill, named by us from Dr. Bishop's sanitarium for the mentally ill. We never teased the unfortunates who wandered the grounds, talking to themselves. We were afraid to. Boys are rarely compassionate. It was a love of fighting, rather than compassion, that caused me to defend a French war orphan, adopted by Henri St. Pierre, the secretary of the YMCA. The boy's knee breeches led to his being taunted, and so I championed him in rough and tumble. Leon Dostert grew to fame as General Pershing's personal interpreter in World War II, and as the developer of the instantaneous translation system used at the United Nations. He's dead now.

There was another young foreigner who required occasional defending, a skinny Dutch boy with a big name—Cornelis Evertse Groenewegen. His father was the head gardener at the Raymond Hotel. This gave us the run of the great barn where the horses were kept. Later the father had charge of the planting on the new UCLA campus at Westwood. The huge eucalyptus viminalis that today line Westwood Boulevard were raised by him as seedlings in five gallon cans. During my early years at UCLA I used to seek him out in the Botanical Garden and talk of past times. As he aged, the old Dutchman came to look like a masterpiece by Rembrandt.

The wide terrace in front of the Raymond Hotel, looking down on the golf course and the town, made an ideal parking place at night when we had given up hunting rabbits for fairer game. It was a secure world whose crime was mostly ours. Why did Old Lady Black persist in drying walnuts on a table in her backyard, thereby inviting us to help ourselves? Why did Old Man White have his tangerine tree right next to our wall? "I don't mind him taking a few," he complained to my parents, "but can't he climb without breaking the branches?"

Another neighbor had a fondness for drink. We used to spy on him drinking alone in his backyard, shout "Boozy" at him, and then run. Those were the years of Prohibition. The doctor prescribed port wine for my mother when she became anemic. I used to sneak down cellar and smell the heady fragrance of the cork. Glue sniffing, marijuana and the like were undreamed of then, at least in South Pasadena.

I rode my bicycle with dash and daring, skidding, crashing and terrifying children and dogs. I was always going to Perky's bike shop on Mission Street for repairs. He gave us free graphite for our chains and sprockets. A favorite ride was uphill to the swimming pool at Brookside Park. The downhill ride was along Orange Grove Avenue, lined with great houses and wide lawns and globed street lights, the acme of elegance.

Another long ride was out Huntington Drive to the San Marino junction where a spur track led to the Huntington estate and the new library under construction. We liked to play on the boxcars standing on the siding. For all we knew, one of them might have held "The Blue Boy," newly arrived from England.

My father drove a 1914 air-cooled Franklin. In those days before service stations, we had our own gas tank in the backyard, next to the hutch that held my pet rabbit, "Jazz." My job was to fill the car's tank once a week with Red Crown, straining the gas through a chamois. Next my father traded up to a 1916 Marmon with cream-colored wire wheels and Goodrich Silvertown cord tires. His initials, G.H.P., were scripted in gold on the maroon doors. I was allowed to dust the car each morning before my father drove to work in Los Angeles. As my feet could barely reach the pedals, he would back it out for me. One morning I decided to run it back in the garage. It was abruptly halted by the workbench on the back wall.

I found my father in the kitchen, wearing overcoat, hat, and gloves, having a last cup of coffee. "What's the matter?" he asked, his big brown eyes searching my troubled face.

"I creased the fenders," I managed to say.

"You what?"

"I creased the fenders."

He looked puzzled and followed me out to the garage. There he solemnly inspected the damage. I awaited his wrath. Instead he said, "Don't worry. I was planning to have the car painted."

Thus did I find acceptance of my proneness to error, as well as love and recognition, and as I grew up I learned that I must give to others what had been given to me.

I had two good teachers other than my parents. One was the town's librarian, Nellie Keith. She recognized my hunger for books and let me take out as many as I could carry. I read fast, a book to a Hershey bar. Years later, I dedicated my first book of essays to her memory.

My other yea-sayer was the third-grade teacher of Marengo School, a soft spoken, steel-gripped Kentucky mountain woman named Mattaline

Garnet Crabtree. No wonder her friends (I learned later) called her Martha. She was not altogether permissive. When I dipped the pigtails of the girl in front of me in the inkwell on my desk and she cried bitterly, Miss Crabtree descended like an avenging angel, lifted me out of the seat by my hair, marched me up the aisle and thrust me under her desk. When I bit her ankle, she locked me in the closet, forgetting that I could open windows and climb down fire escapes. Years after, our friendship lasted until her death at a very old age.

I am glad that my parents were Quakers. They practiced tolerance, making no distinction in people's race, religion, or color. It was years before I learned that there were Jews. In our town, people were just people. Our Lithuanian cook, Japanese maid, and Canary Islands gardener were part of the family.

Tramps got the message, and I'd sometimes come to breakfast and find at the kitchen table a smelly wanderer whose knock on the back door had led to an invitation to enter and be fed. And there was the scissors grinder, a tiny old Cornishman, who came once a year and in return for sharpening our cutting implements was given breakfast and a dollar. He ate and then worked with his hat and coat on.

Although we were a wealthy family, I didn't know it. I never knew it until we weren't. I mean the Depression. My allowance for chores was fifty cents a week, and I dressed as rough as any kid from the other side of Fair Oaks. I was the youngest of three brothers, all different from each other and from our parents. I admired my brothers even as we grew apart. The oldest followed our father into horticulture and went off to South Africa right out of college. There he became an authority on citrus fruits in that land so alike in climate to southern California.

His parting gift to me upon graduation from high school was his 1920 Ford. I promptly stripped it of fenders and top and painted on the back in red OXY'28, and drove it off to my freshman year at Occidental College. Its demise was spectacular. I guess I was influenced by the movies. I used to go a lot when I was a kid. The first movie theater in South Pasadena was The Gem, and it cost a nickel. We called it The Germ. William. S. Hart and Harry Carey were my heroes. I also liked Sessue Hayakawa, a Japanese a lot handsomer than Gay Sugimoto. The Gish sisters were my darlings. When a cousin, Paul Powell, directed *Pollyanna,* starring Mary Pickford, in a local scene, school was dismissed so we could all watch.

When the Ford decided not to run anymore, a friend and I got it somehow to a high point in the Monterey Hills and pushed it over. Down it went, shedding parts at every boulder, to crash in a clump of toyon. Merry Christmas!

My other brother taught me to play the saxophone, and I became a musician for several years until I decided that my future lay in literature. Although my brother and I never went beyond dance music, today one of his sons is a symphony violinist, and so the chain of life keeps growing.

My father was a fisherman and taught me to cast in the surf and to troll off coast for albacore and in Big Bear Lake for trout. Newport was an idyllic beach before 1920. People went there for surf and sand and the mud-flatted bay where cockles were to be had for the digging. Newport was unfashionable: in fact except for Coronado, Santa Barbara, and Oak Knoll, all of southern California was happily unfashionable. Today, the bay at Newport is packed with yachts and people, and the tide bears their empty cans and bottles out to sea.

When I look back at the land I see only change. Southern California has become a vast, homogeneous metropolis. People's lives are geared to TV. Programs of entertainment, sports, and commentators mean that most viewers are experiencing the same things at the same time. Although reconciled, I do not wish to participate.

Three years ago our high-school class held its fiftieth reunion. Name tags weren't much help to dimmed eyesight. The old guard was there, including Harry Ward Ritchie, Pat Kelley, Roger Weldon, Malcolm Archbald, Ralph Kuhlman, Charles Ledgerwood—and Cornelis Evertse Groenewegen, all six-feet, two hundred-plus pounds of him, retired from a long fiscal career with the Federal government.

If there should be a seventy-fifth reunion, we decided to appoint Jimmy Carpenter, the best preserved of us all, as our delegate. He wasn't one of the class. He was our math teacher and baseball coach. At eighty years of age he looked good for another twenty-five.

None of my parents' contemporaries are still alive, nor many of mine. A few years ago I called on an aged couple who had bought the house near where we lived on Marengo Avenue. They had prospered from humble beginnings in South Pasadena after the turn of the century when the French woman had been a dressmaker and the English man the chauffeur for a family across Garfield Avenue in San Marino. During the Depression they bought up numerous bank foreclosures, refurbished the houses, and thus accumulated a tidy income from rentals.

A housekeeper admitted me. The old man lay paralyzed. His eyes knew me and filled with tears, his lips tried to form words. I sat by the bed and held his withered hand and thought of the years when all the fruit was sweet. The old lady was in the parlor, watching a soap opera. Her eyes were bright, her lips moved soundlessly. She paid no attention to me. The housekeeper apologized. "She won't leave the TV. They haven't seen each other for years."

I wandered around the old neighborhood. The big eucalyptus had been topped, the open zanja covered. The trunk of the wisteria vine had grown to the size of a man's body. I had buried our old collie at its base. In the biggest live oak someone had built a tree house and platform. A small boy looked down and waved.

"Would you like to come up?" he asked politely. "It's not hard. I nailed steps to the trunk. See?"

"I used to climb that tree," I said.

"Has it been here a long time?"

"Maybe a hundred years."

"Gee!"

"Do you ever ride a bike?" I asked.

"Sure."

"Do you read books?"

"Sure. I've got my favorites up here."

"Any Zane Grey?"

"Who?"

"The one who wrote *Riders of the Purple Sage.*"

"I like Tin Tin. Do you know the Tin Tin books? I've got five of them and Mom says I'm going to get another for my birthday. Do you want to look at them with me?"

"Maybe someday. I've got to go now."

"Where do you live?"

"In Arizona."

"Do you have a horse?"

"No," I said, "but I might get one if gas gets scarce again."

We laughed and I drove off, feeling that the old town was in pretty good hands.

Prejudice, Hate, and the First World War
M.F.K. Fisher
Whittier

As I see it now, our non-Quaker family started out in Whittier with several strikes against us. When I was a child there, though, I was unaware of almost everything except being sturdy and happy. I still have no idea of how much and how often my father, Rex, may have been rebuffed and rebuffed as editor of the *News,* as well as known companion of men who played poker, drank strong liquor, and even went to mass. As for my mother, Edith, she took out whatever social desires she may have had—and they were indeed puny, for by nature and training she was asocial—in working valiantly for the Woman's Club and the small mission which later became the Episcopal church, and in exchanging long cheerful letters with her Eastern relatives . . . and in running a kind of boardinghouse for anyone even remotely related to her. As long as she lived, anyone whose uncle on his mother's side had married a second cousin of Grandmother's sister-in-law could and did come to stay with us for anything from a week to several months, although it was a real ordeal for Mother to ask two "other people" to dinner. Some of the relatives were staid and stuffy, but there were fortunately a lot of them who could safely be called eccentric or, now that my candor cannot hurt Edith, downright crazy. They were the leaven in the loaf, and only rarely did my father suggest in a mild way that perhaps it would be nice to have some of his own brothers or nieces around for a few days. I think he knew that his wife's feverish need to open her house to her own clan was a sign that she was, in truth, lonely in her local world of polite but distant Quaker ladies. . . .

Of course my sister Anne and I knew nothing of all this. Painter Avenue was a wonderful street, gummed over with tar which melted deliciously during the first heat waves in May and then settled into a cozy warm ooze which felt good on our feet. And tar meant the steamroller, the most exciting mobile object in my lifetime, until I heard my first and last real calliope in about 1917. Probably the ground was smoothed or scraped a little first. Then, awesomely, the steamroller would rumble into view. We stood almost prayerfully on the front porch and then, as we grew older and bolder, on the sidewalk, and watched it move up and down our block. It was like a gigantic snail, but of course noisier, with a man up in its shell to wave now and then to us. It was faultless in the way it rolled the tar, our tar, into the flattened streetbed. It always went forward, and perhaps did not even have a reverse gear: I am ignorant of anything but its irrevocable progress past our house, a jolly Juggernaut.

We stood as long as we were allowed, probably almost dozing on our feet, hypnotized by its enormous and ruthless behavior, but I am sure that our jaws were not dropped, for we had our backs to the house and were chewing on the tar that had been spread earlier that day, and strictly forbidden by both Grandmother and Edith, a double hazard.

Tar with some dust in it was perhaps even more delicious than dirty chips from the iceman's wagon, largely because if we worked up enough body heat and had the right amount of spit we could keep it melted so that it acted almost like chewing gum, which was forbidden to us as vulgar and bad for the teeth and in general to be shunned. Tar was better than anything ever put out by Wrigley and Beechnut, anyway. It had a high, bright taste. It tasted the way it smelled, but better. And it was challenging, for unless we could keep up the heat and the juice and the general muscular involvement, it would flake off and turn our teeth a spotted, betraying black . . . black as tar. Dangerous game!

One time after we had flagrantly and plainly cheated, Mother said coolly to me at the dinner table, after we had eaten the first course with propriety and were waiting to see what came next (for Anne and I had been too busy on the sidewalk that afternoon to quiz the kitchen), "Mary Frances, I would like you to show your father your teeth." I steeled myself, and bared my little fangs at him. Things were still as church. Then Rex gave a great good laugh, and said, "TAR! Delicious! Best thing I ever chewed! But it looks awful on teeth!"

Later we did discuss the dubious sides of turning our backs, and the knowledge that we were cheating, and all that, but the reaction of my father made it easier for Anne and me to accept our capitulation to Obedience, and within a comfortable time the steamroller stopped its majestic smashing and we had a paved street, which made even ice chips less tasty.

Down on the corner of Philadelphia and Painter, near enough for us to see at night from the sleeping porch which we gradually had to ourselves as our parents started a new batch of children in another part of the upstairs, there was a big light strung over the intersection, and when a man had climbed up to it to clean it, he would drop out a long grayish tube of some kind of clay which made fine chalk. The sidewalks were sketchy in the town then, but we had a lumpy one going along our block, over the bulging roots of pepper and camphor trees. Later I found it hellish to skate on, but for hopscotch and artwork it was very good.

Across the street lived Old Lady Ransome, and her house still stands in its genteel green-and-white remoteness. Now and then my mother would put on a hat and gloves and go across to pay a call, and the two women would come out on the wide cement porch behind the hanging baskets of smilax ferns and perhaps wave to us. Anne and I went there only a few times, to carry Easter eggs or some such trifle, for Mrs. Ransome was crippled, and in pain.

Next door to her lived a series of people we never knew, except that during the influenza epidemic in 1918 Mother made us stay in the backyard while two or three coffins were carried away from it, one of a young woman, perhaps not yet twenty, who had waved now and then to us as she walked downtown to work for a lawyer. We did not feel one way or another about the plague, probably, although it interested us that soon after that Father came home at noon and pulled off the gauze mask requested by the Red Cross and said something like, "Bushwah! I can't smoke in it. And my nose is too big."

Next to the sad unknowns across from us, for a magical few years lived the Smiths. He was a lawyer. She had enormous sunken dark eyes, and played the piano very well. I think she was the fairly rich daughter, with what in France would be called a dowry, of the owner of a department store in Kansas City or some such place. Gradually they had two little girls. All four of them were tubercular. The last I heard, at least three of them had died. Mr. Smith's family was very bitter about his having caught the terrible disease from her, and her family felt the same way about him, and Mother worried a lot about their dilemma, but Anne and I simply enjoyed them. We went on wonderful picnics, for one thing. And I remember sitting under Mrs. Smith's beautiful grand piano and holding onto one of its legs while through my body ran the force and delicacy of the music she knew and played well. I think now it was Schubert, Mozart.

On up the street lived the Maples. They were and probably still are important in Whittier, and I remember them as a handsome large family. They were intelligent and well bred, and went to local schools and then away to Western colleges. Mr. Maple was the banker. On the top floor of the large house, into which I never once stepped, lived Mrs. Maple's mother, a small and apparently fearsome woman who looked down all day on the corner of Painter and Hadley from her high windows, but never waved or nodded.

I remember walking to the Bailey Street School when I was about five and a half years old, with the oldest Maple girl, Caroline, who was wearing her first long skirt. This was in about 1913, and it was plainly an important step for her to take. Two or three girls accompanied her enviously, still with skirts flapping above their shoe tops, perhaps nine inches from the ground. Much later in our lives I met Caroline a few times and liked her very much, but always felt some of my childhood awe of her having grown up that long before I did.

I was supposed to be a good friend of her little sister Josephine, but it never worked. Both of us tried for years to like each other, because our mothers thought it would be nice for one reason or another; we went to little parties, and had mutual friends, and remained consistently cold and disinterested.

Josephine had blond hair and was solidly built, as a child. She was rather malicious, I think, and I remember that once when I was tagging along shyly behind Red Sutherland, my first and only love in school until I was well on toward marriage, Josephine in a small gang of my friends spread the word that I had blown a kiss to Red's back or head as he marched on bravely in front of me. This hurt me. I would have liked to blow a kiss to him, but would never have done so. It also insulted me: such a childish gesture, turned into such a lascivious one! I was no dolt, but rather a sensitive, proud princess riding behind her knight, whether or not he cared. (He did not.) I felt defiled, no matter how naively.

The real thing I still have against Josephine, even now, although by now we well might like each other without cavil, is that once she whispered meanly to a school friend about my mother's looks. This I found, and still find, hard to forgive, and it gave me my first ugly taste of real hate. It must have been in 1918, because Mother was bending over my new sister Norah in her pram at the bottom of the front steps, where the baby lay in the sunshine. Skirts came to the floor or more daringly the ankle then, for a woman of my mother's age and social position, the first of which was about thirty-seven and the second, precarious. She was probably pregnant with my brother David, and her ankles were puffy, and as I watched her tuck the soft white covers about the baby I heard Josephine titter to my other school friend, "Look at her big fat ankles." Ah, there was a flash of rage in me, still felt!

It was the custom for the little girls of one or another neighborhood to meet on the sidewalk in front of their houses and walk to Penn Street School together, in a morning troupe that sometimes held fifteen or so, and I suppose the boys did the same. We never rode bikes, except after school and on Saturdays, and skates were out of the question because of the chancy sidewalks. We walked.

That morning of the slur on my mother's beauty, I knew we would stop for at least eight friends before we got to Penn. For perhaps the first time in my life I was so conscious of being angry that I knew I could not go with them, and especially with the sly, secure, tittering traitor who had mocked Edith Kennedy's ankles. Mother had suddenly become real and beautiful to me. I wanted to embrace her wildly, which we never did in our family, especially in those early days, and then run out onto the sidewalk and hit Josephine in her blond smug face until all her teeth popped out and her skin turned black and her eyes died.

This would not do, plainly. Instead I had a bang on the side of the baby's pram, turned away roughly from my mother's tender if preoccupied goodbye, and ran around to the back of our house and down the alleys, alone all the way to school. And I was swinging higher than anybody when my own crowd came onto the playground before the bell rang.

Across the street from the Maples, and down a block toward us, so that the house would be only a little north and across from the low brown cottage so full of love and music where the Smiths coughed and rotted, the Fays stayed for several years. Mrs. Fay was very grande dame, and always dressed formally for dinner, although they were poor as Job's turkey, according to my mother. When my parents went there, Mrs. Fay simply slung her train over one arm as she carried in the vegetable dishes, I was told later with laughing admiration. They did not even have a hired girl, and Mrs. Fay washed her lone child Eleanor's long hair and pressed her middy skirts' countless pleats.

Eleanor was very nice to us, and today might have been called a babysitter, on the rare times when Rex and Edith and the Fays would drive into Los Angeles in our Model T for a dinner with wine at Foix's or Marcel's or the Victor Hugo. My sister Anne and I never liked her much, one way or t'other, but I cannot remember why, for she read to us and was not sly or a tattletaler. Later the Fays moved away and she was sent to a fashionable school, and occasionally we heard that she had done things like made a debut (to what, in southern California?) and get married. Caroline Maple kept in touch with her for a long time, and passed news along to my mother, but it did not seem to move any of us. The Fay we remembered, with varying degrees and reasons, was her father, Charles, always thought of as Charlie.

All I can say now is that he was thin, not as tall as Father, and ineffably distinguished. He wore shabby hunting clothes the way most men dream of doing. He was from Boston, and I loved to hear him talk, although I don't think he ever addressed more than a remote greeting to me. Often he came in for a nip of sherry or beer or a rarer whiskey, before he went on up the street to change into his dinner clothes for the evening ritual of the thin fare he could provide, and I would listen with delight from a nearby room as his elegant high voice hung in the air. My parents were under his spell too, and when he was with them they spoke with more wit, more attention to their own fineness.

He and Rex often went hunting, during several years, and unloaded dead doves or quail from the back of the Ford, late at night. Rex always carried his own weapons, but said that Charlie did the shooting and he was bird dog. Then they stopped going away together, and it was most probably coincidence that about then the Fays left Whittier and never came back, but later I learned that Rex had refused ever to hunt again after a weekend with Charlie in Antelope Valley, where countless sportsmen stoned and clubbed the trusting little fawnlike beasts to death, and then sometimes stripped them of their skins, and mostly left them dead or dying, and went on clubbing and laughing and swigging from their flasks. Before that we had often eaten antelope when Charlie Fay brought us a piece, but from then on we never did, and as far as I can remember, this unwritten taboo covered all game like venison, bear, the occasional wild kid that still turned up in California hills. We did eat birds, but only when people gave them to us, and although my father never shot again, later he liked to go away on fishing trips, mostly for trout, so that he could be with men he enjoyed. (I know he and Charlie parted as friends.)

The only other thing I remember about the Fays, except that he was probably the first man I ever realized was attractive, is that between their small parlor and the dining room hung a curtain made of long strings of eucalyptus buds. I thought that was truly elegant. I think there were colored glass beads now and then on the strings of the scented little nobs, and I would have loved to wrap myself naked in the clicking tinkling spray that hung down with such mystery between the two small, crowded, ugly rooms.

We never had any such modish fripperies at home, if one overlooks an elaborate edition of *Sesame and Lilies* by Ruskin, and there were a couple of other local status symbols I pined for, but not too strongly, in those days. One was a brass vase, at least two feet tall, in which stalks of pampas grass would stand. This should be placed in a corner of the living room, or perhaps in the entrance hall. If possible, the frothy weird seedpods or whatever they are should be tinted pale lavender and pink and yellow. I have no idea where I got this vision, for we went into almost no homes in Whittier.

There was an old lady who lived out near Jim Town and had an avenue of pampas grass which she sent to a great convention somewhere in America, and Rex interviewed her once, and there was a story about her in the *Saturday Evening Post*. The highway to Los Angeles was lined in those idyllic days with silvery olive trees on her big ranch, and when we drove past the avenue of thick, tall grasses that curved away from it we slowed down to look at them, plumy and beautiful and even famous. But a brass vase filled with them? Where did I find this dream?

And of course it seemed a shame to me, for several years, that we did not have hanging baskets of smilax ferns on our small front porch. Other people did. Nice people did, especially nice old ladies, which probably I thought my mother to be and took for granted that Grandmother was, at least socially. Mother was adamant. She hated, for one thing, to have to remember to water anything. For another, as she confessed to me many years later, she had always considered smilax middle-class and vulgar, especially in hanging baskets, because she had been told that the only way to keep them flourishing was to give them diluted human urine. This haunted her, perhaps with some titillation, for I remember her pointing out especially beautiful fountains of smilax on other people's porches and then laughing scornfully.

South of the Fay house, one or two doors, lived a tiny, ancient Kentucky colonel and first two devoted daughters and then one. Once there was an automobile parade past our house, on Memorial Day, and he rode in an open Pierce Arrow in his Civil War uniform, not seeing anything, but fixed in a regal salute. Sometimes he sat on his front porch in a wheelchair, like Old Lady Ransome and Mrs. Worsham, but we knew enough not to bother him either. I think Mother liked the daughters, but they were still very unhappy about the Civil War and what it had done to them, and Mother was very busy.

Next to the Colonel, in a modest cottage compared to his faded yellow barn of a house, lived two little girls for a time, and they were friends of ours. Their mother had migraine headaches, which one of them later developed, and their father worked on the *News,* I think as a reporter. Helen and Alice the girls were, and Helen was almost too old for Anne and me, and already prone to biliousness and withdrawal. Although they moved away, they continued in the same school as we did, and that was fine, because Alice was a girl one wants to see again.

Between them and us was a big ugly house where for a few years lived the Cutlers. There were several children. The oldest girl, Ethel, occasionally stayed in our living room at night when Mother and Father went out, which was increasingly rare as our family grew bigger and Rex grew busier and Edith grew heavier and more social. There was a sister about my age whose name I have conveniently forgotten. She was the first person I saw in Whittier.

All our furniture was being moved from a dray into the house. I stood far to the north of the small front lawn, against a spindly hedge which later fattened. On the other side, in the middle of her own scrap of Bermuda grass, stood a little girl sucking her thumb with one hand and fondling her private parts with the other. We looked at each other several times, for I was interested in what she was doing, but we never spoke, and the process of moving into the house was basically a better show. That night when I was lying in my bed in the new room, a wonderful, big, screened porch like a bird's nest high at the back of the house, my mother came to kiss me and welcome me there, and she asked me if I had noticed what the little neighbor was doing. I think I had almost forgotten, but I recalled it, and she said that she did not want me ever to bother myself that way, because it would make me nervous. I wondered what that might mean, but did not question it for years.

The Cutlers took a Sunday paper, and so had funnies, which Grandmother did not allow in our house, and Anne and I became tricky at an early age in evading the Blue Laws. Ethel would bring them over in the afternoon, and we would meet at the far end of the long pergola of Cecil Brunner roses which led to our garage; Anne and I and a few of Ethel's siblings there, all of us loaded with heavy Bible picture books. We would lie down close together on our stomachs on the grass between the two car tracks of cement, with our five or six heads pointed away from Grandmother's room, and Ethel would read every delicious caption of every page of the funnies as we kept our Sunday books open in front of us. We knew, as if in secret language, the Katzenjammer Kids, Mutt and Jeff, and another saga about a very tall, thin, willowy character in a prison uniform whose name I now forget. There was also Krazy Kat, which I did not really enjoy for years, except for all those bricks that could close any gap in his conversation.

It seems strange that the Katzenjammers did not suffer from the War, when German measles were called Liberty, as also were hamburger steaks, and when somebody threw half a brick through our side window near the piano.

This was because Mother was playing, and she and Rex and Uncle Evans were singing, some German student songs in variously bad accents, no doubt bolstered by either beer or white wine and a common tenderness for one another. I cannot remember that a curtain was ever pulled in our house anywhere, so there in broad electric light were the editor of the town daily, his wife who had once lived in Germany itself, and her uppity professor-brother from the East, laughing and singing in the enemy's own tongue! Somebody lobbed the brick rather timidly into the subversive group: it went through the glass, all right, but most of the shattered staff stayed in place, so that the next morning when Anne and I came downstairs after our innocent slumbers, everything was fairly tidy, and by that night a new pane had been installed. I feel certain that Edith cried, for she wept easily and well, although hardly as often as she wished. The German music was put away. Uncle Evans went back to his law classes and Rex to his desk, each mum for his own reasons.

For a while after we went to Whittier there was one bakery going, run by a German, and usually at Christmas our turkey would be stuffed and taken down to be roasted in his undying oven. I think this happened a few times with large pots of beans, too, which stayed there overnight. The baker left town in 1916, to fight at home, and his brother-in-law took over.

The day before his grand opening, he sent home with Rex a great platter of gleaming sweet cakes, called Butter Flies because they made the butter fly, his new ad would say in the paper. We had a special treat that afternoon, and sat around in the dining room and drank pitchers of milk and ate the delicious surprise.

Grandmother tasted one, pronounced it good, and then dismissed it scornfully as a bribe. Edith, who was a helpless gourmand as well as a mild cynic, could not resist eating several cakes, while she murmured coolly to her husband that they could not possibly keep to this standard and would soon be like all other bought stuff, not fit to have in the house. Anne and I devoted ourselves to keeping far enough within the bounds of courtesy not to be noticed, while we got away with more delicacies than we had ever eaten before. It was a fine occasion, on which I think my father drank a beer and sat watching us from behind a cloud of slowly exhaled Bull Durham smoke.

Not long after that, though, the second German baker left town, and this time it was because we had entered the war and it was being said that he had put ground glass in some of his excellent bread. It was a sad thing, and my mother held her hand over her brown eyes, and then withdrew to her darkened room.

There was one other commercial war casualty in our town: our butcher, who had lived there for many years but with a German name, disappeared after several weeks of harassment and gradual bankruptcy, because a little boy, locally famous for his disobedient and ornery ways, had stuck his finger in the sausage slicer. Rumor said that the butcher went right on making and selling sausages from that machine, with the flesh of an AMERICAN CHILD!

There were, most of the time, two Jews who ran the town's variety store. They seemed to change, perhaps all in one family but spending a winter in turn, for their health, from some place like Chicago. They were always small, quiet, and kind, and I loved to go into the store for something like shoelaces or a paper of pins. I think that once a little daughter came to Penn Street School for a few months, but I do not remember seeing her in the store. Jews were simply not there, in Whittier. They did not really exist, except within themselves I hope. Their temple must have been long miles away. Nobody spoke to them. I cannot imagine what they did for proper food if they were Orthodox. I prefer not to think of their isolation.

Catholics were a step above Jews, socially, and one or two below the

Episcopalians. This was largely because we were all white, instead of having a few Mexican communicants. Rex had one very good friend, a Catholic, who ran a garage in Whittier, who finally was frozen out of town (as my father was supposed to have been by 1913 or so). He moved to Santa Ana or Anaheim, or some place like that. He was never recognized as a friend by my mother, who took a consistently dim view of her husband's offbeat intimates.

After the Catholic left town, Rex bowed to pressure and became a Mason, which may or may not be important to his picture. By then he had learned what a small religious community can do to a human being. All in the name of the Lord, and it is probable that in Masonry as in Rotary and the Salvation Army he believed there was enough fairness left to counteract the bigotry all these institutions have been accused of. It is one of the many things we never discussed, later. I do not know if we would have been able to. We were a hot-tongued and articulate family, and by the time Time itself had cooled us, it was too late: we were dead, or physically deaf, or spiritually numb and wary.

There was a small Catholic community in and around Whittier, mostly Mexican and illiterate, and some of my friends in school, therefore, were Catholics, but we never bothered about rituals like going to Sunday school together, or comparing Friday menus. We learned to read and write, at school, and we played wildly and thoroughly, and then parted every twilight, content as calves going to their own barns from a common meadow.

My mother was not used to having people of different-colored skins near her, and was shy about it, but Rex had it heavily on his mind that the living conditions in Jim Town, out around Pio Pico's rotting house on the banks of the Rio Hondo, were not right for man nor beast. He found that the Catholic priest in Whittier was the townsman most in touch with the people there, and they began to work together. I am sorry that I cannot know what they got done, in that Mexican ghetto of so long ago. Certainly it is not the kind of action that would possibly result today from the friendship and concern of two good men, but at least it sufficed for a pair of renegades, and they continued a long life of golf, mild tippling, and zeal; both of them social mavericks but shrugged off, if not actively condoned, by the good Quakers.

Much later, and perhaps as a result of this suspicious activity of the priest and the editor, the Friends installed a small mission in Jim Town, and Rex asked its earnest heavy-breathing pastor to give all of us Spanish lessons. It was doomed to quick failure. Mother gave up at once, and retired to her genteel romance with everything John Galsworthy ever wrote but especially *The Forsyte Saga*. Anne and I were wild Indians at that period, and could not long tolerate the endless afternoons with Señor Cobos and his fat little daughter Amparo, as we sat politely and drank lemonade and tried to understand the difference between "Thee" and "You" (if we had only been Quakers!). Finally Rex went alone to Jim Town and sweated over Spanish verbs, which were suddenly fun for him when he began escaping to Guadalajara, once a year or so. I have often felt sorry about being so stupid with Señor Cobos.

Later I studied Spanish hard and happily in school, and when I was much older I went to tedious night classes in adult education to recall some of it, and I can still read and hear it with pleasure. Of course I have never been hurt, except perhaps indirectly, because of another language I love besides my own. Nobody ever threw a piece of brick through a window because I was singing "La Cucaracha" or "Plaisirs d'Amour." But my mother never sang a German song again, after that night in about 1917—nor spoke a word of the language she had learned in several years in Germany, except when one of us would sneeze and wait happily for her Gesundheit!

The Double, Double Line
Michael Petracca
Hollywood

A stretch of Sunset Boulevard, just as you get into Beverly Hills, used to be called "Dead Man's Curve" because fatal wrecks happened there all the time. Before they installed the raised center divider, and without the steep velodrome cant it has today, the Curve was a lode of gory still photos, the kind they showed us in high-school driver's ed, in an attempt to scare us wild teens into driving safely. Some behavioral hack probably got a federal grant to develop the crude aversive technique, but it had a flaw. We loved the photos. A pretty deb impaled and hung out, like wet wash, on a telephone spike; ma and pa and junior and babs in what was once a sedan, a scene that more closely resembled a melting chocolate sundae than a family on an outing: we would have paid good money to see this stuff. We never associated the dead meat in the pictures with ourselves.

My father broke the law at the Curve, on a clear, windblown fall Sunday, ten years before my high-school driver's ed class. We were on our way back from my weekly pony ride by the big Owl Rexall in West Hollywood. I was eating Lik-M-Aid in the back seat, pouring the powder onto the saliva-sticky back of my hand and licking it off slowly, absorbed in the simple joy of its sweet-sour grainy roughness. I wasn't paying attention to Pop's driving. I was barely tall enough to see out the window.

Pop must not have been paying attention, either. He said, "Godfrey Daniel, what now?" when we heard the siren behind us. We pulled off Sunset and onto a side street overhung with trees. Leaves brushed past my window.

A tense silence in the car. The officer's heavy bootfalls outside the car got louder and then stopped. Pop rolled down his window. The cop said, "Can I see your license, sir?"

While he fumbled in his coat, Pop asked, "What did I do, officer?"

"You crossed the double, double line, sir."

I was barely old enough to read my own name, let alone study the motor vehicle code, but it was clear my father had broken someone's rule. Pop had always been the summit of authority figures, and I never considered that someone might be able to boss him. This sudden role reversal hinted at a world without absolutes, where power currents can change direction capriciously, like dry leaves in a Santa Ana. The new perspective was unacceptable to me. A kernel-sized "No!" took root in my solar plexus, grew in intensity and pitch as it reached my larynx, blossomed into an ululating drop-drill wail of deafening volume by the time the policeman handed Pop's wallet back to him.

The cop craned his neck around the window post and winked reassuringly at me, which caused me to go into convulsions and make hideous choking noises. I spilled my Lik-M-Aid on the seat cover.

Undaunted, the cop said, "Wait a second." He dug his hand into a trouser pocket, then reached out and dropped a quarter onto the upholstery beside me. From my vantage point deep in a tantrum, the coin seemed somehow out of place, like a tiny silvery cruiser from another galaxy. Its incongruity worked to cut me off in mid-mewl; after all, twenty-five cents can buy you a rapturous afternoon with two Scrooge comics and money left over for a righteous Lik-M-Aid bender. I pocketed the cash.

I wiped my upper lip dry with my jacket sleeve. The cop tore the citation from his tablet and gave it to Pop, who was smiling now, no doubt relieved that he wouldn't have to drive me to the Kaiser clinic to have my voice box cauterized. As Pop started the Buick's engine, the policeman gave me these final words of advice: "Keep an eye on that father of yours. If he crosses the double, double line again, you give me a call. You're on the department payroll now."

Cheap but effective PR. For two bits the LAPD had bought themselves a supporter for life . . . or at least until my last semester in high school. And even in those progressive, loving sixties, when everyone wanted to Off The Pigs, I remained a loyal ally of L.A.'s Finest—that is, until the night two redneck deputies pulled me out of Thrasher's old Austin America with the multicolored shelfpaper flowers pasted on the door panel, tore apart the interior of my friend's car looking for drugs, and when they found none— nary a roach nor a seed nor a stem—pushed me hard across the hood, my feet spread-eagled on the asphalt, and said, "What's this?" They had uncovered the small ratchet wrench I used to tighten the Austin's fan belt, which was always slipping.

I started to answer, but one of them said, "Shut up, you little longhair fuck. We found this under the front seat and damn if we're not going to have to cuff you and take you in for grand auto and driving with a concealed weapon."

The unprovoked cruelty of my former brothers in crime prevention, along with an instantaneous vision of the holding area at the Garden Heights jail—the reverberating concrete austerity, the appalling acrid stench of vomit and urine in the drunk-tank drains, and filthy unshaven churls giggling sadistically as they turned me out—gave rise to an unpremeditated response in me. A kernel-sized "No!" took root as it had years earlier, and this time, by the time it blossomed in my larynx, I was already in convulsions and making hideous choking noises. The incongruity of a full-blown fit of weeping hysteria in a high-school kid daunted the deputies. I must have appeared close to a massive stroke which they'd have to explain to their captain at the station, "Gee whiz, sir, we were just havin' a little fun with the hippie, heh-heh, we never thought he'd go and *die* on us . . ."

They let me up, "Go on, get out of here, you little fairy crybaby," and gunned off into the early morning darkness. I sat in my car and shook, and I shook all the way home.

The socket wrench incident undermined my early reinforcement with the quarter and left me with some new and ugly preconceptions about cops, which still weighed heavily when I met Sergeant Freitag after my bedroom almost blew up. It didn't help that his face was in a perpetual grimace, as though he smelled fresh dogshit where he went. I fully expected him to whip out his riot stick without warning and start clubbing me across the back of my neck while he accused me of trying to asphyxiate myself to make my mother look incompetent as a child raiser. But when Sergeant Freitag turned out to be courteous, attentive, soft-spoken, direct and intelligent, my initial attitude toward him changed, as did the way I perceived him physically. Over the course of our initial meeting, his grossly heavy eyebrows took on a fierce and determined set, his upturned nose a noble pride, his acne-scarred complexion a ruddy glow. You couldn't help but like the guy, or at least feel sorry for his face.

Sergeant Freitag said, "You'd better start from the beginning. I need as much information as you can give me, if we're going to find out who did this. Do you know anyone who would want to kill you . . . or give you a good scare?"

"Can I sit down?" I asked. "This could take a long time."

"Certainly, sit."

I collapsed into a chair by the dining table and shoved aside the pile of books and paper that had been sitting there, untouched, for weeks. Sergeant Freitag commented, "Student?"

"Senior," I said.

I told him about my problems with my senior thesis. He said, "Believe me, you're fortunate, and I don't just mean by avoiding the gas explosion as you did. I'd give anything to read for the fun of it." He picked up a volume of Browning from the table and held it in front of him, " . . . literature, like *The Ring and the Book* here. There's so much to say about it, if I had the chance, if anyone would listen . . ."

"You know Browning?" I asked, forever amazed at the way life reveals porkers to be poets, but more often vice versa.

"The Victorians are my specialty—or were. I was an English major once, too, and I was going to grad school, but Vietnam kind of interrupted my plans."

They nailed him in 1967, he said, and he came back two years later with limbs intact but a fractured soul. "It took me a while to recover. I had what they called a 'situational chemical dependency.' Mostly pills, tranks, it was the only way I made it through my last year of combat duty. After the war I landed at the detox center at the V.A. hospital in Westwood. When I got out I was clean but broke. I needed a job, and being a cop seemed like a natural. It kind of uses the same skills as 'Nam, except right and wrong are so much clearer when you're after crooks on the streets."

"Malaria is probably much rarer in L.A., too."

"True," he said. "Being on the force hasn't been a bad job, but I don't have much time for literature any more . . . a real waste. I even had a topic I wanted to pursue: how the Victorian poets revised the whole idea of truth, a constant reminder that throughout history the poet has been the source of truth, and not history itself. It's like . . ." He stopped and looked around the room, and his eyes lit on my ceramic drinking mug, a cheapie Japanese import decorated with a wraparound Escher print. Blue fishes were dissolving into diamond-shaped negative space, while diamonds of white negative space were evolving into fishes. "It's like . . . do you know Escher?"

"Sure, I'm familiar with his work." I had a black light poster of some lizards in a castle when I was seventeen.

"Browning here," he said, raising Browning above his head in the manner of a demolition worker hefting a sledge hammer, "does to the whole notion of truth and authority, what an artist like Escher does with fishes, or lizards." His eyes focused, unblinking, on a point in space somewhere between his face and mine. "The author becomes the truth, and the truth becomes its creator. They are inseparable. You can see the same thing happening all through nineteenth-century letters, and not just in poetry . . ."

Sergeant Freitag was talking nonsense, but it was legitimate academic nonsense, the same pure-land critical speculation with which I had been trying to approach Eliot for months, and failing. He had seen in Browning the very inseparable melding of artistic self-consciousness and art that I was trying to point out in Eliot. He was extemporizing on the creative process with passionate lucidity that had long since been wrung out of me, by meetings with faculty members on my thesis committee, each of whom had a different philosophical slant. Sergeant Freitag had not yet been used as a battleground in departmental holy wars, trampled and scorched by warring factions of crusaders for literary Truth, and so he yearned for nothing more than to pursue the very scholastic life I have come to detest.

I observed, "Strange situation. Fraught with ironies. You want to do research more than detective work, and to avoid literary research I'm doing detective work."

"You're doing a damn poor job of it, too, if you don't my mind saying. At least Browning won't get me killed."

"Give him time," I said. "Look, I'll make you a deal. You help me out of this mess I'm in, and I'll help you get into grad school. I know everyone."

"I can imagine," he commented waggishly. He reflected for a moment. "I don't know, it's been five years since I got back from the war, maybe I'm ready for a career change now. We'll see . . . but first, let's get your life safe."

"Admirable *imprimis!*" I exclaimed, showing off the delightful inflated vocabulary of the 3.7 English major. "I know I'm not going to be able to sleep at all tonight. Check out that window, the frame is all bent. Anyone could stick a hand in there. There's no latch left. And if somebody does try to break in, my phone's next to the window, so if some killer was right outside, he'd be able to hear me call."

"Common sense," Freitag said. "Just dial nine-one-one and then whisper into the phone."

"I'm scared they're not going to be outside, they're going to be inside already."

"You might stack up some Coke bottles or something like that by the window. They'd have to make so much noise getting in, over the stereo and everything, they'd wake you up."

"Terrific. Coke bottles. Is this the latest advance in crime prevention technology?"

"No, but with a place as small as yours, a couple piles of bottles usually works better than those electronic setups people pay thousands of bucks for. Crooks can disable an alarm system with one snip of wire, if they're pros. And your crooks are definitely pros."

"You have a terrific way of putting a guy at ease. I guess I'd better start drinking Coke."

"It's the real thing," he said.

Chochis and the
Movies at Sanfer
Mary Helen Ponce
Pacoima

I remember when as children we attended movies in the nearby town of San Fernando, where of the two movie theaters, Mexicans were welcome in one, the San Fernando Theater. The other, El Rennie Theater, catered to Anglos and was off limits to the *chicanada* of Pacoima and Sanfer. It was not until World War II and soon after that Mexican-Americans (as we were then known) were allowed to patronize local movie houses and restaurants. Many barrio men were wounded, killed and decorated while fighting for their country, the good ole USA. It was not considered patriotic to turn away non-whites in uniform so we were let inside. However, by the time we were admitted to the Rennie Theater we had already chosen to attend el San Fernando Theater, where the owner, Mort, was friendly and made us feel welcome. Mort was Jewish, and tolerant of other minorities. He was a good businessman, but more than that, he was kind to Mexican people. For the Mexican-Americans of Pacas and Sanfer, the place to go for fun on a Sunday afternoon was el Towne, on Brand Street.

The "draw" to the special Sunday matinees were the weekly serials. We took the long bus ride and then stood in line, eager to see the latest escapades of the blonde heroine of *The Perils of Pauline,* and the curvaceous girl who was Nyoka of the Jungle. Both young women were usually caught up in adventures that had us sitting on the edge of our seats, gasping from excitement. The movie would end with Pauline and Nyoka on the brink of death as they waited to be rescued by the handsome hero who later

213

reappeared in other episodes. When the words "to be continued next week" flashed on the screen we sank back in our seats, exhausted but exhilarated. We exited the theatre, and on the way to the bus stop, we talked of nothing else but the coming episode, and of our plans to return the following Sunday.

My friends faithfully attended the movies. I went once in a while. Most of the families of Pacoima (like ours) were of the working-class, with large families and little money to spend frivolously. We rarely had spending money, other than a few pennies and *cincos* earned from returning bottles to La Tienda de Don Jesus; yet my father was forever fixing our house, putting up a new fence, and my mother made sure we had "church clothes." Perhaps what we had were different values.

I remember some of my friends lived in run-down homes yet always had spending money, and went often to the movies. Not until I was older did I realize our parents' first priorities were to feed, clothe, and provide a comfortable home for us. There was little money left over for fun. When on Sundays I saw my friends walking to the bus stop on the way to the "show," I was filled with envy but only for a minute. In time I was more grateful for our home with the white picket fence and well-tended rose bushes.

Although none of my friends dated or went steady, by the time we were twelve or so, we made arrangements to "sit" at the movies with someone we liked. One year, George Sanchez, or Chochis as his mother called him, asked me to go with him to a matinee. I wasn't too thrilled as Chochis was *un gordito*. The fact that I too was chubby was of no consequence to me. I mean we didn't have to be *gordinflones*.

It was fun to "sit" with George. He ate all during the movie. Popcorn, peanuts and candy. He would load up before the movie, during intermission, and just before the movie ended. To be with him was to partake in a continuous feed. Food was happiness for Chochis, and for me, happiness was sitting with him.

There was a certain amount of security in being with Chochis. He was content to stuff himself all during the movie so that he never had time to get fresh with me. All he ever did was put his arm around me. One arm on my shoulder, the other entwined around a big bag of buttered popcorn. While the other girls were busy fighting off *los frescos,* I munched contentedly throughout the entire movie, mesmerized by the antics of Pauline and Nyoka, secure with an array of Baby Ruths, Milk Duds and Snickers.

The movies included war news of World War II. These were in black and white, produced by Pathe News. Scenes of battles, soldiers and tanks flashed on the screen: fighting men of the USA! Although we were interested in the fighting overseas, the war seemed far away. The war news appeared to be another movie, part of the entertainment offered to youngsters on a Sunday afternoon.

One time during intermission a short propaganda movie was shown. This included a funny jingle, which the audience was urged to sing. The words evade me now, but sounded like this:

Stinky Jap, off the map

Benito's jaw, oh ho ho

The song was an allusion to the enemy, the Japanese and Mussolini. We sang several verses, all funny and clever. I stopped eating long enough to sing along. I liked to sing and didn't want to miss either the words or beat. We sang and sang. The theater rocked with shouts of laughter and jeers. Aha, ha ha.

I remember thinking it was wrong to be making fun of the Japanese. We were not exactly blonde and blue-eyed. We were brown. Light and dark brown, but nonetheless, brown. *Morenos, trigueños, prietos.* Not white enough to be accepted in the predominately white Rennie Theater but able to laugh at others who, like our ancestors, had fought a war against this country, men who were mocked and called "dirty Mexicans," not "dirty Japs."

When this "short" was not screened again I was grateful as I felt uncomfortable laughing at other minorities. My parents were not racist, and neither were we kids. I think Mort disliked the movie too, as we never saw it again. As I said, he was a nice man.

In the Center
of the Outskirts
Leonard Nathan
El Monte

Already as a boy Pindar felt that this unimposing town
of his, the walls along which he walked day after day,
the springs from which he drank, a street here and
a square there, were profoundly linked with the past,
with the gods and demigods . . . By force of circumstances,
therefore, he grew up in an atmosphere of spiritual
riches, and this to a poet is probably far more
valuable than the quality we call genius or talent.
  Bruno Snell, THE DISCOVERY OF MIND

I wish I could say that I found my poetic vocation in Arcadia. I can't. I found it in the neighboring town of El Monte. El Monte was no-wise remarkable, except for its claim to have the only lion farm in the world. Like other southern California valley towns in the early thirties, it was gradually and unintentionally passing from a rural community into something else, undecided as yet but full of one-story stucco houses and small businesses, with a chain five-and-dime and two modest movie palaces.

Years before my parents moved there, I spent summer weekends in El Monte with my cousin Bob, playing cops-and-robbers in the stockroom at the back of his folk's dry goods store, and Saturday noons going to the lo-cal plunge (except when it was closed by a polio scare). After, our eyes cloudy with chlorine, we downed a fat hamburger and a malt. Then it was time to betake ourselves to a triple feature—Tom Mix, Bob Steele, and Hoot Gibson. All this for fifty cents apiece, including popcorn and a Baby Ruth. In those days, Bob's folks kept a few chickens and geese, and Sunday mornings we collected eggs still warm from the hens.

I was twelve when we made the move from Los Angeles to El Monte. There were still hayfields at the west edge of town, only one long street from our new house, the only house on the block. A fifteen-minute walk in the other direction lay El Monte's main drag, Valley Boulevard. Between were six or seven blocks of stucco houses, each with its tidy lap of lawn and one-car garage. On the fringes of this stucco center were wood-framed

217

houses, remains of an earlier, farming phase of the town, their paint peeling, porches sagging a little. And it was all so still. Walking with me from my house to Valley Boulevard on a hot afternoon, you might have the impression that all El Monteans were resting behind drawn blinds. Only the cries of the children in the park broke through the silence, but even these sounds were muted. I think we were quieter in those days.

And what in all this could summon up poetry? Pindar would have found no myths among us. It wasn't closeness to nature either. Nature in El Monte had been tamed. What other places ever made lions into a farm crop? Besides, if nature had addressed me, I probably wouldn't have heard. I was a lazy, unventuresome boy, full of triple-featured fantasies—heroic deeds, beautiful girls rescued. It was easier to dream than to read—till I found Shelley in a high-school anthology.

Why Shelley? Perhaps it was that, like El Monte, I was small and boringly familiar while Shelley was vast and exotically remote; or that, like El Monte, I was plain and prosaic while Shelley was gorgeously obscure. If I could have personified El Monte, I would have found its eyes like mine, too close together, its face freckled and its ears too big. Shelley, by being every wonderful thing that El Monte and I were not, gleamed beyond our pitiful limits as a summons to transformation.

How else explain the morning I found myself standing before the bathroom mirror reciting iambic pentameters—my own—filled with high-sounding if disconnected words? A strange place for poetic inspiration, true, but everyone knows that a bathroom with a lock on its door is a sanctuary and that a mirror is just the place to study self-transformation. And I believed that transformation, though its effects didn't seem to be in the realm of the visible.

Meanwhile, in its own modest and unintentional way, El Monte was encouraging what Shelley had begun. About this time, the high school had hired a new journalism and English teacher. But it had got more than it paid for (about a $1,000 a year). In Vernon Patterson it got an ex-soldier, ex-poet, ex-novelist, ex-Hollywood script writer now turned teacher. It also got a persuasive social conscience. In a dirt poor time, in a place where racial hatred was built into the system, Patterson badgered the local service clubs till they supplied equipment to go with the baseball diamond he laid out in the Mexican ghetto outside town. What I got—and just in time— was someone who knew that poetry was not a private enchantment, but the disciplined craft that made enchantment into communication. Once he saw what I was about, he bought me—out of the thousand a year—a little book of prosody, in case I missed the point that poetry was also work, not escape from work. A hard critic of self-indulgence, he never let me forget that a long labor of love lay between what I was writing then and what I might do some day.

But he was not all critic. He was a wonderful storyteller, bringing me the lore of a bigger, more complicated world than the one I knew. On long walks at dusk through the quiet streets, I heard about great cities, about the "Great War," about great personages. I heard also for the first time, as did perhaps El Monte, that a life given to art was different from other lives— more dangerously intense, more passionately isolating. Keats was the example, though Shelley would have done as well.

That was all wonderful. But more wonderful still was the long yellow roadster that pulled up beside us one of those quiet dusks. Its driver was beautiful, her hair the color of her car. Pat gave a shout of surprised greeting and the next thing I knew I was in the front seat, squeezed between two larger-than-life people, listening to larger-than-life talk. It seemed that she was an ex-wife and an actress. I don't remember anything they said. I was too absorbed in sensation—the green glow of the dash, perfume blending with the aroma of new leather, the music of happy, intelligent voices, and the car itself, more speedboat than car. And over all this, big pastoral stars were brightening, shining on the plainness of El Monte as on the majesty of the great cities. If, as some thinkers have it, poetry is articulate wonder struggling with contradiction, here surely was the stuff to make a poet.

When the time came for me to leave El Monte, I was not sorry. I was eighteen and going to another great and, as I understand it, just war. And by now I had become a small-town intellectual snob, a self-appointed misfit to whom the war seemed a noble way of departing from the place he scorned. A few months later, marching through the freezing alien stubble of a Georgia training camp, I got homesick for El Monte. But when at the end of the war I returned, it was not to stay. After a season of discontent, I left for college. Still, college was a few hours away, so I often came home on weekends, but only to pace the town as though it were a cage, and a cage that was getting smaller and smaller each visit.

El Monte was in fact quietly growing. The lion farm was gone, and light industry was moving into the fields, the stucco houses spreading wherever they could. But I only saw this after putting real distance between us. Now I was at Berkeley and the returns were fewer. And more disorienting. Once, a wrong turn off the freeway landed me in what had been a riverbed, now wall-to-wall houses sprouting a thick crop of TV aerials. When I understood where I was, I panicked a little, suddenly seeing past and present in one place, like one transparency superimposed on another. More recently, it took me less time to get from Oakland to Los Angeles than from Los Angeles to my old house. I lost my way in a maze of unfamiliar streets. At one point I turned and there was an airport. El Monte had no airport! Or hadn't when I'd last looked. For all I know it may now also have Cajun cookery and a fresh-pasta shop. The world is moving ever faster and El Monte with it. The town may be passing me at this very moment.

So perhaps I'm not as far from it as I like to think and therefore closer to what I was when the town and I shared the delusion that we were the center of the universe. I think I can see my smaller self clearly enough from here. Of course, I'm tempted to give him some good advice.

But what kind? If the child is father of the man, it is the man who should be seeking counsel. The man, however, can't think of any good questions. As he stares out the back window, he sees the boy kneel in the empty lot behind his stucco house to find, half hidden by the shadow of a grass blade, a strange seed, which he picks, feels (it is furry), then pries open with his fingernails. Out shoots a vapor and, poof, the future arrives and I am here composing this, looking at the boy still kneeling. A very sharp image, but distant and opaque. It could be the posture of prayer, submission, readiness, or all of these in some unstable combination. But this also is true: the boy is sitting here writing it all down, inventing a self to go with the look of sixty-two years of living.

Saint Aloysius
Danny Romero
Watts

T wice a year the parish held fund-raising bazaars. They were on weekends in October and May and were the backbone of the finances for the grammar school and church. They were held on the blacktop of the schoolyard. There were never any rides, but plenty of food, and games of chance and amusement. It was the duty of the parents of the schoolchildren to contribute some of their time in the organizing and actual running of the bazaar.

My father ran the jingleboard. He carried metal rings on a metal rod with a magnet at one end, and bellowed out the prices for the rings. They were bought, or rather rented, by the patrons of the board and thrown at a table filled with coins and bills. When one landed clearly on a coin or the face of a bill it became yours. He picked up the ricocheting rings from off of the ground and table with the magnet. He was the perfect barker for a carnival somewhere out of a fifties movie, making up little rhymes and jingles as the day went on, more and more enticed by his words as the evening went on. He was quite adept at the game himself, having been running the board for ten years by the time I entered that school.

There were other games too. The goldfish pond where a person threw Ping-pong balls, three for a quarter, at a table filled with bowls of the fish swimming in colored water, some of their orange tails seeming whispery thin against the background of blue-, red-, or green-colored water. Mrs. Tabor, whose daughter was in my first-grade class, was always the one to run this particular booth.

There was another fish pond at those bazaars. My mother, I remember, always worked at this one. It was a booth covered in front with cardboard. Portholes were cut in the cardboard, and children for the cost of a dime were given bamboo poles with a string tied to one end and a fishhook at the end of that string. The poles were lowered into the portholes and my mother tied cheap toys onto the hook and tugged at the string. Thereupon the child would retrieve the pole, string and hook from out of the hole and take his prize. It was the only sure winner in the entire operation.

When I first began school there at Saint Aloysius I had a sister in the eighth grade, a brother in the sixth, another sister in the fourth, and finally my brother Felix in the second. I remember being at the bazaar with my oldest sister that first year. At that time it was still felt I needed to be with someone older and being with my sister and her friends had its drawbacks. I had to use the girls' restroom, the boy's being far too dirty, rowdy and violent for the six-year-old child I was. Even later when I was old enough(?), wise enough(?), dumb enough(?) to use that restroom it remained a place of fear and uncertainty. It was a place of flooded floors and overflowing toilets, sweating Mexican men and Seconal swallowing, zombie-eyed cholos passing the pills and cheap wine. It was the scene of the first sight of knives cutting flesh, bottles breaking skulls and the strangeness of being fearful but curious, of being scared enough to cry but not wanting to miss a thing that tears might blind me from.

One Saturday afternoon in those first formative years I walked with my then buddy Jeffrey Leon. We bought *raspadas* from Mr. Salazar and his boy scout troop and crushed the confetti eggs we had spent all week preparing on the heads of our classmates. Now within the scrutiny of our parents we snuck peeks as best we could under the miniskirts of the seventh- and eighth-grade girls and the teased-hair high-school cholas. We knew there was something up under those skirts and between those long legs which everyone talked about and desired and which would be ours to partake of someday, though we didn't know at the time what it was for sure.

Bingo games were held in the Old Hall throughout the weekends. It was the only parish hall, but always referred to as the Old Hall. In the cafeteria the food prepared by the parish mothers was sold: corn dogs and buñuelos, tamales, tostadas, tortas and tacos, and burritos and menudo always for the morning after. When they were setting the booths up for the weekends it was probably some of the best times that were ever had during the school year. During recess and lunch breaks the children of the school stood within the booths acting out what each knew or thought the weekend would be like. The yard would be filled with strange cars and trucks and the men of the parish building the booths, leaving little room for any football, basketball or sockball.

On one such weekend while I was in the third grade I asked my father permission to visit a friend's house who lived close by. It was the first time ever being allowed and I was getting older, more responsible perhaps. My friend Alfred and I went and looked at his older brother's *Playboy* magazines.

I used to love the mariachis who would play all decked out in their black suits and wide-brimmed sombreros, the guitarron thumping and the shrill trumpets getting louder. My father loved them too.

Sometime in the early Seventies they stopped having these fund-raisers, though I have heard they have started them up again. My nephew now goes to that school. They ended because of the violence which always erupted. Cholos squaring off with each other in the crowd of people. I remember the fight that ended the show for years. The church and school lying somewhere on mutual ground, it was more than likely the bad boys from Florence against their counterparts from Watts. I stood and watched it all. It was the third night in a row. Sticks, knives and beer bottles filled the air.

I can remember the panic and fear which engulfed me. I was alone for what was probably the first time on the streets. No brother, no sister, mother or father within reach, just lost in a crowd more than a thousand strong. I heard the commotion starting, growling, and getting nearer. Glass broke and curses flew. People screamed and cried. Father Jose in his heavy Castillian accent stood in the middle of it, speaking in a combination of both English and Spanish and called upon the Lord to help settle the matter.

Some of my family was there though I didn't know where at the time. I heard firecrackers which I later learned was gunfire. I saw one dark, skinny *vato* walk by me with the bottom of a beer bottle firmly imbedded in the side of his head. I felt sick. People ran scared. More people stuck around to see how it would turn out. The sheriffs then came to bust some heads themselves. Everyone left then, including myself, for fear of being arrested. I walked home alone at night for the first time, the sirens speeding towards where I had just left. School. Church. Someone died. The Neighborhood. Perhaps it was the *vato loco* with the beer bottle bottom for a crown. I felt a fear I hoped I would never feel again.

Life Among the Oilfields
Hisaye Yamamoto DeSoto
Redondo Beach

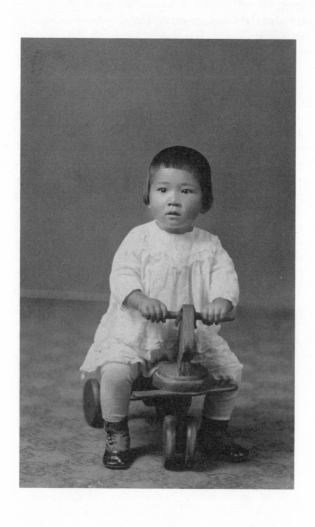

They rode through those five years in an open car with the
sun on their foreheads and their hair flying. They waved
to people they knew, but seldom stopped to ask directions or
check on the fuel, for every morning there was a gorgeous
new horizon . . . They missed collisions by inches, wavered
on the edge of precipices, and skidded across tracks to the
sound of the warning bell.

—*F. Scott Fitzgerald*

T here has been some apprehension this year about the possibility of
another depression such as overtook this country in the autumn of
1929. I was eight years old at the time and was unaware that there
were people then who were leaping out of windows to their deaths. But
our family was never distant from poverty, so we probably did not have
that far to fall.

Over the years, however, I have managed to piece together this or that
homely event with the corresponding dates—the Flaming Twenties, the
Volstead Act, Al Capone, Black Thursday—and realize that there were
signs of the great debacle around us all along.

My mother has given me four pennies to take to school. Two cents are
for me to spend, but the other two cents are for candy for my little brother
Johnny at home. At noon, a little Japanese girlfriend and I cross over to the
little grocery near the school so that I can make my purchases. After due
deliberation over the penny Abba–Zabbas, which are supposed to resemble
the bones worn through their noses by the black figures on the checkered
wrapper, the long white strips of paper pebbled with pastel buttons of
graduated hue, the large white peppermint pills, the huge jaw-breakers
with the strange acrid seed in the middle, the chicken bones covered with
golden shredded coconut, the bland imitation bananas, the black licorice
whips, I settle for two white wax animals filled with colored syrup, one for
me and one for Johnny, and, always one for a bargain, eight little wrapped
caramel and chocolate taffy squares, which come four for a penny. The man

behind the counter, white-haired and kindly, gives me one wax candy and four chews, then hands the same to my little friend.

Before I can protest, my friend dashes off with the candy clutched tightly in her fist, the candy which I am supposed to take home to my brother. I sputter my inadequate English at the storekeeper and give furious chase to my friend, who knows what the deal is. But, running like the wind, she has already escaped. The rest of the school day I spend seething about this introduction to incredible treachery and worrying about what to tell my mother.

It does not occur to me to forego eating my share of the candy, to take it home to my brother.

It was at the same school, Central School in Redondo Beach, that I once watched in wonderment as two thin tow-headed children, a boy and a girl, delved into one of the trash baskets filled with lunchtime litter. They came up with a banana skin which they gravely shared, taking turns scraping the white insides of the yellow peeling with their lower teeth.

But I don't know why I was attending Central School, when I had begun kindergarten at South School, since we were still living at the same house with the enormous piano and orchard. I do know that I went back to South School subsequently, where, at the beginning of the second grade, I encountered obstacles in being admitted to the proper classroom. On the first day of that school year, I was among the milling children lining up to march into the building. When I tried to line up with the second-grade children, a teacher steered me over to the first-grade column. I did not command enough English or nerve to argue, but meekly joined the first-graders and prepared to go through the first grade all over again.

After some weeks, though, I must have made enough noise about it at home, because my mother was upset. Since the same bus serviced both Central and South Schools, unloading first at Central School, she counseled me to get off at Central School, there to see if the second grade wouldn't accept me. In trepidation I obeyed, but there, too, I was consigned to the first grade. I sat woefully at the rear of the room that day, like one suspended in limbo, while Central School tried to figure out how to handle this deluded Oriental shrimp with second-grade pretensions. As it turned out, probably because of my grass-roots revolt, South School found out that I did indeed belong in the second grade. The bus driver came after me in his own car later that day and transported me to South School, where I was finally delivered to the second grade. I was secretly so delighted to be in my proper niche at last that I took steps to make myself known to the teacher. Taking my reader up to her, I asked how to read the word "squirrel" which I knew very well. I guess this was like pinching myself to make sure there was order in the world again, the seconds of his personal attention constituting the confirmation.

When I was still in second grade, we moved to our last location in Redondo Beach, going a little distance south to a farm among the oilfields. We were not the only oilfield residents. There was a brown clapboard house diagonally across the road, first occupied by an Italian family whose home garden included Thompson seedless grapes, then by a Mexican family. At the far end of the next oil tract to the west, next to a derrick, lived an older gentleman in what I recall as more of a tent than a house. Once, a few years later, after we had moved inland, we stopped by to visit with him and found him tending a baby in a canvas swing set up outside his canvas-and-wood abobe. It seemed to be a grandchild left in his care. He showed us the special canned milk he fed the baby. Each can came completely wrapped in plain cream-colored paper, so it seemed a more elegant product than the condensed Carnation milk we used.

There was a white family in the corner of a diagonal tract, where we played with the children. A Japanese family with two little ones farmed in the middle of a tract to the north, and I remember one day watching the father smear a poisoned red jam on little pieces of bread in order to kill the rats in his barn. Beyond, I remember visiting a blonde schoolmate named Alice, whose older sister was named Audrey.

Our house, bathhouse, barn, stable, long bunkhouse, outhouse, water tower and kitchen garden were set down adjoining a derrick along the country road. Derricks then were not disguised by environmental designers to be the relatively unobtrusive, sometimes pastel-colored pumps that one comes across nowadays. Constructed of rough lumber, tar-smeared and weathered, they were ungainly prominences on the landscape. They reared skyward in narrow pyramids from corrugated tin huts and raised platforms whose planks accommodated large wooden horseheads nodding deliberately and incessantly to a regular rhythm. Each derrick had its rectangular sumphole, about the size of an olympic swimming pool. The reservoir of rich dark goop, kept in check by sturdy, built-up dirt walls, might be a few inches deep or nearing the top. Occasionally a derrick caught fire, but I remember only a couple of times when, off in the distance, we could see the black smoke rising in a column for days.

We must have lived day and night to the thumping pulse of black oil being sucked out from deep within the earth. Our ambiance must have been permeated with that pungency, which we must have inhaled at every breath. Yet the skies of our years there come back to me blue and limpid and filled with sunlight.

But winter there must have been, because there was the benison of hot *mochi* toasted on an asbestos pad atop the wood-burning tin stove, the hard white cake softening, bursting, oozing out dark globs of sweet Indian bean filling. Or Mama would take out from the water in the huge clay vat a few pieces of plain *mochi* which she would boil. The steaming, molten mass, dusted with sugared, golden bean flour, would stretch from plate to mouth, and the connection would have to be gently broken with chopsticks.

It must have been a chilly January, too, when my father, with horse and plow, dug up the ground. After the earth was raked and leveled, he would pull after him the gigantic pegged ruler which marked off the ground for planting, first one way and then across, so that seen from the sky, the fields would have been etched with a giant graph.

Some of the preparation was done in the empty bunkhouse at night, the bulging, thin-slatted crates of strawberry plants arriving from somewhere to be opened up, each damp plant to be trimmed of old leaves and its clump of earthy roots to be neatly evened off with a knife.

Each plant was inserted into the soil where the lines on the ground intersected—first a scoop of dirt out, the plant in, followed by a slurp of water, the dirt and quick tamping. Once in a while, before the strawberry runners started to grow, we could find tiny red berries to pop into our mouths.

Then, with the horse again, my father would make long furrows between the plants. Others, including my mother, would go crawling down the rows with wooden paddles with which to mound the dirt up around the strawberry plants; then they would plug in the roots of the runners at suitable intervals. Regular irrigation would smooth the channels between the rows and, voila, there would be the strawberry fields, row upon row thick with green leaves and white blossoms and, by early summer, gleaming red berries.

Our fields stretched to the east end of that particular tract, to another road whose yonder side was a windbreak of fir trees, but there was an interruption in the center, a long corrugated tin building with a neat sand-and-gravel yard. Also sand and gravel was the compacted narrow road which sliced the tract in half lengthwise and which must have been for the convenience of the oil company. (We used our end of it as a driveway.) The building was visited from time to time by inspectors of some kind but was usually kept locked. I remember entering that building once, but its contents were mysterious and mechanical.

I do not know how reliable my memory is in conjuring up a giant hangarful of gas pump-size gauges that stood at attention like robot troops.

My mother learned how to drive among the oilfields. The whole family, which by then would have included three brothers and me, went along in the open car while my father instructed her in the fine points of chauffeuring. Chugging around with her at the steering wheel was for me a harrowing experience, and I insisted on being let off when we arrived at an intersection near the house. I walked home by myself, relieved to be on terra firma. In later years, my mother even drove trucks, but she never seemed to have learned how to get across an intersection after a stop without the vehicle undergoing a series of violent jerks and spasms that were terribly disconcerting. Besides, as one endured the eternity it took to traverse the intersection, one knew the whole world was laughing at the spectacle.

It was among the oilfields that we first subscribed to an English-language newspaper. I remember the thud of the newspaper arriving on Sunday morning. First out to the porch, I would open up the funny papers and spread them out right there, to be regaled by nouveau-riche Maggie and Jiggs arguing over his fondness for corned beef and cabbage; Barney Google and the dismal, blanketed excuse for a horse named Spark Plug; Tillie the Toiler at the office with her short boyfriend Mac whose hair grew in front like a whiskbroom; the stylized sophisticates of Jefferson Machamer. There were several assortments of little boys who were always getting into mischief. Hans and Fritz, the Katzenjammer Kids, usually got away with murder but sometimes would get caught by the Captain or Mama and soundly spanked, to wail their pain as they felt their smarting behinds. The little rich boy Perry, in his Fauntleroy suit, associated with a rag-taggle gang. There was also a chunky little guy named Elmer, with a baseball cap that he sometimes wore backwards. Was it Perry or Elmer who had a chum who was always saying, "Let's you and him fight!" who was always offering to hold coats so the fight could commence? The only comic strip I had reservations about was Little Nemo, a little kid who seemed to spend an inordinate amount of time wallowing in a welter of bedclothes, surrounded by a menagerie of ferocious animals from (I gathered) his nightmares.

We still used kerosene lamps then. One of my jobs was to remove the glass from the lamp and blow my breath into it, so that I could wipe off the soot inside with a wadded newspaper. I remember my mother saying how disillusioned she was to come to America and find such primitive conditions. In rural Japan, she said, her family had already had electricity running the rice-threshing machinery.

Our staples included 100-pound sacks of Smith rice; the large *katakana* running down the middle of the burlap sack said Su-mi-su. The sack must have cost less than five dollars because I seem to hear my mother exclaiming some years later about the price going up to five. We had five-gallon wooden tubs of Kikkoman soy sauce, wooden buckets of fermented soybean paste, green tea in large metal boxes, lined with thick, heavy foil, with hinged lids. There were quart jars of red pickled plums and ginger root, Japanese cans of dark chopped pickles. The house was redolent with the fragrance of some vegetable or other—cabbage, Chinese cabbage, white Japanese radish—salted in a crock and weighed down with a heavy rock.

But we also bought bread from the Perfection Bakery truck that came house-to-house, fish and tofu and meat from the Italian fishman, who would break off wieners from a long chain of them and give them to us as treats. In summer, the iceman brought fifty-pound chunks of ice which he hefted to his leather-clad shoulder with huge tongs, and we always rummaged around the back of the dripping truck to find a nice piece to chomp on.

We used butter but also white one-pound blocks of oleo margarine which we made butter-colored with a small packet of red powder, mixing and mixing so as not to leave orange streaks hiding inside. Coffee came in a red can dominated by a white-bearded gentleman in a white turban, long yellow gown sprinkled with flowers, tiny black slippers that curled up at the toe. Salt was always in a blue carton with the girl under the umbrella happily strewing her salt into the rain. The yellow container of scouring cleanser pictured a lady in a white poke bonnet chasing dirt with a stick.

Medicines were bought from a tall Korean gentleman who spoke fluent Japanese. He brought us ginseng in pale, carroty roots and silvery pills. There was the dark dried gall of a bear for stomachaches; fever called for the tiniest pills of all: infinitesimal black shot that came in a wee black wooden urn in a teeny brocaded box.

The financial world might have been on the verge of collapse, but I was wealthy, well on my way to becoming a miser. In my little coin purse of Japanese brocade, I managed to save four shiny dimes which had been given to me over a period of time by friends of the family, particularly by one childless man who once even brought me a pair of shiny roller skates.

The day that cured me of money was a horrible one, on which I came home from school with one of my splitting headaches. Neither my parents nor I connected my increasing headaches with the fact that, as I learned to read English, I used to read all the way home on the schoolbus (especially *The Blue Fairy Book, The Red Fairy Book, Tanglewood Tales*). It was not until much later, after Redondo Beach, that I was discovered to be seriously my-opic and the miracle of glasses banished my headaches forever. But, in the meanwhile, the headaches grew worse and more frequent, so that I often, close to nausea, had to take to bed as soon as the bus dropped me off.

I tried to crawl into my crib (I was such a midget that I slept in a baby bed even when I was in the second grade), but my mother stopped me. "Where did you get all that money?" she demanded. I had left my little purse under the pillow and she had found it in making my bed. Perhaps my illness did not make me a convincing defendant. Mama, alas, did not be-lieve me and confiscated my life savings. I guess it *was* a suspicious hoard for a mere child when a grown man might make ten cents an hour at a reg-ular job. I think I learned then and there the folly of saving and have man-aged to keep insolvent ever since.

I can evoke the strains of only two songs of that era. Radio must have been coming into its own but my only brush with it was once when we visited our cousins among the vast strawberry fields of Carson. My cousin Kaz had wired his crystal set to the socket of the light bulb that hung from the ceiling and he let me use the earphones to hear a little bit of Amos and Andy.

Another time when we were visiting with my aunt and uncle there in Carson, one of the boys came rushing in to get some pennies for bread. In great excitement, he announced that there was a bread war on, that sliced bread—a relatively new development—was selling for a cent a loaf.

Either my cousin Isamu or Nor would come to help us during the summer, and it was Nor who was not shy about using his nice baritone. I remember him crooning one of the songs.

> Skeeters am a hummin'
> 'round the honeysuckle vine,
> Sweet Kentucky babe . . .

The other song was sung by my best friend Isoko, whose family had moved to a tract on the other side of the highway to the south. That area there seemed to have several Japanese families living the length of a dirt road with tall eucalyptus trees fending off the wind from the west. Isoko, an only child, and I became inseparable at South School, Japanese school, prefectural and village picnics, and home, except when she would go off to the city to stay with her older cousin Asako, whose mother operated a bathhouse. When she came back, she would be insufferable for a time, talking about buying dresses at Mode O'Day (much as someone today might drop the name of Givenchy) and singing,

> There's a rainbow
> 'round my shoulder . . .

which her cousin had taught her.

As I have said, I cannot recall that the great depression immediately plummeted us into a grimmer existence. It was only years later that I remembered overhearing adult talk of a man who was a pillar of the Japanese community, who farmed a stretch beyond Isoko's house. For some reason I see him as forbidding, as a disciplinarian with his children. Probably the most prosperous Japanese farmer around, he one day went to bed with his shotgun and blasted his head open by pulling the trigger with his toe.

Likewise, living alongside derricks and sumpholes did not interfere with our daily routine. If we could not ignore their considerable presence, we accepted them, worked and played around them, and made respectful allowances for the peril connected with them. We might venture onto the derrick platforms, but investigations were conducted gingerly to avoid contact with the pounding pistons and greasy pulleys, except that we sometimes tried to ride the long steel bars that moved back and forth.

Once a pigeon or two entrapped by the thick oil of the reservoir was served up at dinner. Was it my cousin Isamu who, appalled, objected as my father crouched to pluck the feathers of the bird? A coyote that wandered in too close was kept caged under a cabbage crate for a while, but I don't know what eventually became of it. We made kites from Japanese newspapers and sticks, using boiled rice as glue, and flying them in between the derricks, a-flutter with rag strips tied together for tails.

Only once did we come face-to-face with oilfield danger, when my folks were working in the far fields to the east, near the road with the windbreak of fir trees. Little Jemo, probably three or four at the time, was playing on the earthen embankment of the sumphole nearest there when he fell in. His frantic yelling must have brought Mama and Papa running. They told us later (Johnny and I must have been at school) that they had siphoned gasoline from the car to clean the tar baby off.

Indeed, Jemo seems to have had the most traumatic of childhoods during our stay among the oil wells.

One evening my two brothers and I race home from the neighbors. We have about reached the far end of our stable when we hear a car coming up the road. We separate to opposite sides of the road and continue running, my brothers on the side nearest our property and I on the other. The car speeds by and all of a sudden, there is Jemo lying over there on the shoulder of the road.

He does not move. His eyes are closed. His still face is abraded by dirt and gravel. I run the fifty or so steps past the stable and tall barn. The house is set back from the road, from where I, terror-stricken, scream my anguished message, *"Jemo shinda, Jemo shinda!"*

My mother must be putting supper on the table, my father perhaps reading the Japanese paper while he waits. My unearthly shrieks summon the father of the friends we have been visiting. He comes running up the slope to the scene and is carrying Jemo's body towards our house when Mama and Papa finally dash out to the road in response to my cries.

As it turned out, no limbs were broken. He was only stunned, probably flipped aside by the car's front fender. But his concussions and contusions had to be attended to at the hospital in Torrance. When he came home, he was clothed in bandages, including one like a turban around his head and face. When we took him back for a checkup and Papa afterwards bought us a treat of vanilla ice cream and orange sherbet in paper cups, I had to spoon-feed him with the little balsa spoon as we rode home.

My folks thought the hit-and-run driver of the car ought to pay something towards the hospital costs. The *hakujin* neighbor who had come running up the hill was acquainted with the couple in the car, who lived way down the road in a two-story house. He must have seen the car go zooming by, as it frequently did, before the accident and had some kind of foreboding. Else how had he, farther away, reached the scene before my parents even?

My father and the neighbor conferred, and the neighbor offered to try and negotiate a settlement of some kind for us. He came back shaking his head; the couple had refused to accept any responsibility for Jemo's injuries. They said it was all Jemo's fault.

Mama and Papa were indignant. Mostly, it was because such coldness of heart was not to be believed. The couple had not even had the decency to come and inquire after Jemo's condition. Were we Japanese in a category with animals then, to be run over and left beside the road to die? My father contacted a Japanese lawyer in the city, who one day came out to talk first with us and then with the couple. He, too, returned with bad news: the couple absolutely denied any guilt.

But the scenario was not played out as simply as I have written it. This is more of a collage patched together from the fragments of overheard conversations, glimpses of the earnest expressions on the faces of my father, our neighbor, the young lawyer in the dark suit, their comings and goings, my own bewildered feelings.

So that must have been the end of the matter. I have no recollection of the roadster whizzing by our place after that. The couple must have chosen an alternate route out from the oilfields to the highway.

When I look back on that episode, the helpless anger of my father and my mother is my inheritance. But my anger is more intricate than theirs, warped by all that has transpired in between. For instance, I sometimes see the arrogant couple from down the road as young and beautiful, their speeding open roadster as definitely and stunningly red. They roar by; their tinkling laughter, like a long silken scarf, is borne back by the wind. I gaze after them from the side of the road, where I have darted to dodge the swirling dust and spitting gravel. And I know that their names are Scott and Zelda.

The Republic
Of Burma Shave

Richard Katrovas

San Diego County

If it were something one could actually see, I'd have seen most of it before the age of seven. It isn't; I didn't. The very word is as something made almost entirely of sugar that dissolves, leaving a faint aftertaste, in the acids of the mouth. This figure, of course, is a convention for memory, and the nexus of America and Memory—for this moment in history when Self is the supreme commodity—is childhood. In a rare fit of lucid resolve, I decided recently that I would cure myself of that peculiarly American sickness, the critical stage of which is a morose attachment to memories of childhood; however, I still watch enough television to know just how unrelenting media can be at keeping us childlike, that is, uncritically receptive. I also know that to break a fever one must ride it out.

As a child, I was as uncritically receptive as the next, and though I was born in the early fifties, smack dab in the middle of the Baby Boom and the Golden Age of Television, I did not spend as many hours as most in front of a screen. Mind you, I *loved* television, but the circumstances of my life not only made it impossible for me to watch as much as I desired, but also created an inverse relation between myself and television relative to what I now realize was, and is, the norm: I experienced it not as a means of transport from a static environment but rather as a fixed point, a touchstone.

By 1960 there would be, including my parents, seven of us, my youngest brother arriving in March of that year. We'd been on the road since before I could remember, changing cars every couple of months and staying in motels at roughly forty-eight hour intervals. I viewed America (or the vestiges

237

of its Platonic shadow) through the window of the backseat of a car, and I also viewed it through another window when we stayed in motels. My relation to what I viewed through both windows was one of uncritical receptivity, yet whereas what passed the car window seemed distant, redundant and uncaring, the world I viewed through the TV screen was close, varied, and constantly concerned with *me*. No matter what seedy little motel in what ugly little town in what boring state we found (lost) ourselves, Captain Kangaroo and Little Miss Sunbeam would be there, waiting.

I remember leaning onto the passenger-side seat which my mother will always occupy in my memory, and asking, "What's a merica?" I was seven months from my seventh birthday. The sky was dark. Two younger brothers and a younger sister were sprawled around me, breathing through crusted nostrils, and a third younger brother lolled in the most comfortable space in the car, swelling my mother's stomach. My father was in his long-distance coma behind the wheel. The gray rabbits bounding across the road at the vague limits of our high-beams, and the furry blood-splotched pancakes of the ones which didn't make it were no less real to me than Captain Kangaroo's Bunny Rabbit—that mute, bifocaled puppet who made a lucrative career of tricking carrots from the Captain—but were certainly less engaging.

"What?" my mother whispered.

"What's a merica?" I asked again.

This may seem a naive question even for a six-year-old to ask, but I hadn't attended a single day of school yet, and wouldn't for another couple years. My mother had taught me to read a few words from comic books and to write numbers, but as prelude to my widely and irregularly spaced lessons she had never made me sit with my right hand over my heart reciting, after her, the Pledge of Allegiance. I'd probably heard of mericas in a song sung on TV late at night in a Holiday Inn just before the shows stopped and the bugs swarmed all over the inside of the screen:

> A merica, a merica,
> God shade his gray sun tree . . .

First things first. I'd find out what mericas were.

"Just a word," she mumbled, half asleep. Of course, this wasn't enough.

"But what does it *mean?*" I whispered-whined. Her eyes opened slowly. Her fingers, laced over her ninth month, began to drum lightly.

My mother was a beautiful woman. She was beautiful enough to be on television. As I stared at her shadow-softened profile, I saw that peculiar smile take shape which meant she was about to say something to me without really talking to me. It was a thin, crooked smile which meant her voice would be more breath than words.

"The Republic of Burma Shave," she breathed, letting her tired, dark beautiful head roll toward the window glass where she would keep her forehead pressed against the coolness till dawn.

I turned my cheek and rested it on my forearm which lay across the top of the seat. A rasping body curled just behind me so I couldn't sit back, but I didn't much care because the one talent all of us had developed was to achieve relative comfort in what cramped space was finally allotted when the chips, as it were, had fallen for the night. I realize now that everything I am, for better or worse, depends on that moment, which was many, many such moments: my mother pregnant and sleeping upright; my father achieving Zenlike oneness with the road; my siblings breathing as from the clogged center of the earth; the hum of rubber over asphalt vibrating up through a ton of steel, plastic, glass and flesh. My dreams were reruns.

I had only the vaguest sense of how others lived. The Nelsons, Cleavers and Ricardos lived in their own places like the people in the houses we passed in our car. Even Fred and Alice ("Mom, what's a honeymooner?") had a little place, though it looked pretty drab, a bit like motel rooms in the desert, which I hated because some of them didn't have televisions or, if they did, only got one fuzzy station.

Two days through California desert with a burlap bag strapped to the grill . . . we filled it with orange pop and the water ever after was tainted with a sugary mildew . . . another day through mountains and into snow.

Just out of the mountains ("Don't worry, there's a secret button that'll let us *float* down!") we stopped in a little town that was glazed with frost. We waited in the car while my father was "doing business." He came out of an old, brick building holding new license plates wrapped in wax paper, then took us to a motel on the outskirts of town. I knew I'd be going back with him later. I no sooner got the TV on than he made me wash up with him and change into fresh clothes. Back in the car he told me that when we got inside my name would be Mike.

I liked that bank as soon as I saw it because it had revolving doors. My father introduced me to a man in a brown suit and made me shake his hand. The man's smile reminded me of a game show. My father sat in a chair across from him and they talked like they knew each other, though I knew they didn't. My father put me on his knee, which I hated, but I knew that when my father told me I was someone else my only job was to keep my mouth shut. So I sat there balanced on his hard knee, seeing the man as my father saw him, admiring how, though he was leaning back away from his cluttered desk with his elbow propped on his chair arm and cigarette smoke swirling from his fingers around his head, he seemed to *wear* that desk. I wanted a desk like that, with a black telephone and lots of papers and pens.

At one point my father made me stand up so he could reach into his back pocket for his wallet. He plucked several cards from the good-smelling leather, and then a neatly folded rectangular piece of paper that, opened, had numbers printed on it here and there. The man smiled and nodded, then pushed something in front of my father. My father wrote on it, shook hands with the man who, at the same time with his free hand, gave something that looked like a wallet to my father. I knew as we passed through the revolving glass door that I could stop being Mike, though it didn't really matter. There wasn't much to it.

Snow fell fast that evening. My mother went into labor. Her weeping and writhing scared the younger children. I was scared, too, but I didn't cry. My father told me to watch the kids while he went out to see if there was a hospital close (there was no phone in the room, only some kind of buzzer that the office could use if a call was coming in). When he opened the door I glimpsed, in yellow-bulb light through wind-whipped swarms of snow dust, white mounds where cars had been. I told the kids to lie on the floor. I spread a blanket over them to muffle their whimpering. My mother seemed foreign and terrible. I didn't dare approach the bed. I turned on the TV. She screamed louder, making noises I'd never heard. I turned the volume as loud as it would go, draped a sheet over the cabinet, and squatted under the glowing tent. The noises my mother made were drowned out by a roaring laugh-track, but the screams weren't. I ran into the bathroom, locked the door, turned out the light, put the seat down on the toilet and pressed my cheek to the seat, mumbling *please, please . . .*

Just as the Pledge of Allegiance was not part of my backseat curriculum, neither was prayer. My pleading was raw and random. I was awakened by a pounding on the door and my father's furious voice. I opened the door. He pushed me aside, lifted the seat and pissed. The kids were still under the blanket. My mother writhed slowly and moaned gently, flushed and sweating. My father had turned down the sound on the TV. I heard a quick, sharp *honk*. My father lifted my mother, ordered me to open the door, and carried her to the cab. The cab's chains crunched them away and I watched the red taillights dissolve in the snow-swirled, late-night traffic at the outskirts of wherever we were. I turned to the sleeping, blanketed lump left in my charge, and, as I closed the door on a cold wind, began to weep silently. I switched off the overhead light, stepped over my brothers and sister, and curled up in front of the television's gray glow. It flickered through my eyelids and in a moment I was empty and peaceful, drifting to sleep on the violin-thickened strains of an old movie.

Artaud said somewhere that "he who does not bring back from the plunge into a fertile unconscious the sense of an atrocious nostalgia is a pig." I have often wondered how television has affected the unconscious of my generation. I don't much care about the evolution of archetypes, and my regard for questions centered on collective perceptions of ideal-types is subordinate to what I believe is a more fundamental question concerning how an individual's remembered feelings manifest in the present; I mean, when I make that plunge and return, soaked and reeling, perhaps the nostalgia I feel for people, places and things of my past is so tainted by that other conscious past, that other life, that the quality of feeling I unconsciously possess, say, for Lucille Ball is equal to that which I possess for the beautiful young woman who was my mother. It's a chilling proposition. None of us knows what his or her Rosebud will be, but Citizen Kane's pathos may be lost to a generation whose period of innocence was cloven into two worlds of consciousness both of which may bear equally upon the unconscious, for what dreadful charm is inherent in a person dying with the image of the NBC peacock frozen in that infinitesimal black space where his last synapse had sparked and faded?

The point is, from the moment I was old enough to watch television, which was before I could talk, I lived two lives, one of passive receptivity, the other alternating between active hostility towards my siblings and passive participation in relation to my parents. In neither were significant decisions made, but whereas in the former I learned quickly what to feel and when, in the latter there were only vague clues. Lucy taught me how to love her; I laughed when the TV laughed. My mother never taught me to love *her;* she was ironic and unpredictable.

Considering how different my childhood was from most, I believe that if not for television I'd probably have been just a little less antisocial than those fabled children raised by wild animals ("Mom, did Tarzan go to school?"). Television gave me *some* sense of what was "normal," and it even informed me as to what were normal problems.

My mother listened to *Queen For a Day* from the bed, pale and quiet, staring at the ceiling. My new brother was asleep in a bed we'd made from a bureau drawer. *Queen For a Day* was one of my favorite shows, though I found it puzzling. Women took turns telling how messed up their lives were, and the studio audience voted, by clapping, for the one who seemed the most messed up. I liked the part where they clapped. The winner got prizes and wept for joy. "Democracy in action!" my mother had exclaimed more than once, never explaining what democracy was; but this time she just lay there staring off. Several years later, when my father would be in prison and she'd be dying of an undiagnosed muscle disease, I'd see her like that often, though I'd be spared by dubious good luck the pain of her final pain and wretched dying.

I remember clearly that the queen for that day was a "housewife from Miami" whose husband was in an iron lung. That one gave me fits, but I didn't dare ask about iron lungs. My mother seemed in no mood for questions. I briefly tried to imagine it, but I couldn't really come up with anything. It certainly *sounded* like a winner! The audience went crazy, the needle of the little speedometer that appeared under her chin jerked to its limit, and the man with the little moustache who ran the show gave her kitchen appliances and a vacation to California and she wept for joy.

It was my job to keep the kids from messing with the baby while our father was out doing business. The kids accepted my authority because I was larger than they and quick to exhibit the inherent advantages of that fact. The burden and privilege of authority were mine, and I carried both aspects with less than regal grace. I was a brutal older brother. This new one, though, I would never brutalize. He was mine. I would raise him to the age of seven when I, thirteen, and the brother a year and a half younger than I would be taken away by our father and finally adopted by his sister and her husband in San Diego. Sixteen years from the moment I left him I'd face a twenty-three-year-old up-and-coming Cadillac salesman whose every utterance would seem obsequious and loud. He'd ask me, in his North Carolina twang, "Well, what's the bottom line on this poetry business, bub?"

But now I was a guardian angel fending off the alien hordes. My mother kept asking me to bring her glasses of water. The baby was sleeping, and she'd lift her head with much effort to cast a weary glance at the pink, swaddled product of her previous night's pain. I would never know how my father got the two of them out of the hospital so quickly, nor, of course, at the time was it within the realm of my natural considerations. I possessed fairly vivid recollections of the two previous births, and in neither case had my mother languished in professional care.

My vigil over the new citizen was interrupted only by the theme music of *The Three Stooges*, the zippy strains of which made my heart race and washed away even this solemn new sense of responsibility. I shoved the three-headed bundle from in front of the screen, and stationed myself six feet from the action, half-lotus. This was my seminar on violence, and my siblings were the nervous rabbits on which I'd perform by rote my assigned experiments. The brother a year and a half younger than I, the one who would be adopted by the same good folks who'd adopt me and therefore was the only one of my family I'd grow into adolescence and adulthood knowing, would become a career navy man and a staunch supporter of a strong defense. This, of course, was inevitable.

After the last pie had struck the last stoogey face and the credits began to roll across the screen to that adrenalin-pumping theme song—"Three Blind Mice" done double-time—I faced my second-in-command with my fist extended perpendicular to his chest, and ordered him to strike down on it. "Come on, hit it!" With side-glancing trepidation he did so, and braced for the inevitable stiff-armed three-hundred-and-sixty-degree arching hammer-fist that found its mark on the bull's eye-cowlick in the middle of his crew cut. I supplied my own stoogey sound effects and laughed hysterically. He whimpered off to a corner of the motel room, the seeds of a military temperament taking root in his four-year-old soul. The last time I saw him, his ship, a nuclear powered aircraft carrier, had docked in San Diego where I was living again, and he took me on a tour of the thing. He conducted the tour amicably and with pride, but seemed under all the spit-shine like a man itching to kill something, something big. I understand from reliable sources that he watches very little television, but spends much of his professional life stationed in front of a radar screen. He was, and no doubt still is, quite patient.

I was not very patient. After *The Three Stooges,* programming entered the wasteland of news and talk shows, and that always made me irritable. I'd turn the sound all the way down and twitch about the room for the couple of hours till prime time. Now, though, I resumed my station by the drawer, reaching in once in a while to touch the small sleeper.

The weather had calmed outside. My mother lifted herself with much effort, and took the baby from the drawer and nursed it sitting upright in bed with her eyes closed. My father came in stomping snow from his soaked black shoes. My parents' eyes met and my father smiled broadly and arched his eyebrows. This was a facial gesture I would come to hate, but now it signaled good news so it made me excited. I knew it meant we had a new car and probably a bigger one than the last. He was holding two white bags which made me very excited. I could smell the french fries and see the grease stains at the bottom of the bags. My heart began to pound. We'd not eaten since the night before. He doled out the burgers and fries, and my siblings took their rations and moved as far from me as they could. They didn't want to be close when I was in a feeding frenzy. From the moment I ripped the wrapper off my burger my mouth was filled beyond its natural capacity, and I finished just as the others were settling into their nests. My second-in-command was savvy enough to lock himself in the bathroom. The other two, my sister and former-youngest brother, three and two respectively, chewed their burgers and nibbled their fries by the bedpost together, never taking their eyes off me. I left them and their booty alone this time. From the tone of my father's voice as he spoke to my mother, we were in for a period of prosperity. There would be burgers and more burgers.

Television can be torture to a hungry child. Though I'd never seen a Television Chocolate Cake in real life—the black frosting swirled in hundreds of perfect little wavelets from top to base—I knew that a good mother was one who made them that way. The few times we'd stayed in one place long enough to occupy an apartment or kitchenette, my mother cooked very little and then almost strictly from cans. Only twice she'd baked cakes and both times the frosting was flat, thick and boring.

When we were really hungry, desperately so, and my father was out doing business, we'd wait in a motel, lethargic, watching television. Once I started crying while watching a commercial for Duncan Hines, and my brothers and sister started crying after me, and then our mother was weeping with us, and all our eyes were fixed on that frosting-swirled monument.

A few years later, while my father was in prison for his first three-years stretch and the five of us and our mother lived in relative comfort on a hundred and sixty-four dollars a month from Welfare, my friends would ask me where my father was and what he did for a living. I was told to tell them he was away at school learning a trade. That was usually enough to stop the questions. In that neighborhood, a lot of fathers were away at school learning a trade.

My father's only talents were bouncing checks and ripping off car dealers. However, his dream was to be a legitimate business man. "Legitimate" was an adjective he used often, and his dream of legitimacy soured years later into schizophrenic fantasy. The last time I saw him he was drunk, and proceeded to relate to me the shrewd manner in which he'd recently acquired offshore drilling leases in the Gulf of Mexico. Before I left his sleazy motel room, he pressed a personal check for thirty thousand dollars into my palm.

The Millionaire was coming on just as my father started packing us up. It took the *Queen For a Day* theme much farther. It was a more romantic, more civilized fiction. The plot formula was simple: a multimillionaire covertly searched out a person who was down on his luck and sent a butler to give that person a check for a million dollars. The antithesis of the Horatio Alger formula, it was, among other things, a hyperbolic metaphor for what a few years later would be called the Welfare State. On a much smaller scale, *Queen For a Day* seemed downright neighborly; its intimate game-show format within which a kind of Christian-fundamentalist witnessing took place was like a local church sending Christmas groceries to the Widow Jones. *The Millionaire,* with its pontifflike source of centralized, quiet power had an old-world grandness. In regard to his relation to money and what he thought one could and should do with it, my father's temperament and background suggested a kinship with the world of the former while his false self-image was a dream hatched in the precincts of the latter. He traversed the continent subsisting on the small though myriad payoffs a good lie told many times may garner. As liars go, he was a one-trick pony: a television character actor who could only play one kind of role, the henpecked husband or the laconic stogie-chomping gangster from Nowhere, or only the voice of commercials for toothpaste and shaving cream.

The car was large and awesome, the best we'd ever had. The *cry* in Chrysler seemed inappropriate to such a chrome-bespangled, fetching thing, though the bright vowel at the heart of the word suggested the frank and sporting glare of the thing's waxed newness. My father packed up what little we carried with us, and after several hours of the kids bouncing on the slick vinyl and all of us inhaling the heady scent of a new car's interior, night came on, clear, cold and precise with stars that seemed to follow us. The younger ones slept in a bunch on the seat under army-surplus blankets that smelled of mothballs and the loneliness of closets, and I curled up in the space at the top of the backseat covered with my father's jacket that smelled of his sweat and aftershave. The curved window was an observatory when I lay on my back, and when I turned on my side to see the faint glow of our taillights on the snowbanks at the side of the road, to see also the pearl necklace of traffic, far away, from where we had traveled, my position was one that felt like destiny. Though, of course, I had no such concept in my life, the memory of the feeling that filled me as I lay, shifting my vision between the broad field of stars that followed us and the faint lights of distant traffic, is the measure by which I now understand the word. It has little to do with where one is going, and nothing to do with where one has been. It's the supersentient moment of trust in blind movement toward anything and nothing, the dry whir of artificial heat and the steady whine of new tires through slosh.

I lay counting the stars of a moonless sky, fixing one a long time and promising myself that tomorrow night I'd find the exact same one again. As I stared at my star, which was neither a faint nor a particularly bright one, an ordinary star I knew I'd lose forever after this night no matter how long or hard I stared, I visualized the letters of the first words I'd ever recognized as words: my mother would read aloud the little signs, one by one, until the last, when all of us, from my father to the two-year-old would yell in unison those words printed in bold caps. The wisdom of the land thus appeared to us on the highways of America.

And we were off again. Their stomachs full, my siblings slept as one. In the darkness of the car, I closed my eyes and dreamed a waking dream of television cakes and burgers as my American mother held a future salesman to her breast. In the Republic of Burma Shave the sins of the father can be taken to the bank, and every mother's son gets an even break.

Songs My Mother Taught Me
Wakako Yamauchi
Imperial Valley

I was eleven in the summer of 1935. My father was farming then in the valley of the Santa Rosa, San Jacinto, and Chocolate Mountain Ranges called Imperial Valley near the Mexican border of California. The land was fertilized with tons of chicken manure and irrigated by the All American Canal that flowed out of the Colorado River. Planting started in late September: tomatoes, squash, cantaloupe. All during the winter months, it was thinning the seedlings, weeding, building brush covers for them, repairing the covers after a storm, and starting the smudge pots to ward off the frost. In early spring, it was harvesting the crops. By May, after the broiling sun had reduced the plants to dry twigs, the plowing began. Then the land was flooded to start the weeds and fallen seeds growing, after which there was another plowing to destroy these sprouts, and once again fertilizing, furrowing, and preparing the land for late September planting.

At best, the entire process kept us alive and clothed. There were five of us: my father, Junsaburo Kato; mother, Hatsue; sister, Nami, fourteen; brother, Tetsuo, thirteen; and myself, Sachiko. Why my father kept at this unrewarding work, I never knew or questioned or thought about. Maybe there was nothing else he could do. Maybe he worked in hope that one day that merciful God (to whom we prayed, before whose lacquered shrine we burned our incense) would provide the miracle crop that would lift us to Japan, rich and triumphant.

My father was a quiet man. If he suspected this was the whole cloth of his life, that he would live and die this way, he never showed it. He never revealed his dream for us, his children, in America, or articulated his own dreams. But sometimes when he was in his cups, when the winter rain drowned his hopes for a good harvest, he would sing the saddest and loneliest Japanese songs. My mother spoke often of returning to Japan, of smelling again the piney woods, tasting the exquisite fruits, of seeing her beloved sisters. The stories of her Japan came on like a flashback in the movies—misty, wavering, ethereal, and her beautiful eyes would grow soft.

Summer is unbearable in the valley. The sun beats on miles of scrub prairie and the air is deathly still. One listless day succeeds another, without incident, without change. The farmers who had had some luck with their harvest usually spent their summer north along the coast in San Pedro where a colony of Japanese resided permanently, occupied with fishing and canning. On a small island off the mainland called Terminal Island, most of the Valley people rented cheap houses and spent the summer fishing off the scummy San Pedro wharf, clamming, crabbing, and swimming in the Pacific. My mother said it was hard to believe these same waters broke on the shores of Japan.

The harvest of 1935 was a good one. That summer we started north in early July, after we popped off the firecrackers my father had bought for Tets. They loved firecrackers; I can't remember a year that we didn't have some, no matter how poor we were. Usually, though, they couldn't wait until the 4th, and they'd fire off a few each night, until there was nothing left for the 4th. So on Independence Day we often sat outside and watched the neighbors' fireworks a quarter mile away. Sometimes my mother made iced tea with sugar and lemons while we waited for the dark. That year we had enough to string out until the actual celebration.

After the 4th, we packed our old gray Chevrolet and drove 300 miles north to Terminal Island. It was always a hot tiresome trip and when we finally drove up to the drawbridge that spans the narrow channel, and recognized the Ford plant to the left, we let out whoops of delight. My father quieted us with a grunt. He hated noise.

There was already a group of people from the Valley, townspeople we knew from the Buddhist Church. We rented a small four-room house for the summer.

The days were filled with vacation fun. We trapped crab at the piling of a demolished pier. When the sun went down, we boiled the catch in large galvanized tubs and ate the sweet meat, our skin chilled on one side by the night air, and seared on the other by the campfire. There were roasts; I can still taste the succulent meat and the bitter ash. There were hot days in the sun, blistered backs, and the good pain. In the evening, the older folks sat on front stoops or wandered from house to house looking to start a card game or a session of *go,* and we were allowed to play outside until darkness blurred our faces and hide-and-seek became too hazardous. We went everywhere with friends, huge contingents of raucous children and adults. Every day was a holiday, far removed from the isolated farm and its chores and the terror of another blighted year.

But there was a subtle change in the family. I don't know if Nami or Tets felt it. If they did, they said nothing. Or maybe I too would not have noticed if Sayo, my summer friend, had not called attention to it. Sayo was two years older, and wiser, more perceptive and knowledgeable than I. She wrote poetry and read masses of books and knew all the latest Japanese songs and the meaning of the lyrics. She said, "Your mother plays the same record again and again. Why is she so sad?"

I said, "Maybe she likes the song. Maybe she wants to learn it."

It was true. My mother joined our excursions less and less. Often I found her sitting at the kitchen table writing, nibbling at the stub of a pencil and looking past the window. It was also true that she played the Victrola and usually the same record over and over: *"Mujo No Tsuki,"* which Sayo said meant transient moon. She translated the lyrics for me:

Samishiku kyo mo	Today too
Kurete uki	Passes in solitude
Yuhi wa toku	The evening sun is distant
Umi no hate	Beyond the rim of the sea
Dare ga yobuno ka	Who is it that calls
Sagasu no ka yo?	Who, that seeks me?
Namima ni sakebu	The sea birds that
Hama chidori	Cry from the shore

It was all true. But I couldn't always remember to think about it while everyone else appeared so happy. I laughed with them and fought with them and pretended, like Nami and Tets, that nothing was wrong.

After one of those quarrels at the beach, I returned home alone. Nami and Tets always sided against me, and though I had a well-honed tongue for my age, I couldn't match the two together. I begged my father to come home with me, but he was playing cards with some cronies and he waved me off like an annoying fly. I walked home alone, sulky and morose, and went to the rear of the house to brush the sand off my feet. Mrs. Griffin, the landlady, lived within eyeshot and she was very particular about sand in her threadbare rug. We called her *Okorimbo,* which is a diminutive for Angry One. *Okorimbo*'s face was permanently creased in a pattern of rage. She spent the daylight hours at her window, and when she caught us heading toward the front door, she rushed from her house, her ragged slippers flapping, screaming, "Go to the back, to the back."

I was rubbing sand from my legs when I heard soft voices. My mother had company. Not wanting to be seen, I crouched behind a privet hedge. There's a humiliating routine a Japanese child must endure from adults: the pat on the head, the examination, the appraisal, "How tall she's growing! She will be beautiful some day. She looks very bright!" Then: "Not at all, very small for her age, homely like her mother, not very smart, no help at all around the house, lazy . . ."

Within fifteen minutes, the visitor left through the rear door and passed very close to the hedge where I was hiding. I could smell the polish on his shoes. I recognized him as Yamada-san, the young man from northern California who earlier that spring had come to the Valley with a group of laborers. He was a *Kibei,* a Japanese born in America and reared in Japan. My father had hired him to help us with our good harvest. Yamada-san was different from my father—handsome and younger. He came to the dinner table in a fresh shirt, his hair combed back with good-smelling oil. My father, like most farmers, wore his hair so short that neither comb nor rain (nor sun) changed its shape. Yamada-san had eyes that looked at you. When you talked he committed himself to you. My father's eyes were squinty from the sun and he hardly saw or heard you.

My father had been dissatisfied with Yamada-san. For a man of few words, I was surprised how strongly he spoke.

"Someone like that I wouldn't want around here long. He's a bad example for our Tetsuo," he said.

"How can we finish harvesting without him?" my mother had asked. "He works hard, Kato, you know that."

"You see how he is—plucking at that frivolous mandolin all the time—like he was practicing for the pictures or something. The clothes he wears—those two-tone shoes, that downtown haircut, the fancy cigarettes. Like a woman! Do you want Tetsuo to get like that? So he works hard. So? He stays only until harvest is over. I won't tolerate him after May! I don't want him in the house except at meal time. Tell him."

"Kato, I can't tell him this."

Some of what my father said was true. But I watched Yamada-san's sure body move effortlessly and I knew he worked hard. He was not like a woman. He had a quality of the orient my father did not have. He was the affirmation of my mother's Japan—the haunting flutes, the cherry blossoms, the poetry, the fatalism. My mother changed when he was around. Her smile was softer, her voice more gentle. I suspect this was what my father disliked more than the man himself—the change he brought over the rest of us.

Though we loved to listen to Yamada-san's mandolin, loved to touch the pearl frets and pluck the strings, we began to avoid him. He sensed the change in us, and thereafter confined his visits to mealtimes. He lived in the cabin my father had built for Tets, but Tets didn't like sleeping away from the rest of us, so it had stayed unused until now. I pictured Yamada-san sitting on his cot reading by lamplight, or mending his clothes, or singing his songs alone. We pretended not to hear the lonely music that came from his quarters; we pretended not to notice how each missed him.

Immediately after the harvest, Yamada-san packed his things and shook hands with us. My father drove him to the bus station. I went to the vacant cabin. The cot was in the corner with a naked mattress on top and the bedclothes neatly folded at one end. He'd left an empty jar of pomade on the table.

I saw Yamada-san one more time before summer was over.

One evening Sayo and I crept away from the other children and walked to the dunes where the sea figs sprawled to the edge of the surf. The sky was still pinkish from the dying sun and a warm wind blew in from the west. I only saw his back. He was standing against the wind, facing the sea. When he heard us, he walked away without turning, flicking the stub of his fancy cigarette to the wind.

As summer drew to a close, my mother's malaise would not be ignored. She spent a lot of time in bed. Nami and my father did the cooking because the smell of food sent her retching to the bathroom. My father finally called Dr. Matsuno. It was a frightening time for me because I remembered years before when my mother was very sick and had to stay with friends in town. They had recommended the blood of carp, so a live carp was kept in a tub on the back porch for her. My mother told me she put her mouth directly to the living fish. When she didn't improve, a white doctor was called. He diagnosed the illness as typhoid and we all went to his office to get shots. I was very frightened. I thought often of her dying and my heart would contract.

We waited disconsolately on *Okorimbo*'s ratty couch not saying a word to one another. The doctor had closed the door behind him. When he finally emerged, he told us there was nothing to worry about. "She will give birth in late March," he said.

The next day we strapped the luggage to the top of our car and started the dismal trip back to the Valley.

The baby grew steadily in my mother's belly, distending and misshaping her body. The black hair she wore in a smooth coil at her neck grew crisp and faded. Broken strands hung from her temples like dry summer grass and brown splotches appeared on her skin.

She withdrew from us. I couldn't coax a smile from her. My father was kinder than he'd ever been, but everyone seemed to retreat to a separate place. I wanted someone to make room for me, someone to tell me what was going on, to assure me everything was all right. But things were far from right; no one would let me in. I was too afraid to ask. It was as though each prepared to fight this monstrous condition alone, with silence, and will it back to its dark origin.

I looked for someone to turn to. I chose the highest source.

In December, the Jodo Shinshu sect of the Buddhist church headquartered in Los Angeles sent down a new minister to stimulate religious life in the Valley. The previous man was a bachelor, too handsome and too popular for his own good. Many members of the Ladies' Auxiliary desired him for their daughters. He may have asked for his own transfer.

There was something disconcerting about the new minister, Reverend Umino, his eczema, his full lips, his obesity (in contrast to ideals of austerity and self denial), but he appealed to me just because of these very human traits. I thought if God could accept so ordinary a man for His emissary, there was a good chance He would listen to *me*. I thought if prayer and faith could heal the sickness in our house, I would build a faith matched by no one, and I would pray with every breath I drew. So with limited knowledge of ritual, I prayed to my eastern diety in western methods. The request was always the same: Sweet Buddha, let us be happy again. Let there be six living people in our family. I was afraid something terrible and unmentionable would happen to my mother or the baby. After a while the prayers became so abbreviated, only Buddha could have understood them. I slipped them in all the activities of school and home—while turning pages in my reader, while cleaning lamp chimneys, "Six, six, six . . ."

On the morning of the birth Nami shook me awake: "Sachiko, wake up! Something's happening!" We ran to my mother's room. She lay twisting, clutching the metal bars of the bed and breathing in short gasps. Tets stood beside her, his head low, his tears dropping silently to the floor.

"Papa has gone to get Mrs. Nakagawa," she said. Mrs. Nakagawa was the midwife who delivered most of the Japanese babies. She lived in town, her husband was an accountant, and they were both religious Buddhists. "Go quickly to school, be good children and take care of the little one," she said. She touched my face.

It was the first time in a long time she had touched me. I screamed, "Mama, don't die!"

"Don't worry," she said.

At school I was unable to concentrate. I loitered behind everyone so I could whisper privately into my joined palms, "Six, six, six . . ." I spoke to no one. Two or three times the teacher peered into my face and shook her head.

Once home, I went directly to my mother's room and watched until I caught the movement of my mother's breathing. The baby was lying next to her.

Buddha had saved this infant for me, Kenji was very special. I loved him, cared for him, changed his diapers, pretended he was my own. I spoiled him. But he took only my mother's milk and when it was gone, he would refuse a bottle. Then he'd fret and cry and Nami and I took turns carrying him, rocking and teasing him until her milk returned. Times when we were already in bed, my mother would get up and carry him off to the desert. I listened to her footsteps on the soft sand, terrified they would not return. The more he cried, the less she liked him; the less she liked him, the more he cried.

She grew despondent from this perpetual drain on her body and her emotions, and slipped farther and farther from us, often staring vacantly into space. Every day I rushed home from school to take care of the baby so he wouldn't start my mother's terrible strangled sighs.

One evening after supper, Kenji began his crying again. My mother snatched him from his bed and walked rigidly away, bouncing him erratically and vigorously. I followed her, begging her to let me carry him, assuring her that I could quiet him.

"Go back!" she snarled. I was frightened but I would not turn back, and half running, I followed her to the packing shed. By this time Kenji, shocked by the unnatural motion, had stopped his crying. My mother too, had calmed down, but she saw a hatchet my father had left outside his toolbox, and she lifted it. While I stood there watching, my blood chilling, she lay the blade on the baby's forehead. I began to cry, and she pulled me to her and cried too. She said, "My children are all grown. I didn't want this baby—I didn't want this baby . . ."

I know now what she meant: that time was passing her by, that with the new baby she was irrevocably bound to this futile life, that dreams of returning to Japan were shattered, that through the eyes of a younger man she had glimpsed what might have been, could never and would never be.

I turned to prayer again.

Sunday service was largely a congregation of children and adolescents. Adults were at the fields preparing for Monday's market. Whereas the previous minister geared his sermons to the young, using simple parables and theatrical gestures, Reverend Umino never talked down to us. He spoke on abstract philosophies in rhetoric too difficult to follow. Peculiarly responsive to shifting feet and rustling hymn books, he often stopped abruptly, leaving the lectern massaging the festering eczema on his wrists. The church people who lived in the city and had the most influence didn't like him, but I didn't care. I only hoped he'd sense my need and put in a special word for me.

The spring harvest was meager and market prices low. My father couldn't afford the hired help of the year before. Tets and Nami helped wherever and whenever they could. My father would rise before daylight and work on until dark. He grew morose and short with us.

That summer there wasn't enough money for a vacation. Sometimes my father would drive us out to town and give each of us fifteen cents for the movies: ten cents for admission and a nickel for popcorn. I loved the movies, but I couldn't enjoy them, I was so worried about my mother and Kenji. Most of the summer we played cards. The baby grew rapidly in spite of the lack of breast milk and mother love. He responded to his name, slouching like a giant doll in an attempt to sit up. My father went to the burning fields to parcel out the land for flooding.

Then one day toward the end of August, it happened. As it had its beginning in August, so it found its end then.

A hot wind blew in from the desert, drying the summer grass and parching throat and skin. Tets had gone out to help my father with flooding, controlling the flow of water at the water gate. My father was at the far end of the field repairing the leaks.

I was playing with Kenji who was sitting in a shallow tub of water. He loved water. It was one of the few ways to keep him happy. With one hand he grasped the rim of the tub and with the other he pawed at a little red boat I pushed around for him. My father bought the boat for Kenji shortly after he was born. Nami was reading an old Big-Little book, carefully turning the brittle pages. My mother had prepared some rice balls and a Mason jar of green tea for my father's lunch and since Tets was also in the fields, she divided the lunch in two separate cloths and sent Nami and me to take them to the men. We went together, first to Tets, then to my father.

My father had seen us coming and waited for us by the scant noonday shade of a cottonwood tree. We sat together quietly while he ate his rice balls. A rice ball is to a Japanese what a sandwich is to an American, a portable meal. It's a molded ball of rice sprinkled with sesame seeds and salt and inside there's usually a red pickled plum. My mother once told me it was the mainstay of Japan's Imperial Army, the symbol of her flag: the red plum with the white rice around it. Nami poured tea for my father into a small white cup decorated with a few gold and black strokes—a tiny boat, a lone fisherman, a mountain, and a full moon.

The sound of my hungry father devouring his lunch, gulping his pale yellow tea, the rustle of wind in the cottonwood leaves, far away the put-put of a car, these lonely sounds depressed me so, I wanted to cry. Across the acres of flat land, the view to the house was unbroken. It stood bleached in the sun in awful isolation. A car turned up the road that led to our house.

I shaded my eyes. Far in the distance I saw the small form of my mother waving frantically and running toward us. I pulled my father's sleeve and the three of us ran to her. I could see she clutched our baby. His arms dangled limply. My heart fell.

The front of my mother's dress was stained with water. "I left him only a minute and I found him facedown in the water! I've killed him, forgive me, I've killed him!" she wept.

My father tore the baby from her, turned him upside down and thumped his back. He put him on the ground and blew into his mouth. The car that had entered our yard lurched over the fields. Reverend Umino, perspiring in his black suit and tie, jumped out. "Come, we will take him to a doctor," he said. My father looked dazed. He carried the naked baby into the car. He brushed away the dirt and grass from our baby's face. The Reverend drove off, steering the car like a madman, reeling and bouncing through the fields toward the road to town.

When Tets came home, we all cried together. Waiting for my father that afternoon, my mother roamed from room to room, holding Kenji's kimono to her cheek. We followed her everywhere. Outside, the tub sat with its four inches of water and the toy boat listing, impervious to our tears. From habit, I said my prayers, "Six, six, six."

The Reverend brought my father home in the evening. With his handkerchief he wiped the dust from our family shrine and lit the incense. He chanted his sutras while we sat behind him, our heads bowed. He stayed a while longer murmuring to my mother, assuring my father that everything would be attended to. My mother gave him clothes for the baby: diapers, pins, a small white gown he had never worn, a slip. The Reverend received them with both hands. He put a palm to my mother's shoulder and left.

There was only a small group in the chapel, those few who were unable to go away for the summer. The flowers that surrounded Kenji's white coffin were the last of summer and their scent along with the smoking incense, filled the room. Candles flickered in tall brass stands and the light glittered on the gold of the shrine. In the first pew reserved for the family, we five sat huddled, at last together in our grief. Reverend Umino's sutras hung in the air with the oppressive smoke. He began the requiem: "An infant, child without sin, pure as the day he was born, is swept from the loving arms of parents and siblings. Who can say why? Trust. Believe. There is an Ultimate Plan. Amida Buddha is Infinite Mercy. The child is now in His sleeve, now one with Him . . ." In his elegant vestments, the tunic of gold brocade, the scarlet tassels, with his broad chest heaving, Reverend Umino swabbed at his swarthy neck. "Providence sent me to this family at this extreme hour. I was there to witness the hand of Amida . . ." And the Reverend went on to tell the story of that dreadful day in flawless detail. The assembly wept.

Pictures of that day, the days of the gestation, the summer before, the terrible days following the birth, reeled before me. Someone in the congregation sobbed. Scratching at his eczema, the Reverend motioned the group to rise. My father helped my mother to her feet. She gripped my hand. It seemed to me if my tears would stop, I would never cry again. And it was a long time before I could believe in God again.

CONTRIBUTORS

- **Michael Blaine** is the pseudonym of a poet who teaches at a major university in southern California.

- **Clark Brown** lives in Chico, California. He has published a novel, *The Disciple,* short fiction, essays, criticism, poetry, and translations. His story "A Winter's Tale" was a 1984–85 Pushcart Prize selection.

- **Christopher Buckley** presently lives and teaches in West Chester, Pennsylvania. He is the author of four poetry collections, the most recent being *Dust Light, Leaves.*

- **Frank A. Cross, Jr.** was raised on farms in Lancaster and Chowchilla. A Vietnam veteran, he now farms 160 acres of cotton, corn, and wheat near Chowchilla.

- **Art Cuelho** is the author of many books and pamphlets, and is the publisher of Seven Buffalos Press in Montana. He is Azorean-American and some of his work has been translated into Portuguese language here in America and on Terceira Island, Azores.

- **Hisaye Yamamoto DeSoto** has written for one publication or another since age fourteen. In 1986 she received the "Lifetime Achievement Award" of the Before Columbus Foundation. She is the author of *Seventeen Syllables: 5 Stories of Japanese-American Life.*

- **Richard Dokey** lives in Lodi. He has several collections to his credit, among them the much lauded *August Heat* and his recent short novel, *The Mountain.*

- **M.F.K. Fisher,** a long-time resident of Glen Ellen, California, is the author of numerous books, including *As They Were, The Art of Eating* and *Not Now But NOW.*

- **Gerald Haslam** has recently moved to Penngrove, California, after many years of living in Petaluma. He has written several short story collections, including *Okies and Snapshots: Glimpses of the Other California,* and is an advocate for California literature.

- **Valerie Hobbs** presently teaches composition at the University of California, Santa Barbara. She has published stories in *The New Renaissance* and *The Kansas Quarterly.*

- **Bill Hotchkiss** teaches English in Oregon, but makes his summer home in northern California. He is a poet, novelist, short story writer, editor, and occasional critic, with more than thirty books to his credit.

- **James D. Houston** is the award-winning author of five novels, including *Love Life* and *Continental Drift,* which he completed with the aid of an NEA writing grant. Among his several non-fiction works are *Californians: Searching for the Golden State; The Men In My Life and Other More or Less True Recollections of Kinship;* and *Farewell To Manzanar,* co-authored with his wife, Jeanne Wakatsuki Houston. He lives in Santa Cruz, where he occasionally offers workshops at the U.C. campus there and sits in from time to time with local country/western bands.

- **Richard Katrovas,** now living in New Orleans where he teaches, is the author of two poetry collections: *Green Dragons* and *Snug Harbor.*

- **Maxine Hong Kingston** is author of *The Woman Warrior, Chinamen, Hawai'i One Summer,* and *Tripmaster Monkey—His Fake Book.* After many years of living and teaching in Hawaii, she now lives in the Bay Area.

- **Genny Lim** is a native San Franciscan. She is a playwright, poet, and performer. Her historical drama, *Paper Angels,* received wide acclaim in New York, where it was awarded the Villager Award for Best Play in 1982, and was aired on American Playhouse nationally on PBS in 1985. Lim is co-author of *Island: Poetry and History of Chinese Immigrants on Angel Island,* which received a Before Columbus Foundation American Book Award.

- **Reginald Lockett** is the author of *Good Times & No Bread.* He teaches at City College of San Francisco and lives in Oakland.

- **Devorah Major,** poet and short story writer, is Director of the Poetry-in-the-Schools Program. She lives in San Francisco.

- **Valerie Miner** is the author of four novels, including the much-praised *Murder in the English Department.* She lives in Oakland.

- **Catherine Mulholland** earned a B.A. at Berkeley in 1945 and an M.A. at Columbia University in 1947. The mother of three grown children, she writes regional history and has authored two books, *Calabasas Girls* (1976) and *The Owensmouth Baby: the Making of a San Fernando Valley Town* (1978). She makes her home in Chatsworth, California.

- **Leonard Nathan,** distinguished poet, translator, and critic, is the author of ten books, the most recent being *Carrying On: New & Selected Poems* (1985).

- **Louis Owens** teaches English at the University of New Mexico. He is author of two books and more than fifty fiction and non-fiction pieces.

- **Michael Petracca** teaches composition at the University of California, Santa Barbara.

- **Mary Helen Ponce,** mother of four children and guardian of one cat, is the author of the prose collection *Taking Control.* She teaches at California State University, Northridge, and at UCLA.

- **Lawrence Clark Powell** was born in Washington, D.C. in 1906, grew up in southern California, and has made a long career as librarian, educator, and writer, primarily at UCLA and the University of Arizona. Since 1970, he and his wife Fay have lived in Tucson where he continues to write about the Southwest.

- **William Rintoul** grew up in Taft and now lives in Bakersfield. He is the author of two short story collections, and three non-fiction books on California oil history.

- **Danny Romero** is presently a janitor who works the night shift in Oakland. During the day, he writes short stories.

- **Floyd Salas,** poet, novelist and short story writer, teaches private writing in his home, boxing lessons at Berkeley, and poetry at San Quentin.

- **William Saroyan,** one of the country's major writers of this century, wrote more than fifty books and plays, including *My Name is Aram, The Time of Your Life, The Daring Young Man on the Flying Trapeze,* and *The Human Comedy.* He died in 1981.

- **Thomas Simmons,** a poet and essayist, has had work in such journals as the *Atlantic,* the *New Republic,* and *Southern Review.* He writes regularly for the travel section of the *New York Times.* He lives in Palo Alto.

- **Gary Soto** has written four poetry collections, two prose collections for adults, and a children's book. He is married to Carolyn and is father to Mariko. The three make their home in Albany, California.

- **Domenic Stansberry's** first novel, *The Spoiler,* was published this past year. He lives in Spokane, Washington.

- **Wakako Yamauchi** is a playwright and short story writer who lives in Gardena, California.

ACKNOWLEDGMENTS

- *Splitting Extraversion* is an original recollection. Copyright © 1988 by Michael Blaine.
- *A Christmas Story* was first published as *This is the Month, and This the Happy Morn* in THE CHICO NEWS AND REVIEW. Copyright © 1981 by Clark Brown.
- *Flat Serve* is an original recollection. Copyright © 1988 by Christopher Buckley.
- *Chowchilla Summertime, 1956* is an original recollection. Copyright © 1988 by Frank A. Cross, Jr.
- *My First Kill* is an original recollection. Copyright © 1988 by Art Cuelho.
- *Life Among the Oilfields* was first published in the RAFU SHIMPO year-end Supplement, December 1979. Copyright © 1979 by Hisaye Yamamoto DeSoto.
- *Going in Naked* is an original recollection. Copyright © 1988 by Richard Dokey.
- *Prejudice, Hate & the First World War* is a chapter taken from AMONG FRIENDS (North Point Press, 1983). Copyright © 1983 by M.F.K. Fisher.
- *The Horned Toad* was first published in NEW ARTS REVIEW, 1983. Copyright © 1983 by Gerald Haslam.
- *Ojai, 1959* is an original recollection. Copyright © 1988 by Valerie Hobbs.
- *South Wolf Creek* is an adaptation of the poem by the same title, published in THE GRACES OF FIRE (Blue Oak Press, 1974). Copyright © 1988 by Bill Hotchkiss.
- *The Dangerous Uncle* was first published in THE MEN IN MY LIFE (Creative Arts Book Company, 1987). Copyright © 1987 by James D. Houston.
- *The Republic of Burma Shave* was first published in TELESCOPE: A JOURNAL OF LITERATURE AND THOUGHT, 1985. Copyright © 1985 by Richard Katrovas.
- *The Quiet Girl* are pages from THE WOMAN WARRIOR (Alfred A. Knopf, Inc., 1976). Copyright © 1976 by Maxine Hong Kingston.
- *A Juk-Sing Opera* is an original recollection. Copyright © 1988 by Genny Lim.
- *How I Started Writing Poetry* is an original recollection. Copyright © 1988 by Reginald Lockett.
- *Little Girl Days* is an original recollection. Copyright © 1988 by Devorah Major.